Advanced Introduction to Law and Psychology

Elgar Advanced Introductions are stimulating and thoughtful introductions to major fields in the social sciences, business and law, expertly written by the world's leading scholars. Designed to be accessible yet rigorous, they offer concise and lucid surveys of the substantive and policy issues associated with discrete subject areas.

The aims of the series are two-fold: to pinpoint essential principles of a particular field, and to offer insights that stimulate critical thinking. By distilling the vast and often technical corpus of information on the subject into a concise and meaningful form, the books serve as accessible introductions for undergraduate and graduate students coming to the subject for the first time. Importantly, they also develop well-informed, nuanced critiques of the field that will challenge and extend the understanding of advanced students, scholars and policy-makers.

For a full list of titles in the series please see the back of the book. Recent titles in the series include:

Advanced Introduction to

Law and Psychology

TOM R. TYLER

Macklin-Fleming Professor of Law and Professor of Psychology, Yale University, and Affiliated Research Professor, American Bar Foundation, USA

Elgar Advanced Introductions

 Edward Elgar
PUBLISHING

Cheltenham, UK • Northampton, MA, USA

Published by
Edward Elgar Publishing Limited
The Lypiatts
15 Lansdown Road
Cheltenham
Glos GL50 2JA
UK

Edward Elgar Publishing, Inc.
William Pratt House
9 Dewey Court
Northampton
Massachusetts 01060
USA

A catalogue record for this book
is available from the British Library

This book is available electronically on Elgar Advanced Introductions: Law
(www.advancedintros.com)

Printed on elemental chlorine free (ECF)
recycled paper containing 30% Post-Consumer Waste

ISBN 978 1 83910 972 0 (cased)
ISBN 978 1 83910 974 4 (paperback)
ISBN 978 1 83910 973 7 (eBook)

Printed and bound in the USA

Two events inspired me to try to collect my thoughts about the field into this volume. The first is the request by Elizabeth Mertz that I write a chapter on law and psychology for the Research Handbook on Modern Legal Realism. The second is the offer from Daniel Markovits and Cristina Rodriguez to give a lecture on law and psychology for their class on the foundations of American legal thought at Yale Law School. These opportunities led me to think it would be valuable to summarize my perspective on the field for a broader audience. Mark Fondacaro and Valerie Hans gave me valuable feedback on the content of the book and Doris Lambertz and Michael Brownell helped me with issues of clarity and organization. The opinions expressed and any errors are on me.

Contents

Preface

This volume reflects my perspective as a researcher who was initially trained in social psychology. Over my career I have had the opportunity to teach both undergraduate and graduate students in psychology departments. I have also taught law students. Like many psychologists I began my career doing research addressing theoretical issues in psychology. Over time my interests led me to focus increasingly upon real world applications of research in areas like policing and the courts. After teaching at several law schools as an adjunct professor I ultimately accepted a full-time appointment teaching at Yale Law School.

The goal of this volume is to provide an introduction to the field of law and psychology at a level suitable for advanced undergraduate, graduate level or law school classes. To do so the book discusses the primary topics central to the field.

There is a natural marriage between the individual-level focus of psychology and the individual-level framing of American law. Our Constitution and Bill of Rights, for example, talk about individual rights. In civil courts people can petition for the redress of their personal grievances, which are generally framed around injuries to specific people. With criminal justice, the focus is also on individual criminals: their character, their motivation, their likelihood of being responsible for a crime, and the appropriate punishment for them if they are found guilty.

In considering law and psychology it is important to emphasize that the field is not organized in terms of the academic discipline of psychology. A textbook on psychology would present a framework organized around core psychological concepts. The field of law and psychology, in contrast, is framed in terms of issues that matter in the law and that, at the same time, have a psychological component. Law is organized around a multi-discipline effort to address core legal questions.

Despite the limitations that both sides of this interdisciplinary marriage sometimes perceive, the growth and vibrancy of the field of law and psychology suggests that there is more than enough in this partnership for both sides to find it valuable. The purpose of law is to guide human interactions and this depends upon an accurate understanding of human psychology, so the legal community benefits from psychological input. Psychology as a field speaks to human behavior and it is important for psychologists to translate their theories and research findings into social policy implications. As a consequence, psychologists need and want to use their knowledge to address important societal issues. Managing those issues is the core function of law and government.

It is my hope that I can communicate the excitement that has sustained my enthusiasm for the field of law in psychology through decades of teaching and research in this area. Over the years, which have involved, cooperation and conflict it has always been clear that, like any good marriage, the partners need each other and benefit from their association. This volume recognizes past areas of mutual gain as well as identifying possible future areas of productive cooperation.

Introduction to Law and Psychology

This volume reflects my perspective as a researcher who was initially trained in social psychology. Over my career I have had the opportunity to teach both undergraduate and graduate students in psychology departments. I have also taught law students. Like many psychologists I began my career doing research addressing theoretical issues in psychology. Over time my interests led me to focus increasingly upon real world applications of research in areas like policing and the courts. After teaching at several law schools as an adjunct professor I ultimately accepted a full-time appointment teaching at Yale Law School.

The goal of this volume is to provide an introduction to the field of law and psychology at a level suitable for advanced undergraduate, graduate level or law school classes. To do so the book discusses the primary topics central to the field.

There is a natural marriage between the individual-level focus of psychology and the individual-level framing of American law. Our Constitution and Bill of Rights, for example, talk about individual rights. In civil courts people can petition for the redress of their personal grievances, which are generally framed around injuries to specific people. With criminal justice, the focus is also on individual criminals: their character, their motivation, their likelihood of being responsible for a crime, and the appropriate punishment for them if they are found guilty.

In considering law and psychology it is important to emphasize that the field is not organized in terms of the academic discipline of psychology. A textbook on psychology would present a framework organized around core psychological concepts. The field of law and psychology, in contrast, is framed in terms of issues that matter in the law and that, at the same time, have a psychological component. Law is organized around a multi-discipline effort to address core legal questions.

Despite the limitations that both sides of this interdisciplinary marriage sometimes perceive, the growth and vibrancy of the field of law and psychology suggests that there is more than enough in this partnership for both sides to find it valuable. The purpose of law is to guide human interactions and this depends upon an accurate understanding of human psychology, so the legal community benefits from psychological input. Psychology as a field speaks to human behavior and it is important for psychologists to translate their theories and research findings into social policy implications. As a consequence, psychologists need and want to use their knowledge to address important societal issues. Managing those issues is the core function of law and government.

It is my hope that I can communicate the excitement that has sustained my enthusiasm for the field of law in psychology through decades of teaching and research in this area. Over the years, which have involved, cooperation and conflict it has always been clear that, like any good marriage, the partners need each other and benefit from their association. This volume recognizes past areas of mutual gain as well as identifying possible future areas of productive cooperation.

1 Overview

1.1 The origin of law and psychology

Hugo Münsterberg's classic book *On The Witness Stand* (1908) is often said to mark the beginning of the modern field of law and psychology. Münsterberg, a psychologist teaching at Harvard, conducted the first experimental research in this area. He staged a mock assault in his class during which he was attacked by an unknown assailant. As the attacker rushed out of the room, students in the lecture hall were told to write down statements about what they had witnessed. This was an early version of what psychologists call a "free recall" task. The result: the students made many mistakes, including some thinking that the attacker (who was actually a student) had a knife. The conclusion drawn by Münsterberg was that eyewitnesses can be in error.

This is one of the first efforts to apply empirical research to legal issues in the United States. It is certainly the early effort of highest visibility because of Münsterberg's prominence in psychology. In addition to teaching at Harvard he was President of the American Psychological Association in 1898. His work was quickly attacked by John Henry Wigmore who was an important legal scholar and Northwestern law professor who taught in the field of evidence.

This early conflict foreshadowed both the promise and the challenges of this field. Münsterberg over claimed when presenting the implications of his findings for law, failing to recognize the ways the law managed the issues he raised, and Wigmore put him on trial by cross-examining his arguments. Thus, from its beginning, law and psychology was marked by high profile law–science conflict, the type of conflict that continues in some areas to this day.

Designating Münsterberg's work as the beginning point of legal psychology depends on making a distinction between intuitive lay psychology and experimental research-informed psychology. Prior to the 20th century, lay intuitions and commonsense ideas about human psychology (human nature)—played an important role in designing law and government. Theorists like Plato based their views of law and governance on their intuitions about the nature of human beings, a pattern that continued until the beginning of the 20th century.

As one example, Montesquieu's seminal treatise, *The Spirit of the Laws* (1754), is credited with inspiring America's founders to include the concept of a separation of powers into our government. Montesquieu suggested that this form of government was necessary because human nature drives people to seek to gain power over others. Contrasting Plato with Montesquieu illustrates the problem of relying on intuition. Plato argues for the benefits of giving "wise" leaders power to make decisions for the community, while Montesquieu says that too much power corrupts, so a balance is needed. These two intuitions about human nature that have opposite implications yield different conclusions about what people are like, and how that should be reflected in institutional design.

In my introductory social psychology class I used to begin my first class by asking students to agree or disagree with a series of folk psychology wisdoms. For example, "birds of a feather flock together," but "opposites attract." Students soon realized that they were viewing contradictory statements as all being true. The plethora of such sayings allows almost any observed behavior to be described with a convenient aphorism, and highlights the problem of relying on "common sense" to explain behavior.

The seeming obviousness of folk wisdoms leads to a popular culture that views psychology as merely common sense, a field that does not use scientific methods that cannot make general statements about people because everyone is unique, that does not yield repeatable findings, that cannot make precise predictions, and that does not help society (Lilienfeld, 2020).

Prior to the 20th century, all concepts of human nature were based upon intuition and commonsense interpretations by individual observers. Those observers were sometimes insightful and sometimes quite wrong in their understanding of human psychology, but none utilized systematic research methods to test their theories. Montesquieu attempted to develop a theory about aggregate features of different societies such as their climate or their size. However, he did not include data for the psychological part of his theory and did not systematically interview any people.

The systematic empirical research approach, reflected in the writings of Münsterberg, marked a shift toward an evidence-informed understanding of the person. A shift could not occur before the development of the concept of experimental methods that enabled the scientific study of people. This began with the growth of experimental psychology around 1880–1915, the period during which it was first recognized as an academic field in Germany. Münsterberg was trained in experimental psychology in Germany, and actively studied perception, in addition to working in law and psychology.

During the same period, Charles Peirce introduced the concept of random assignment (1877–78), the work of people like Karl Pearson (1900) developed statistical methods, and Pfungst (1911) recognized the idea of observer bias/double-blind studies. These developments provided the necessary background for approaching issues in psychology from the perspective of a researcher, and using that viewpoint to study legal questions empirically.

Around the same time, in his book *The Common Law* (1881) Oliver W. Holmes expressed ideas about the value of empiricism in law by suggested that, in the future, law would be placed in the hands of experts in statistics and economics. An early example of such empiricism was the Brandeis brief (*Muller v. Oregon*, 1908), in which statistical evidence about health was used to argue for limits on the work hours of women. This early work in law led later in the 20th century to the Legal Realism and the Law and Society movements, both of which use research to explore how the law actually functions in everyday society, often contrasting that reality to legal ideals. These movements combined multiple fields, including psychology, but were primarily led by sociologists and anthropologists. Scholars from these disciplines utilized a variety of approaches to empirical studies of law, while psychologists primarily focused upon experimental methods.

The use of empirical research to address legal questions continued to expand along with the broader development of social science after World War II. As part of this expansion, the field of legal psychology has become vibrant and multifaceted, supported by diverse researchers, academic journals (*Law and Human Behavior; Psychology, Public Policy, and Law*), and a national association (the American Psychology-Law Society, which is Division 41 of the American Psychological Association). While it has continually expanded, law and psychology has not been the dominant social science perspective in the field of law. Law and economics revolutionized legal scholarship in the post–World War II period and continues to be the primary social science influence upon law today. However, over time, law and economics has moved from a theoretical field to a more research-based endeavor with the advent of behavioral law and economics. This has blurred the boundaries of economics with those of psychology in areas such as judgment and decision-making. Today, some of the concepts and methods of psychology and economics are closely related.

What is particular to psychologists is their focus on understanding the mental state of people: their beliefs, attitudes, and feelings. The classic psychological paradigm contains two key ideas. First, environmental events (stimuli) shape the beliefs, attitudes and feelings of people (the internal properties of organisms). Those elements within people then shape what they do (behavioral responses). It is this focus on the subjective, the inner workings of the person and efforts to quantify those workings, which is distinctly psychological. It can be contrasted to law and economics, a field that uses 'revealed preferences,' i.e., infers what people think from what they do without trying to directly assess internal processes.

Through the 20th century, the power in the relationship between the fields of law and psychology has been held by legal authorities, with psychologists seeking leverage to move the legal system toward more consistency with psychological theories and research findings. For decades, psychologists were pleased when their ideas or research findings were mentioned by legislators or judges, even though they often felt they were misunderstood because the legal system reported their ideas selectively or even inaccurately. In other cases, research findings were simply ignored in the interest of supporting existing legal doctrines, or shaping desired policies and practices of legal institutions.

While law has not always taken psychology into account, the history of law and psychology, and law and social science more generally, is one of increasing influence upon and interconnection with law (Rachlinski, 2011). There are many signs of this, including both the fact that law schools are hiring more interdisciplinary faculty and that legal research is increasingly likely to cite empirical research findings (Diamond, 2019). There has been a similar general growth in evidence-informed government and public policy (e.g., the work of the United Kingdom Behavioural Insights Team and the Obama White House Social Science Advisory Group).

I believe that the law is paying more attention to social science at least in part because its findings can legitimate legal authority. Over time, public distrust of law and government has increased, particularly distrust of national level institutions. It may be that legal authorities believe basing decisions on data, or at least justifying legal decisions by reference to data, builds their legitimacy.

Unfortunately distrust in science is increasing and the early 21st century has seen heightened skepticism about scientific research and scientists. The perceived neutrality of science has become affected by partisanship, with conservatives becoming more distrustful of all types of experts, including those studying law and legal institutions (MacCoun, 2015). While this is not an issue specific to the field of psychology, it perhaps reflects skepticism about behavioral science in particular. Psychology has contributed to skepticism about itself by having an internal 'replicability' conflict, with psychologists themselves raising concerns about findings in their own field (Stanley et al., 2018).

Law and psychology continues to push back against the widespread view, shared by members of the public and legal authorities, that many of the questions involved in the field are amenable to commonsense and intuitive everyday wisdom. This is particularly true in America, where there is a long history of populism and anti-intellectualism (Hofstadter, 1963). It would be comforting to imagine that the movement toward evidence-informed law is gaining public and expert support, but that assumption is not clearly justified. There continue to be competing visions of how laws should be created and implemented, with some scholars joining laypeople in questioning the value of quantification (Merry, 2016). Many areas of law have been and continue to be evidence-free zones where little effort is made to ground policies and practices in research findings.

1.2   Evidence-informed vs. intuition-based approaches

What distinguishes evidence-informed approaches from those based upon intuition? When social scientists talk about evidence-informed policies, they mean policies that flow from studies defined by the principles of empirical research. To psychologists this has often meant randomized control studies, in which people are randomly assigned to receive one of several experimental treatments designed to differ along only one dimension. Such a design maximizes the demonstration of internal validity: the connection between the treatment and some effect. Because of the need for control over the treatments, the focus on internal validity has led psychologists to conduct studies in laboratories, where they can manage the environment and create true experimental designs. This approach has led to skepticism by legal authorities, who ask whether findings in an artificial environment generalize to real-world settings. This is the question of external validity: the applicability of a research finding in natural environments.

Evidence-informed policies can be contrasted to ideas that flow from intuitions and everyday knowledge. In the arena of law, people often feel that their experiences equip them with wisdom about what other people are like, what is effective in shaping behavior, and other issues relevant to law. This is especially true of those with professional training and experience, such as police officers, lawyers and judges. Legal authorities are entrusted with large amounts of discretion by the legal system and they want and need to have confidence in their ability to act in rational ways. These feelings of self-confidence conflict with many findings of psychological research, which cast doubt on even experts' ability to be rational even when they are the experts in some area. It is, of course, inevitable that people, no matter how well-intentioned or competent, will make mistakes in some cases. Research findings go beyond that and reveal that there are also systematic errors, such as consistent overconfidence, that affect the work of legal authorities.

Psychological research can help to overcome these human limitations in two ways. The first is by identifying situations in which people consistently make the same errors, so that those situations can be redesigned. The second is by evaluating the degree of error being made, so that decision-makers can adjust their beliefs and actions to appropriately manage the uncertainty around information that has an error component. These approaches are both possible, but only if people accept the results of the research.

The conflict between individual intuition and the scientific method is not confined to legal experts. Scientists themselves fight a constant battle to develop methodologies that can overcome their own tendencies to act in nonscientific ways. For example, the double-blind study hides the purpose of a study from both the participants and the person conducting the testing, assuming that both are influenced by the tendency to see what they want to see (Rosenthal & Jacobson, 1968).

Everyone, scientist and lawyer alike, is challenged by their tendency to rely on intuition and common sense. In the case of lawyers and legal authorities, this challenge is heightened by the traditional lack of training about scientific methods in law school education. Today, an increasing number of lawyers are learning basic quantitative and data analysis skills. However, incorporating the core message of research on the limits of human reasoning and intuition has been problematic in a legal culture accustomed to accepting the discretionary exercise of authority by police officers, prosecutors, and judges.

The contrast between cultures relying on evidence-informed vs. intuition-based policy can be seen in twin crises that have affected American society in 2020: the public health problem of the COVID-19 pandemic and the legal problem of police violence in the form of the misuse of force. In the arena of public health our society has heard, and in many cases heeded, the voice of scientists working on treatments for COVID-19. Those voices have called for the public not to use untested drugs, but rather to wait for the results of controlled trials to determine efficacy. The willingness to wait for the data (in some cases grudgingly) shows that public health has created a popular culture that understands the idea of testing drugs and vaccines before they are made available. The pull of political forces has been present, with political leaders seeking to declare victory by using drugs of unproven worth (or even proven non-worth), but the evidence-informed culture of public health has generally prevailed.

In the arena of law, conflicts involving police use of force are occurring at the same time. Here, a series of reforms have been implemented without waiting for evidence that they work, an approach that has been common in law enforcement. People, including "experts," often act on intuition, implementing policies in the absence of evidence that they work, or even when evidence shows that they will not work. This may occur without any provision for evaluating those policies once they are put in place, so their efficacy is never known.

Examples of intuition-based responses to moral panics in law abound. What unites these examples is that in each the efforts made by legal authorities to address a pressing national concern have occurred without taking into account empirical evidence about what works. In response to fear of crime, America began a vast program of long-term imprisonment in the 1970s. Studies later indicated that much of this effort yielded few crime-reduction benefits (Chalfin & McCrary, 2014; Kleiman, 2009; Paternoster, 2010). In the 1980s and '90s, police departments in major cities responded to the same fear of crime with a broad policy of stop, question, and frisk, a strategy which has also been shown to yield little crime control benefit (Lanfear et al., 2020). Today, political leaders promote programs such as "scared straight" in the face of strong evidence that they do not work (Petrosino et al., 2013). Legislatures enact programs to engage in lifelong control over sexual predators, in the face of evidence that recidivism rates for this crime are very low (Hamilton, 2017). And, to return to the case of police use of force, the federal government responded to a recent conflict over this issue with a major investment in body-worn cameras prior to having any clear evidence that they are effective in shaping officer behavior (Lum et al., 2020; Yokum et al., 2019). These examples are part of a longer list, all illustrating the point that American law has not generally evolved toward a model of evidence-informed policy, a model which is more dominant in other public policy arenas.

Another example of the benefits of an evidence-based culture is that it emphasizes collecting empirical data on structural problems and using it to make proactive efforts to redesign institutions. One organization that engages in fact-finding to obtain such evidence is the National Transportation Safety Board (Sherman, 2018). Their efforts at institutional design are aided by the existence of data. With road safety, dramatic reductions in highway deaths have occurred because researchers and regulators have focused on car and road design. Drivers have remained as good or bad as they ever were, but designing around their shortcomings has led to situational improvements. This approach requires the collection of systematic information about when and why accidents occur. Over time evidence can pinpoint the cause of a problem in a situation because it reoccurs (Sherman, 2018).

In contrast to these examples, the field of law has historically lagged in the arena of evidence collection. Researchers trying to study the police or the courts are often confronted by the lack of data or, where data exists, the challenges of transforming it into a useful format. Basements with file cabinets filled with old case records do not easily lend themselves to systematic analysis. When the issue of police shootings emerged as a national crisis in America, efforts to address it were hampered by the lack of information about how often the police shoot people and under what circumstances. Similarly, crime rate statistics are notoriously unreliable resulting in continual uncertainty about how serious the crime problem actually is in a particular place.

The issue of crime rates illustrates a problem with the political nature of the American legal system. The FBI's crime report data relies upon individual police departments to self-report. Since police leaders are judged based on the level of crime, they have incentives to distort the crime rate in their community. Examples include discouraging people from filing crime reports and reclassifying the nature of reported crimes toward lower levels of seriousness. The neutral collection of information is challenging in an environment where information has political implications. This issue also illustrates how empirical research can correct political biases. The federal government supports an annual victimization survey that estimates the crime rate directly by interviewing a random sample of residents, bypassing reports from local authorities.

To summarize, law has a lot to gain from making greater use of research based findings. One gain is the replacement of intuition with empirical evidence. Another is support for a broader culture of evidence-informed law. This culture includes but is not limited to the evidence developed by psychologists. But psychology is a heavily research based field so it can also provide guidelines for the effective development of research strategies for addressing a wide variety of legal questions.

1.3   Applications of psychology to law

Psychology has been applied to law at several levels. At one level, psychologists are experts in the empirical study of accuracy and error and are similar in this respect to statisticians and big data economists. They use quantitative indicators to assess policy impact. Among social scientists, psychologists are particularly known for designing and conducting experiments. An example is a study by psychologists focused on the question of whether jurors taking notes changes verdicts (Heuer & Penrod, 1994). A unique contribution of psychologists in such studies is to look at the thinking of the participants, as well as what they do, rather than only upon their actions, a typical econometric concern.

Experiments are valuable whether or not they include a component designed to assess thinking. In the case of juror note taking, it matters whether the act of taking notes changes verdicts, and it also matters why that change occurs. Do jurors who take notes have a better command of the facts? Do they pay more attention? Do they take their task more seriously? These explanations for why an effect occurs are aided by interviewing jurors.

A second level of psychological input involves drawing upon psychological theories. As an example, studies do not simply document the error rates of eyewitness reports; they assess why such errors occur. The various types of error are united by theories about perception, the processes by which people acquire, store, and retrieve information about events in the world. In other words, theories explain why well intentioned and highly motivated people make errors.

It is not necessary to draw upon psychological theory to design and conduct valuable research. However, in key areas of law and psychology, having theoretical frameworks has allowed psychology to unite what otherwise would be a set of discrete and seemingly unconnected empirical findings. As we move through different issues in legal psychology, it is important to understand several core ideas within the field of psychology. They reflect different views about how people manage acquiring information and using it to construct images of the world.

One body of theory is built around the idea of the person as a seeker of truth, a naïve or lay scientist. While they may not use scientific methods, people are viewed as being motivated to have an accurate view of the world. Several more recent psychological theories have emphasized limits to this view. One is that much of the information processing people do occurs automatically or through mental short-cuts called heuristics. Using these processes simplifies people's mental efforts but leads to inaccuracies in their understanding of the world. Finally, people are motivated to achieve goals besides understanding the world as it is. They also want to maintain a positive self-image and have feelings of competence and control. Achieving these goals can bring people into conflict with truth seeking and lead to distortions in people's understanding about facts in the world.

1.4   Images of the person

The traditional image of the person that underlies the design of legal institutions has several key elements. It begins with the assumption that people's motivation when dealing with others is to understand the world as it actually is (Hastie & Dawes, 2001; Nisbett & Ross, 1980). This means that, like scientists, people seek the truth. That does not mean that people use scientific methods. It means that they are motivated to get an accurate picture of the facts about the world around them to shape their actions. This model is often called the naïve scientist model, and is a key image of the person in psychology, where traditional learning theories emphasize the motivation to accurately understand the world.

Why do people want accuracy? People need to see the world as it actually is to be able to maximize their overall gains and minimize their losses. Their beliefs need to be accurate. Even a rat is motivated to accurately understand its maze, because that is the best way to find and keep finding cheese.

The second assumption is that people conceive of gains in terms of objective outcomes: money, resources or opportunities. Losses are thought of as including monetary losses and other aversive, painful experiences, both of which people want to avoid.

This core model of human psychology can be expanded in several directions. One expansion that legal scholars have recognized is that people are often motivated not just by personal self-interest, but by what is good for their family, community, or social group. The other important expansion of this fundamental model is the recognition that people care about more than material gains and losses. They also care about their self-image and self-esteem. Disrespect and humiliation have a real cost, and affirmation and respect from others are valued gains.

These distinctions aside, the law has generally been framed around the assumption that it needs to regulate a society of self-interested seekers of objective and psychological gains and avoiders of physical, material, psychological and other costs. This image of the person fits well with the intuitions of everyday Americans. It is hard to know whether the dominance of economic thinking has led to the pervasiveness of this image of the person within American society, or whether economic thinking has been central to law because it reflects the commonsense ideas of our society. In either case, the image of people as motivated by self-interest is the foundation of American law and American society.

A central concern in applying this model to the legal system is gaining an understanding of when people are actually trying to be rational actors who seek the truth as a basis for their actions. The issue is often not whether people behave to maximize their own well-being, but whether the same motivations are at work when people evaluate the actions of others and decide how to respond to them. A typical juror personally gains or loses little based upon how accurately they determine truth in a trial and thereby shape another person's fate.

In recent decades, the image of the self-interested actor that guided so much American legal thinking in the 20th century has been buffeted by the growth of social science evidence about the psychology of the person. One body of research involves the psychology of everyday human functioning. Although people are imagined to be seeking an objective understanding of the world, in reality, people are continually inundated with a barrage of perception and experience, far more than they can completely process. The information people take in is only a subset of what they experience, shaped by the focus of their attention and processed selectively using existing frameworks of knowledge.

People need to constantly make decisions about what matters. A person who remembered everything they experienced would be overwhelmed by data, much of it useless to them in their everyday life. Human life is about triage: what to pay attention to, what to remember, what to care about, and what to ignore or forget. All of these processes involve understanding the world through the prior mental frameworks (schemas) that people possess. This means that people can look at the same event and come away with different memories of what happened because they filter their experiences through different mental frameworks.

These ongoing efforts to manage reality are automatic in the sense that they occur without any awareness on a person's part that they are actively processing the world around them. Vision is a perfect example. As noted, people are constantly selecting what to look at, what to remember, and how to understand all of the information in the environment. Yet, a person simply experiences vision as seeing what is happening around them. Their conception of vision is that they are a camera recording and storing images in their minds, producing a perfectly accurate and complete representation of what occurs. In reality, nothing could be further from the case.

The literature in this area highlights two points. First, the way that people understand the world is selective and incomplete. Second, people are not aware of these processes and imagine that their mental representation of the world is complete and accurate.

1.5   Heuristic vs. systematic processing

Popular psychology has made many people aware that there are two mental processes through which decisions are generally made: heuristic and systematic. This dual-system model is associated with Nobel Prize winner Daniel Kahneman (2011) who distinguishes a fast, automatic mode of processing information from slower, more deliberative processing. On an everyday basis, people use mental shortcuts to simplify many of the decisions they make. Their goal is to make satisfactory decisions that are adequate to their needs and concerns. Careful decision-making takes time and mental effort, and spending those limited resources on trivial issues is counterproductive. People ration their mental energy, saving it for decisions that are important. Otherwise, they use intuitions and heuristics that rely upon a variety of automatic processes.

Social scientists call acting on adequate rather than optimal mental processing "satisficing." While satisficing with heuristics for routine matters is fine, it is important that people can recognize when this approach is inadequate and respond differently. Everyone knows someone who spends too much time deciding what to wear each day or too little time deciding what job to take. The trick to being adaptive is to channel one's limited capacities toward decisions that have an important impact on one's life.

The systematic approach to processing information is more mindful and conscious, and involves careful reasoning. People shift into this mode of thinking when an issue is important to them, seeking to make more accurate, more optimal decisions. However, in any system of reasoning people will still make mistakes.

The literature on judgment and decision-making provides vivid examples of people's departures from rational thinking. People put too much weight on highly salient and easily available evidence, put too much weight on representative cases, and evaluate gains and losses differently. Such shortcuts are common with intuitive, heuristic-based decision-making. Mental effort is a scarce resource and people prefer to devote it to those tasks that matter in their lives, leaving less important issues in the hands of heuristic reasoning and automatic processing.

A core question is the degree to which people in legal decision-making roles, whether jurors, prosecutors, or judges, are motivated and capable of upping their game to make more rational decisions using available data. For example, how much effort is a juror willing to expend to make a decision that impacts only the life of a stranger? How capable is a juror of ignoring heuristic cues, even when they are trying to be rational?

In addition, a rational decision-maker must try to balance the weight they give to information in terms of its importance and its degree of error, since the data presented may itself be suspect. In law this is called adjusting for the probative value of evidence, i.e., its actual utility in determining the truth. People can manage the limitations of their own reasoning both by putting less weight on facts when they are uncertain about them, and by seeking objective information to test their presumptions. A strong decision-maker is good at weighting evidence by its actual information value. The idea that people need an ability to estimate the worth of information is recognized in law, which assumes that people possess common knowledge, i.e., accurate background information about the world through which they understand any particular set of events.

It is believed that applying common knowledge gives people a strong basis for weighting evidence. People are expected to realize that the testimony of an eyewitness who saw someone fleetingly from 200 feet away through a dirty window at night without their glasses on should be treated with skepticism. In theory there is nothing wrong with considering evidence of this type, as long as the decision-maker weights it with a suitable level of skepticism.

The central theme of the judgment and decision-making movement is that, even when people seek to behave rationally, they are often less than rational. For example, we over rely on the testimony of even very poor eyewitnesses such as the one I describe above. Research in this area has had a broad societal impact, and much of this line of argument has now permeated popular culture. The core point is that, while economic models presume that people act in rational ways to maximize their utility and pursue their self-interest, studies of how people actually make decisions present a more complex picture.

These findings have had an influence in law because they have made scholars and authorities alike aware that there are many problems associated with relying on discretionary human decision-making. This is true when the goal is simply for people to maximize their own well-being, but is even more relevant to situations in which some legal authority is evaluating other people.

An important finding of the work on heuristics is the recognition that expertise itself is not an automatic indicator of superior decision-making ability. As an example, research in this area suggests that although professionals in a particular area frequently evaluate themselves as better decision-makers, they are often found not to be more accurate than lay decision makers (Hartwig et al., 2004). The particular danger with the use of experts in the legal system is that expert confidence in the quality of their judgments increases with more experience, but their actual degree of accuracy does not. Consequently the gap between real and perceived capability expands. In addition, experts are especially motivated to defend their claims to discretionary authority by asserting high levels of skill and resisting negative feedback about their performance.

The question of how to evaluate expert judgment is complicated but intertwined with the type of decision being made by legal experts. Many of the problems used in judgment and decision-making research are math or reasoning problems which do not clearly correspond to the tasks involved in judging legal cases (Wistrich & Rachlinski, 2018). To evaluate legal experts we need to first understand what type of decisions those experts are asked to make and to then evaluate how well they can make those decisions.

Of course, evaluations of legal decision-making do not only revolve around the capacities of individual people. A unique human ability is designing systems of decision-making that limit the impact of any particular individual's errors in judgment. An example is using a jury. A jury first deliberates, which potentially allows any misunderstandings a person has about the facts to potentially be corrected. The jury then reaches a joint decision that cancels out the idiosyncratic biases of any given individual. Judges at higher levels hear cases as a group of varying size. The degree to which these procedures actually reduce individual error is something that will be discussed later. The point here is that the legal system recognizes the desirability of creating procedures that anticipate that individuals can and do make mistakes.

Additional procedures can also be helpful in managing human error, for example, requiring decision-makers to provide a justification for their decisions, since accountability promotes better decision-making, as does the use of some form of checklist or set of guidelines. More effectively managing human error in legal settings relies on people in authority being willing to acknowledge and adapt to the limits of human decision-making in one or more of these ways.

1.6   Motivated reasoning

The naïve scientist model suggests that people want to know the world as it is. They may satisfice, spending less time and energy than they could on problems that they think are unimportant, but they still want to get a reasonable approximation of the correct answer. This makes sense since accurately understanding the world as it is underlies making choices that maximize people's gains and minimizes their losses.

A different way of thinking about people is that they have a variety of motivations, only one of which is to understand the world as it actually is. Another motivation involves sustaining feelings they are competent and moral, judgments that underlie people's self-worth and self-esteem. These judgments have psychological benefits.

People need to have feelings of self-confidence and competence to motivate them to make decisions; without such feelings they would be less willing to take risks and less likely to obtain rewards. The balance between self-confidence and an awareness of one's limits is complex, but it is clearly important for people to sustain the self-perceptions that motivate them to act in an uncertain world. People with exaggerated views about their abilities are found to have higher self-esteem, illustrating the benefits of such views, separate from their accuracy (Taylor & Brown, 1988). However, inaccurate self-perceptions can lead people to make bad judgments that have costs.

Yong et al. (2020) suggest that people are motivated to believe that they are coherent and rational decision-makers. The desire to feel coherent is sometimes prioritized at the expense of accuracy since evaluations of oneself that are not accurate can still facilitate having high self-esteem and self-confidence. These authors also argue that rationalization underlies the beliefs, religions, norms, and ideologies that allow groups to develop organizations and to coordinate human actions. This is further adaptive since an appropriate social organization increases people's capacity to function. At the same time social organization leads people to be motivated to adjust both their understanding of reality and their actions to reflect the views of others and the social norms of their groups. The classic Asch study of social perception demonstrated that people are willing to override what their senses tell them is true in order to conform their beliefs to those of others.

In the legal system decisions must be made, even when evidence is unclear or contradictory (Simon, 2019). Both feeling and projecting confidence is an important factor for a legal authority. Everyone involved wants to feel that good decisions are being made. Feeling self-confident supports the decision-maker, while seeing confidence projected by the decision-maker leads others to view their exercise of authority as warranted. The human aversion to hurting others is well documented. The legal system often requires human actors to do things that are experienced as harms, up to and including sentencing people to death. Society as well as the decision makers themselves want to feel that the people given this authority are handling it well.

A particularly harmful type of motivated error is one that occurs without awareness. An example is the impact of a person's biased perspective upon their judgment. Studies show that when people take sides, whether in a negotiation or an adversary trial, they tend to unconsciously process information in ways that favor their own position (Eigen & Listokin, 2012). Both sides view the evidence as favoring their side more strongly than would a neutral observer. This illustrates the way that one's desire to feel in control shapes perception and judgment because people want to feel that they will win and seeing their case as strong supports this belief. Importantly, the people involved do not realize that they are processing information in a biased way. They think that they are being objective.

In Eigen & Listokin's study, law students preparing for moot court arguments were found to overestimate the strength of their side of the case, regardless of which side they were randomly assigned to represent. The more students overestimated the strength of their evidence, the worse they were subsequently found to perform during the oral argument. Their self-confidence did not translate into superior performance.

A second type of motivation occurs in terms of people's views about society and its institutions. On the organizational or societal level, people are motivated to see authorities as just, benevolent, and caring. People do this because it is comforting to believe that the world makes moral sense and people in power will have desirable qualities, something referred to as "system justification" (Jost & Banaji, 1994; Jost et al., 2004). It is, of course, not surprising that those who benefit from existing arrangements have this view, but it is also found among people who might, on objective grounds, be expected to feel that they are the victims of injustice.

The general motivation to justify the system is important, because it undermines the motivation for reform and discourages recognizing acts of injustice by legal authorities. Eyer (2012) suggests that the reason it is so hard to prevail in a discrimination case is because, in order to agree with such a claim, the jury would have to go against the cultural view that the system is just and that advancement is based upon merit (Jost et al., 2003). If people believe in a merit-based system, they know what they must do to succeed. If the system is based upon prejudice or nepotism many people see no way to obtain their goals.

Another example of justificatory motivation is victim blaming. The argument in this literature is that observers do not like to believe that someone can become the victim of harm randomly or without doing something which leads to that victimization. People want to believe that a person can control their lives and that, if they take careful actions, they can protect themselves from harm. A random victimization threatens this belief, so people want to infer that the victim did something (an action that they could avoid taking) that led to the harm (Kay et al., 2005; George & Martinez, 2002).

1.7   Summary

Law and psychology reflects one aspect of a general move toward evidence-informed law. This book details the many areas in which law and the policies and practices of legal institutions and authorities can and have benefitted from greater attention to what psychological research tells us about the nature of the world and the people in it.

2 Scientific evidence and experts

The centerpiece of any criminal or civil case is evidence. Many types of evidence are presented and evaluated by legal decision-makers in the light of their everyday understanding of the world. However, decision-makers may not have the common knowledge to understand and evaluate forensic evidence developed through scientific and technical methods. The legal system recognizes this difference, but the boundaries between general and scientific evidence are not always clearly defined.

The multivolume *Modern Scientific Evidence* (Faigman et al., 2020) discusses the general rules for evaluating scientific evidence, as well as the literature on its many forms, both psychological and non-psychological. Scientific psychological evidence includes research on eyewitness lineups, actuarial predictions of violence, insanity and other forms of diminished capacity, hypnosis, and repressed memories. Examples of forensic evidence from other fields include DNA evidence, fingerprints, bite marks, hair and fiber evidence and ballistics. Forensics also encompasses medical opinions about the causes of injuries and deaths, and the severity and likely duration of injuries.

Traditionally, forensic science involves experts using scientific means to analyze physical evidence like fingerprints. More broadly conceived, forensics involves expert testimony about any evidence-informed field of science. The courts include psychological research findings in this classification, and the American Psychological Association (2013) recognizes forensic psychology as a field. In this discussion and subsequent chapters, we will look more generally at the application of psychological research findings to law or legal procedures. While this includes psychological assessments of capacity or legal competence, those uses of psychology will not be central to this discussion. These issues are treated in more detail elsewhere (see Needs & Towl, 2004; Slobogin et al., 2013).

In this chapter, we explore how scientific evidence, including psychological research, is used in the legal system, examine standards affecting its admissibility, and consider how the adversary system shapes the presentation of scientific evidence in trials. Before addressing these issues, it is important to understand how the American legal system works on an everyday basis.

2.1   The criminal justice funnel

The legal system is divided into two branches: criminal and civil. Although both are important, the criminal justice system is more publicly visible. It can be represented as a funnel or inverted pyramid, with only a narrow subset of the people initially entering the system ultimately ending up at trial. Most cases are dismissed or settled through informal procedures. Although psychologists study both civil and criminal procedures, until recently most of their research has focused on the criminal justice system.

People enter into this system when they are detained or arrested by the police for breaking a criminal law. They become part of a process that can include pretrial detention, bail, and other forms of pretrial surveillance. During this phase there is usually some informal disposition of the case, often as a plea bargain agreement, and sometimes as a dismissal. A very small number of cases ultimately go to trial. A recent analysis suggested that 97 percent of federal cases and 94 percent of state cases do not reach the trial stage. When a trial occurs, it can be either a bench trial or a jury trial. The settlement of a case may include fines, community service/ restitution, and some form of probation or incarceration. A key feature of criminal cases is that they are largely controlled by the state, with legal authorities deciding whether and how to charge a defendant and how to move their case forward. They do so in a system that has some features of community input, including a grand jury which evaluates initial charges and a trial jury which determines guilt and punishment if there is a jury trial. Of course, members of the public can have control in indirect ways. A witness can decline to testify and stall a case or a jury can nullify a law.

The Kerner Commission Report (1968) referred to the series of interactions that people drawn into the system have with different authorities and institutions as a "criminal justice funnel," because at each stage some cases are disposed of in some way and the proportion of people moving forward grows smaller. At the end of the funnel is a small group of people who are incarcerated as a result of being found guilty in a trial and sentenced in a courtroom. Although the various authorities and institutions involved are primarily state actors, the system is typically composed of a set of semi-autonomous state entities, each of which makes many of its own rules and uses its own practices and procedures. For example, prosecutors can influence charging decisions and thereby shape whether a person is likely to be incarcerated, but they usually have no authority over what happens within prisons. Judges can influence what happens in their courtrooms, but they do not control the jails in which prisoners are held before trial, or the marshal services that manages prisoners before, during, or after their appearance in court. Each agency has its own sense of its mission, as well as distinct policies and practices.

When most people think of criminal justice, they focus on the idea of the trial. While they are infrequent, trials represent a highly visible component of criminal justice in our society. Whether in the novel *To Kill a Mockingbird* (Lee, 1960), or the film *Twelve Angry Men* (Lumet, 1957), the trial symbolizes justice before the law to most Americans. With the introduction of cameras into the courtroom, some trials became national media events. The 1995 O. J. Simpson trial in Los Angeles is an example of how a criminal case became a public obsession (Geis & Bienen, 1998). And in 2021 the trial in Minneapolis of Officer Derek Chauvin for killing George Floyd was widely watched and played an important role in encouraging a national discussion on police reform.

Most people are not aware of how infrequently trials are actually conducted and of how prevalent plea bargaining is in the justice system. In the plea bargain framework, the prosecution negotiates a guilty plea with the defendant in exchange for reduced charges and a reduced punishment (Glover, 2015; Smith, 2005). In theory, this system benefits the defendant, who gets a reduced sentence; the prosecutor, who gets a conviction; and the court system, which does not have to allocate resources to conducting a trial (Smith, 2005).

When criminal trials do occur, they have two aspects: the search for truth and the effort to dispense justice. The search for truth involves evaluating evidence, weighing its strengths and weaknesses (establishing probative value), and reaching a verdict by deciding which, if any, crimes the person is guilty of committing. Following this factual determination, decisions about justice lead to a fair punishment for the crime. Psychologists have been very involved in efforts to study both the probative value of evidence, and people's judgments about responsibility and "just" sanctions for a crime. A central concern in much of the past research conducted by legal psychologists is with using evidence to establish the facts that form the basis for adjudication.

Establishing truth in the legal system involves an investigation to gather evidence, and a process in which decision-makers evaluate the quality and implications of that evidence. The primary responsibility for criminal investigation rests with the police and forensic authorities. The assumption underlying investigations is that the police/forensic investigators are neutral and competent. They will bring evidence forward that will be evaluated by judges and prosecutors, who are also neutral and competent. If that evidence is compelling, it will be brought forward to a judicial procedure, such as a trial, where it will be subjected to an evaluation of its credibility. Defendants have lawyers, who also investigate and bring forward evidence.

In reality, the assumptions about this system for establishing truth are mistaken in multiple ways (Saks & Spellman, 2016). Because almost all criminal cases are settled at the plea bargaining stage, very little evidence is subjected to credibility tests at the trial stage. The lack of pretrial mechanisms for testing credibility means that there is very little accountability for investigators. The products of police and forensic procedures are almost never tested in an open and adversarial arena. Instead, the system is heavily based on the presumption that the police and prosecutors will do a good job in producing high quality forensic findings (Lvovsky, 2017). This ignores evidence that there are career and political motivations to act in self-serving ways, which, in criminal cases, typically involve obtaining convictions. Prosecutors, for example, build their careers based on their conviction record, just as police officers gain recognition for their number of arrests (Findley & Scott, 2006; Gabel, 2014). This system is balanced to some degree by the work of attorneys defending their clients through independent investigation.

Because the police are a key entry point into the system it is important to understand how they make investigatory decisions. This question can be studied empirically. For example, Johnson and Morgan (2013) divide the sources of police intuition into four categories: stereotyped perceptions of typical criminal offenders; prior knowledge about specific people; incongruent circumstances; and suspicious nonverbal cues. Alpert et al. (2005) examined observational data on the police, and argued that they use minority group membership to infer suspicion separately from the behavior people are engaged in. However, they did not find that minority status was directly linked to actually stopping people for questioning. Phillips (2020) found that suspect race, manner of dress and timing of the event all shaped suspicion. These studies suggest that extra-legal issues matter in discretionary decision-making, influencing who enters the "criminal justice funnel." Since this entry point is pivotal and, irrespective of what happens later, dramatically shapes the arrestee's life, a better understanding of the psychology of police decision-making is a key future research area.

2.2   Civil justice

The civil justice system is fundamentally different from the criminal system in that plaintiffs have more control over the decisions about whether to proceed through the system, when to quit, and how to reach a reasonable settlement. The standards of proof are lower (often a pre-ponderance of the evidence), and non-unanimous verdicts or smaller juries are often utilized. Private parties are responsible for investigation and they employ private experts to testify at trial. There is no state-based forensic science system for civil cases. The experts in a civil trial work for the private parties involved. This does not mean that scientific standards are necessarily different. A common complaint is that "junk science" finds its way into civil trials through the testimony of career experts.

To some degree the junk science debate is political. Lawyers defending their clients against plaintiffs alleging injuries have routinely raised the idea the defense experts are not credible. An example of a popular book on this topic is *Galileo's Revenge* (Huber, 1991). That politically shaped book highlighted instances of poor science put forward by injured parties, supporting a conservative critique of plaintiff's use of experts. Conversely Oreskes & Conway (2010) highlighted the way that companies create a body of scientific evidence and a group of supportive scientists to defend their interests.

2.3   Forensic evidence in the legal system

In both criminal and civil cases, issues arise when considering the input of scientific experts of all types, including psychologists. The quality of the forensic experts employed and utilized by the state, and of paid experts employed by private parties, can vary widely, and forensic testimony is often challenged in the courtroom. Forensic experts may also play a role in shaping the nature of pretrial dispositions, e.g., by producing and analyzing evidence that determines whether or not to prosecute cases. The pretrial opinions provided by experts are not subject to evaluation through the accountability imposed by cross-examination in a trial. The public assumes that the quality of scientific evidence and expertise is vetted at trials, but since most cases are resolved before trial, such vetting seldom occurs.

The Innocence Project put forensic science in the spotlight when it found that many of those wrongfully convicted received that outcome at least in part due to faulty forensics (Saks & Koehler, 2005). Of the conviction errors they identified 63 percent involved forensic science testing errors. The story emanating from the Innocence Project—that forensic science is flawed—led to reports on forensics by the National Academy of Sciences (2009) and the Obama White House, and an effort in Congress to pass forensic reform. As of 2020 that effort has failed, and the same system that produced the flaws identified by the Innocence Project remains in place.

2.4   Key critiques

The National Academy of Sciences report identifies several problems with forensic evidence in the current legal system. One is the lack of standards for certifying forensic experts. There are no agreed upon qualifications or accepted forms of training for forensic scientists. There are no general standards for laboratories, or for evaluating investigatory procedures. There are no definitive ways of establishing and presenting errors, or even a requirement that this be done. Therefore, the validity of forensic evidence is frequently unknown. In addition, forensic science experts are often under the administrative or political control of law enforcement agencies and prosecutor's offices. They are not independent. In civil cases it is also true that experts are not independent since they work for one side of the case and studies show that this influences their testimony.

The perception that too much junk science is allowed into civil trials via privately hired expert witnesses is central to the *Daubert v. Merrell Dow Pharmaceuticals, Inc.* (1993) decision by the Supreme Court. This decision requires judges to conduct pretrial hearings to evaluate the quality of the evidence that experts may bring into court. The *Daubert* decision goes beyond the "consensus of the scientific community" standard of the earlier *Frye* rule (*Frye v. United States* (1923)) for determining whether something is valid science. Instead, community consensus among scientists becomes one of several criteria used by judges to decide whether to admit testimony into a trial. It is assumed that poor quality evidence undermines juries, but it is also assumed that judges are qualified and able to make correct judgments about the quality of evidence (Hans & Saks, 2018).

2.5   The problem of local control

The origin of our current problems with inconsistent standards for forensic evidence can be at least partly attributed to the local organization and management of American law enforcement. American policing evolved out of informal systems of village watchers, and a framework of law established by our federal model of government. That model resulted in most legal authority residing at the community, county, or state level. Today there are around 18,000 police departments in America. The most common type of agency is the small-town police department that employs ten or fewer officers (Banks et al., 2016). Similarly, local courts handle the bulk of legal matters. The use of forensic science in these departments has evolved through a series of ad hoc efforts to build city and state forensic laboratories and staff them, often with police officers who have little or no formal training. The problems around forensic science, in other words, reflect the general issues associated with a system of local legal authority.

2.6   Admitting scientific evidence and experts

Admitting expert testimony in a trial does not occur automatically; the judge must allow it. A key consideration in determining whether a judge allows an expert to testify is whether additional scientific or technical knowledge is beyond "common knowledge." If it is an expert might be needed to assess the probative value of the evidence presented.

The legal system has long held that people do not know scientific facts, so having an expert educate the jury is a reasonable and sometimes necessary accommodation. On the other hand, experts are not allowed to bring scientific evidence into a trial unless it meets certain conditions. One concern is that the prejudicial impact of the seeming "scientific" character of the evidence would outweigh its probative value. An example is the early response to DNA evidence. Judges believed that jurors saw DNA evidence as essentially error-free, overestimating its probative value. The issue with admitting evidence was not that it might contain error, but that people may not adequately recognize that error, and thus not take it into account.

Under the older *Frye* standard still used in some states, the judge determines if there is a consensus in the scientific community that a particular type of knowledge produces valid results that could help a jury to better understand the scientific evidence involved in a case. Testimony is only allowed into a trial if such a consensus is believed to exist. This standard has been criticized for allowing the introduction of questionable evidence such as bite marks and voice stress, evidence that is only considered valid only within a narrow community of experts who do that type of research.

2.7   Forensic evidence and the *Daubert* standard

The more recent *Daubert* standard, used by federal courts and in some states, requires judges to have a pre-trial hearing to evaluate scientific evidence (Hilbert, 2019). Issues to be considered by the judge include four criteria: (1) What is the basic scientific quality of the research (falsifiability)—i.e., is it a way to produce accurate information? (2) Has evidence of the type presented been subjected to peer review and publication? (3)

Is there a known error rate for the information? and (4) Is there general acceptance of the particular type of evidence in the scientific community?

(Note that one source of confusion in psychology and law is distinguishing "reliability" from "validity." In *Daubert*, the Court refers to research reliability, meaning the scientific quality of studies. In the field of psychology, scientific quality is referred to as validity. Reliability involves the ability to reproduce a finding. The fact that a test will always get the same result does not show that the result is an accurate test of an hypothesis. Validity refers to the ability of a research design to produce results that we believe reflect truth. This difference in terminology has led to ongoing confusion in legal scholarship when referring to research findings. This volume will use the psychological definitions of validity and reliability.)

The *Daubert v. Merrell Dow Pharmaceuticals, Inc.* decision (1993) instructed judges to be the gatekeepers for scientific and technical knowledge. In *Kumho Tire Co. v. Carmichael* (1999), the Court broadened the range of applicability of this principle to include all expert testimony about scientific, technical, or other specialized knowledge that will assist the trier of fact to understand the evidence.

An interesting consequence of these rules is that it matters whether something is regarded as "scientific." A lie detector (polygraph) result is regarded as scientific evidence, and so is subject to the *Daubert* rule. However, eyewitness identification is not, so there is no equivalent rule requiring that eyewitness testimony be subjected to a *Daubert* hearing about the general reliability of eyewitness identifications. The only rule that limits the admission of the testimony of an eyewitness in court is that law enforcement should not be improperly suggestive during the process of identifying the suspect. If legal authorities follow the rules in this respect an eyewitness identification is automatically allowed into trial testimony, without the scrutiny that polygraph operator findings would receive under the *Daubert* standard.

Importantly, in neither case would the scrutiny be applied to the evidence in a particular specific case. The issue is the general quality of evidence of a particular type (labelled "social framework" evidence, Monahan & Walker, 2011). An expert might testify about an area of science that is generally valid but attorneys could potentially raise questions about the quality of that evidence in their particular case.

The legal discussion about evidence is typically about the quality of that evidence, i.e., how often is it in error. It is important to emphasize in this context that it is not relative accuracy that distinguishes an instance of eyewitness identification from a lie detector finding. The issue is whether a scientific technology is involved.

One study of state judges suggests that, in practice, judges at the state level continue to focus primarily on whether there is a consensus in the scientific community and whether there are scientific publications in the area (Dobbin et al., 2001–2002). A more recent study involving a random sample of federal judges suggests that they also consider whether the methodology is sound, and look at known or potential error rates. It is these two latter criteria that address the actual validity of the science and not whether scientists accept it (Meixner & Diamond, 2014).

Specifying peer review and consensus as criteria puts the weight of admissibility on the scientific community. Peer review does so because studies are only published if other scientists think that they have high quality, so an area with many published studies is likely to be seen by scientists as having general validity. Consensus does so for the same reason, i.e., because it shows that scientists generally regard the science involved as valid. In this latter case, while the legal system relies on the concept of consensus, there are no standards for determining when such a consensus exists. Of particular concern is determining the boundaries of the relevant scientific community. Most lie detector operators view their technology as valid science, but many other forensic scientists do not.

The *Daubert* decision was aimed at junk science and career expert witnesses who appear in civil cases such as product liability cases. However, many of the issues raised in the civil arena are also issues in criminal law. The new focus on experts and standards for forensic evidence has revealed the generally poor quality of forensic science in America (Harris, 2012). While forensic evidence is "the essential hallmark of certainty that juries need and society craves" (Gabel, 2014, p. 289), such evidence often does not meet the requirements articulated in *Daubert*, because of the general lack of cohesive standards, mechanisms for quality control, and error rate data. Examples of errors linked to forensic errors abound (Hans & Saks, 2018). A common theme is that experts testify about scientific evidence whose validity has never been tested or, when tested, has been found to be low.

Most recently, Neal et al. (2019) studied the way the courts handle psychological assessments tools. These tools include aptitude tests (e.g., general cognitive and ability tests), achievement tests (e.g., tests of knowledge or skills), and personality tests that are used to address questions such as competence to stand trial or the risk of future violent behavior. They found that only about 40 percent of such tools have generally favorable reviews of their psychometric and technical properties within the scientific community. But their admissibility in court was challenged only 5.1 percent of the time. These challenges were successful around 33 percent of the time. Finally, the authors found no relationship between whether the tools being introduced were considered by psychologists to be of questionable quality and whether they were challenged.

In this context it is important to note that courts have generally not considered testimony by clinical psychologists about the mental health of individual defendants based upon clinical interviews to be scientific evidence. Such testimony has usually been accepted in court without being subjected to a *Daubert* hearing. Similarly, a test used by a psychologist to make an assessment may not be regarded by the courts as scientific in nature, but rather as similar to a clinical judgment.

2.8   Ideal vs. real-life forensics

The poor state of forensic science highlights a broader issue about the quality of scientific evidence. Studies testing validity and establishing error rates are typically conducted under pristine conditions, with the best practitioners and practices. Such studies are then presented in court to establish the capability of a particular scientific technology. This does not mean that all or even most of the forensic scientists and laboratories that currently exist follow those practices and achieve those standards. What is possible under best conditions and what is typical in everyday practice can be very different. It is important not only to ask what a technology is capable of doing, but what it normally does. This distinction is illustrated by the case of DNA, a technology that has been highly regarded for its potentially low error rate. In practice, however, inconsistent or suboptimal lab procedures have produced errors (Cole, 2005, 2006; Gabel, 2014).

When psychologists testify in court they are typically talking about addressing overall problems with a particular type of evidence. Experts are not allowed to apply their general comments to the specifics of the case. An expert can say that people generally overestimate the accuracy of DNA evidence, but they cannot say how much weight should be put on the DNA evidence in the case in which they are testifying. It is up to trial attorneys to highlight issues of evidence quality in the case being tried.

Perhaps the most important issue raised by the increased scrutiny of forensic science in criminal law is that some types of evidence, long admitted in court, actually have a weak scientific basis or poorly understood error rates. A good example is fingerprint evidence. Subjecting fingerprint evidence to *Daubert* hearings has resulted in questions being raised about the quality of this evidence, echoing concerns expressed more broadly in the criminal justice community. The issue here is the accuracy of print matching, in which the examiner matches a latent print of unknown origin to an existing latent print held by the police.

In 2009, the National Research Council raised questions about the lack of empirical studies showing foundational validity and measurement reliability for fingerprint evidence. Forensic experts have testified for decades about matched fingerprints. That testimony has not been supported by an underlying research literature. The actual accuracy of their testimony has been untested and, when more recently tested, found to be open to question (Hoy, 2017). In 2016, the President's Council of Advisors on Science and Technology concluded that latent fingerprint analysis has a "false positive rate that is substantial and is likely to be higher than expected by many jurors based upon longstanding claims about the infallibility of fingerprint analysis" (President's Council of Advisors on Science and Technology, 2016, p. 9). That report notes that estimates of error range from one in 306, to one in 18 cases. Here, the testimony of an expert on the set of fingerprints involved in a specific case might be countered by an expert explaining to jurors the general "overbelief" in the accuracy of this type of evidence.

Judges have been less willing to accept the idea of excluding forensic evidence in criminal than in civil cases because there is a long history of presuming that forensic laboratories produce valid evidence. As Gabel notes (2014, p. 348), "Even when the science is clearly inadequate, judges have been unwilling to rigorously examine it because they are set in their ways and cannot imagine excluding evidence that commonly comes in."

This is illustrated by Meixner and Diamond (2014) in their analysis of federal court decisions. They found that in criminal cases judges were more likely to reject requests for exclusion of evidence when they were raised by defendants' attorneys who were questioning state experts (57 percent when the exclusion request comes from the defendant vs. 26 percent when it comes from the prosecution). This suggests that prosecutors have an advantage over criminal defense attorneys in presenting forensic evidence and supporting it with expert testimony.

As noted, a series of efforts have been made to create national standards and a national institute for research on forensic science, but those efforts have been unsuccessful to date. A key reason for the lack of success is that there are important political and organizational interests supporting the current system, which relies on close relationships between police departments, police laboratories, and prosecutors. Having control over labs gives police departments and local government officials the ability to better manage potentially embarrassing cases.

The system promotes efforts to obtain convictions, thereby supporting the career aspirations of legal authorities, including police officers and prosecutors, who build reputations based on their conviction rates (Garrett, 2011). Further, as Findley and Scott (2006) note "Police investigators are under pressure—from victims, the community, the media, elected officials, and their supervisors—to solve cases" (p. 323) and "public and media expectations can and have resulted in police administrators pressuring police investigators to solve (or in the technical parlance of police, to 'clear') as many cases as possible" (p. 324). This is not only true for police officers "public pressure on prosecutors to convict may even be more acute than the public pressure on police to arrest because the prosecutor's role in society is widely perceived even more narrowly than is the police role in society" (Findley & Scott, 2006, p. 327).

Scientists regard the neutrality and transparency of scientific procedures, and the fact that their outcomes are outside the control of the scientist, as crucial to ensuring that they are not affected by issues besides the evidence in the case. Political actors may look at the same features and see them as liabilities, if the outcome cannot easily be controlled and shaped based on the desires of the authorities. The attainment of accurate outcomes conflicts with the desire to have control over what those outcomes are.

It is important to emphasize that most legal authorities have good intentions, and that it is a formal requirement of law that state actors seek truth. However, like everyone, these authorities are subject to the consequences of motivated reasoning. Their evaluations of people and evidence are influenced by the desire for certainty, the wish to identify the guilty, and the motivation to solve cases.

Legal authorities are also constrained by the nature of the system within which they work. They are political actors, with many prosecutors and judges directly elected by the public. Once in office, they have to cooperate with existing legal authorities to do their jobs. If prosecutors alienate the police then the police may be less cooperative in helping them prosecute future cases. Forensic experts are closely aligned with the police because they are often drawn from the police force and in many cases are embedded within it.

Authorities are also often faced with an overwhelming number of cases to manage in a system with limited resources. The majority of American police departments are very small and lack sophisticated laboratories or dedicated forensic officers. The resources of prosecutors and the courts are similarly limited.

Prosecutors do not control the flow of cases and can be overwhelmed by arrests due to changes in public policy that criminalize widespread activities, as happened in New York City with stop, question, and frisk policing. This can lead them to manage cases in ways that lack desirable safeguards simply to keep up with the workload (Kohler-Hausmann, 2014). In New York City, prosecutors developed a managerial justice model in which they dismissed most misdemeanor cases after the defendant had repeatedly appeared in court for the same offense, unless they committed further crimes in the interim. This style of management was a response to the large number of arrests for minor crimes.

2.9   The adversary culture

The American legal system is an adversary system, under which truth is established by attorneys for the prosecution and defense, each representing one side of a case. These attorneys are motivated to present compelling narratives for their point of view, putting experts on the stand to support their key arguments.

In an adversary system, neither advocates nor experts are motivated to present evidence in a neutral or dispassionate matter. An example of this is a tendency among police officers to focus on a particular suspect early in their investigations and to ignore evidence inconsistent with that person's guilt as they build their case (Findley & Scott, 2006). As the police and their forensic experts investigate, they have incentives not to aggressively pursue issues of uncertainty if it undermines their case. They know that, if they do so, they will be required to explain or justify alternative areas of investigation. Since the state does not want to provide a basis for "reasonable doubt," rather than examining and amplifying doubts officers are encouraged by the system to focus on creating a compelling case against the suspect who will become the defendant. This mindset can also lead to identifications and confessions being shaped by improper procedures in lineups and interrogations.

Expert witnesses often have professional degrees, so one might expect them to be aligned with science and neutrality. However, in trial settings experts are chosen for their willingness to support one side of a case, and not to express doubts. The nature of the adversary system has thus led to the phenomenon labelled "dueling experts," which has undermined the credibility of expert testimony in the American courtroom. In European countries with an inquisitorial system, experts investigate all sides of a case, and present a balanced report to the decision-makers.

The adversary culture makes it challenging to bring science into law (Wells, 2005). The nature of science is to be cautious and emphasize the limits of any conclusions or methodology, an approach in opposition to the desire for definitive statements. Further, it is typical of scientists to suggest that further research is needed to fill gaps in their results. Pointing to the limitations of existing knowledge is a central feature of scholarship, but not a virtue in the adversary system, in which expressing "reasonable doubt" is problematic. For this reason, many scientists who perform primary research are unwilling to act as expert witnesses, leaving the courtroom to paid experts.

The adversary culture is particularly problematic for psychologists because, unlike economics, psychology does not have one grand theory of human motivation. Rather, psychology has a set of overlapping theories and models, none of which is a general model. Furthermore there are interactions between research results and situational factors, leading psychologists to almost always say, when asked if something is true or false: "The result depends upon the situation." This equivocation may seem like a lack of confidence in psychological science, but is actually a reflection of the nature of psychology. Very few findings can be expressed as generalizations that apply to all people or in all situations.

How is it possible for legal authorities to have good intentions but still accept poor forensic evidence in their everyday practices? Consistent with theories of motivational reasoning, the argument by psychologists is that the nature of the system within which legal authorities work encourages psychological processes conducive to this outcome. Simon et al. (2020) refer to this as the adversarial mindset, which has both psychological and institutional elements.

Simon et al. (2020) emphasizes that the adversary system encourages people to engage in distortions that favor their side and disparage the other side. As a result, people unconsciously overestimate the probative weight of evidence that favors them, and underestimate the weight of facts that oppose them. Second, people do this unconsciously believing they are being neutral. Murrie & Boccaccini (2015) note a similar phenomenon and refer to it as adversarial allegiance.

Vidmar and Laird (1983) provide a concrete example. They had people testify on one of two sides of a case. Observers, watching a video of that testimony, detected ways in which those testifying presented their own side of the case more favorably, even though those involved had been told to be neutral and believed that they were being neutral. The process stimulated a set of motivations that unwittingly undermined their objectivity.

2.10   Alternative approaches

Various alternative approaches to presenting forensic evidence have been proposed to help overcome the problems created by the adversarial mindset. One such alternative is the inquisitorial model. In this system a case has an impartial investigator who investigates and presents a balanced set of findings in the trial. This assumes that scientific evidence is better presented by a neutral professional following a disinterested investigation, rather than by two adversaries, each of whom presents a one-sided view of the case vetted via cross-examination.

Thibaut and Walker (1978) propose using inquisitorial procedures in trials when science is involved. They advocate science courts in which trials are bifurcated. In the first stage, an inquisitorial procedure is used to determine the facts. A fact package then goes to a second stage, where it is used in an adversary trial focused on justice.

An alternative to a bifurcated trial is to seek to mitigate some of the impact of adversarial procedures on expert testimony. A real world example can be seen in trials over trademark confusion. In these cases, the two parties conduct surveys providing evidence of the degree to which consumers are confused. In some trials the judge requires the two parties to agree in advance about questions and to conduct a single survey. In this way, the problem of dueling experts is avoided. In theory both sides feel that the evidence from the survey is objective and neutral, because the questions are agreed upon in advance of the findings.

Alternative mechanisms for educating jurors about science have also been suggested. There is a large psychological literature examining the impact of expert testimony on juries. Research suggests that jurors are influenced by such testimony (Levett & Kovera, 2008; Schuller, 1996, 2002), although often not enough to lead them to be accurate in their assessment of the evidence. They are not, however, found to be sufficiently sensitive to evidence quality when they consider expert testimony, so they are sometimes influenced by poor quality evidence (Ivković & Hans, 2003). Jurors are also found to consider a variety of extrajudicial characteristics of experts (e.g., their appearance, their enthusiasm) (Cooper, 2000; Kovera et al., 1999). Further, the ability to understand such testimony is found to be undermined by adversary proceedings (Brekke, 1991). Finally, studies make clear that many of the problems jurors have understanding experts are shared by judges (Chorn, 2019).

One alternative to expert testimony is the use of pattern instructions. These involve a written outline of what an expert would testify to or a statement prepared by the judiciary and either read to the jury by the judge or provided as written material. This is given to jurors either at the beginning or at the end of the trial. Their use recognizes the impracticality of bringing experts into every trial involving scientific evidence. Information provided by these instructions is testimony about the general state of knowledge, but does not address specific elements of any particular case. Consequently, one set of instructions is widely applicable across cases. At this time the effectiveness of pattern instructions is untested.

Psychologists can also help to address issues of forensic science by providing research about pretrial decision-making processes. For example, psychologists evaluate the pretrial procedures used by police officers, like lineups, to determine how to make them more accurate. In civil cases, similar research is needed about how to better utilize evidence in settlement conferences.

A more fundamental contribution of psychology is to highlight the ways in which the widespread handling of cases and forensic evidence via informal procedures, within a politicized and adversarial culture, shapes legal outcomes. As noted, most police officers, prosecutors and judges aspire to do their jobs competently and honestly. However, the institutional framework within which they work introduces the potential for a variety of recurring errors in case processing. Research on expert decision-making makes clear that competent and well-intentioned experts are motivated by the situations in which they work in ways that lead them to make systematic errors of which they are unaware (Kahneman, 2011).

The recent attempt to create national forensic standards is an important effort to improve the current framework, which psychologists can support by providing evidence of errors in the existing system to support the need for such reforms. Another important contribution is making legal authorities aware of the limitations of their own decision-making processes, and the institutional framework that both creates and reinforces those limitations. Law and psychology can be particularly impactful when it steps back from a focus on trials and considers the everyday operation of the criminal and civil justice systems.

3   Lineups and eyewitnesses

From its beginnings, the field of law and psychology has been concerned with the issue of eyewitness identification and misidentification. The accuracy with which people recall the details of a crime they have witnessed was the subject of experimental research by Münsterberg in 1908. Numerous studies since that time have examined people's ability to recall events and recognize others, an area of research that is also central to the psychology of perception. An important reason that legal psychologists focus on this area is that studies of criminal procedure suggest that eyewitness identifications are frequently part of the evidence, and sometimes the only evidence that is available to use in determining a defendant's guilt or innocence.

In this chapter we examine the validity of eyewitness testimony and how problems related to perception, social background factors, lineups, suggestibility, and evidence for video and other modern technologies can lead to error in the criminal justice system.

3.1   The validity of eyewitness testimony

While relatively little information is available about how frequently eyewitnesses are involved in criminal investigations, Goldstein et al. (1989) studied 157 prosecutors in 30 states and estimated that about 77,000 cases per year involved eyewitnesses. Liptak (2011) similarly estimated that there are around 75,000 eyewitness identifications per year in criminal cases.

Studies have been conducted which suggest that eyewitness mistakes are a major factor in producing errors in the legal system. In the United Kingdom, the Criminal Law Review Committee (1971) concluded that cases of mistaken identification constitute by far the greatest cause of actual or possible wrong convictions. Similarly, the Innocence Project, which uses DNA evidence to exonerate prisoners who were wrongfully convicted, suggests that of the first 250 cases considered, eyewitness misidentification played a role in 76 percent of them (Garrett, 2011). Liptak (2011) estimates that around 25,000 of the eyewitness identifications that are made each year are incorrect. This is approximately one-third of the cases in which eyewitnesses are involved. Wells, a leader in the field of law and psychology, notes, "Although these discoveries of wrongful convictions from mistaken identification ... have been a surprise and shock to the legal system and the public, psychological scientists have been less surprised" (2020, p. 1316). This is the case because there is a long history of psychological research raising questions about eyewitness evidence.

When considering the problem of eyewitness reliability, it is important to recognize that such errors not only impact the outcome of trials, but also affect earlier stages of the criminal justice funnel. Identifications are important in the process of investigating crimes, with the police often using a variety of informal means to initially identify suspects for entry into the system. This includes asking a witness for a description that can be used by the police in their search, pointing out someone on the street or in a squad car, and showing photographs or computer images.

Early informal steps can be followed by a more formal lineup, in which eyewitnesses are asked to select the suspect from a group of people. Only if the case ultimately goes to trial does the eyewitness testify. Thus, there are likely many more cases, disposed of by plea bargain agreement, in which eyewitness error contributes to injustice.

The fact that eyewitnesses make mistakes need not automatically lead to the consequence that these mistakes become a major factor in incorrect verdicts. In theory, the legal system is designed with mechanisms to correct for such errors, operating with the presumption that judges and juries recognize the possibility that sincere and well-meaning witnesses can be wrong. Decision-makers have long been expected to use common knowledge to understand the circumstances of an eyewitness's identification and assess its probative value. However, it is now recognized that psychological testimony can contribute to filling gaps in common knowledge about eyewitness validity.

An early concern of many psychologists, a prominent example being Elizabeth Loftus, was with gaining the right to provide expert testimony about eyewitness unreliability in trials. It is easy to see why judges might reject this request, since the assumption has been that jurors can use their common knowledge to weight this testimony and do not need expert help. The landmark case *State v. Chapple* (1983) established the right to have an expert testify in this area. In that case, the failure to allow a psychologist to testify was ruled by an appellate court to be a reversible error. Since then there have been many decisions made by judges allowing this type of psychological testimony, as well as ongoing discussions about its value.

The history of research in legal psychology takes the chronological sequence of the criminal justice process and reverses it. Psychologists first studied trials and only later lineups. An example of this shift is provided by Gary Wells. He began by studying errors that might be identified in trial testimony and later highlighted the importance of establishing better investigatory procedures to improve eyewitness reliability, rather than seeking to mitigate possible errors at trial (Wells, 2020). This shift in focus has led to greater attention to the processes, such as lineups, that affect the pretrial phase of cases.

3.2   Misconceptions about perception

One important contribution of psychological research and testimony is showing that laypeople have a fundamental misconception of the way perception works, which leads them to overestimate the accuracy of eyewitness recall. People think of memory as a series of photographs which are stored and retrieved. In reality, it would be impossible, and not particularly useful, for people to store information about past events in this way. Rather, memory is a process of selection, in which only some information is stored.

People first decide what to pay attention to in their environment. Decisions are then made, guided by prior knowledge and stereotypes, about what to consolidate into memory, so that what is remembered is not a veridical representation of what has occurred. Classic studies in perception show that people fill in events, especially where there is ambiguity, to make them consistent with their expectations and stereotypes.

Once material is in memory, it is still malleable. All memories are being consolidated over time, leading to constant change in the way people remember the past. This is not simple forgetting, since the actual form of memories changes, and people's memories can be influenced by later events. Classic work by Loftus (1979) shows that suggestive questioning during storage can alter memories. She finds that asking a witness to recall an accident alters memories about how fast the cars were traveling, depending on whether the two cars are described as having "hit" or "smashed into" one another. Strikingly, those witnesses questioned about cars that "smashed into" one another were more likely to recall that there was glass strewn on the road, although no glass was present in the video they watched. These altered memories then become part of the remembered event.

Finally, the framework of retrieval shapes memories. In particular, adversarial questioning shapes the nature of the memories that are retrieved. While the dramatic questioning of witnesses is a hallmark of adversary trials, studies show that witnesses are more accurate if they are allowed to give an uninterrupted narrative of the events they remember (Wheatcroft, Wagstaff & Kebbell, 2010).

3.3   Social background factors

Psychological research has also established several additional areas in which jurors lack the background knowledge to appropriately weight eyewitness testimony. Those areas are over-belief, poor situational awareness, and non-diagnostic cue utilization.

The first issue is over-belief in the credibility of eyewitnesses. While people recognize that eyewitnesses can be wrong, research suggests that they do not sufficiently adjust for the unreliability of identifications. In general, decision-makers such as jurors put too much weight on eyewitnesses relative to their actual accuracy (Brigham & Bothwell, 1983).

People also have poor awareness of some of the key situational factors that affect eyewitness accounts. Although people usually recognize that the conditions of an identification (e.g., distance, lighting, weather) can shape eyewitness accuracy, many aspects of their general knowledge about situational influences are lacking. For example, people often do not know that cross-racial identifications are generally less accurate, or that when a criminal uses a weapon the accuracy of an involved eyewitness goes down (Connecticut Eyewitness Identification Task Force, 2012).

Finally non-diagnostic cue utilization is another potential factor causing jurors to make errors when weighing eyewitness testimony. Jurors may rely upon a variety of cues to determine the accuracy of an eyewitness. Studies suggest that they rely heavily upon the confidence expressed by that eyewitness. People are letting the eyewitness tell them how much weight to put on their testimony, rather than distinctly evaluating the circumstances of the identification. The problem here is that research indicates that the actual accuracy of an eyewitness is only related to eyewitness self-confidence under some conditions (Wixted & Wells, 2017). In practice, these conditions have been infrequently met in the past (Loftus & Greenspan, 2017). Sauer et al. (2019) note "the absence of established protocols for systematically collecting and preserving witness confidence ratings in most criminal justice systems currently represents a significant practical hurdle to the effective use of confidence as an index of identification accuracy" (p. 213).

Studies demonstrating overconfidence, poor situational awareness and non-diagnostic cue utilization all demonstrate general errors shaping the average accuracy of memories (Monahan and Walker, 2011). When a psychologist testifies in court, they are permitted to say that, on average, people are less accurate under certain conditions. They cannot know and are not allowed to testify about whether any particular eyewitness is correct or incorrect.

In testifying about background factors, psychologists normally address adjusting for elements that are outside the control of the witness. These involve the circumstances of the initial identification: time viewing the event, lighting, distance, whether there is a weapon, etc. The degree to which the eyewitness paid attention is also important, since witnesses are often not initially aware that an important event is occurring, and may not be focused on the events unfolding around them. They may be talking on their phone, diving for cover, or trying to run away. Everything that shapes the degree to which an eyewitness can be accurate is an estimator variable. These circumstances are what the jury needs to appropriately adjust for.

3.4   Lineups

Psychologists involved in legal cases have been skeptical of the ability of expert testimony to counteract the weight of (often dramatic) eyewitness testimony. The alternative is to try to make sure that eyewitnesses make accurate identifications earlier in the process, during the initial investigation. Lineups have been an important area of focus for this work.

How is eyewitness identification information typically gathered in criminal investigations? At a crime scene a witness may initially be asked to recall the event and describe the person they saw committing a crime. At that point or later they may be asked to look at an array of faces on a computer screen or in a mug book, or even have people on the street pointed out to them. If a suspect is apprehended, witnesses may participate in a lineup in which they are asked to identify the suspect from among a group that normally includes the person of interest and a number of fillers. In a lineup the witness can do one of four things: identify the suspect; identify someone who is not the suspect (a filler); identify no one; or say they are not sure. Research on lineup design has the goal of making such eyewitness judgments as accurate as possible.

There are widespread differences in how police officers approach the lineup task and how careful they are about conducting these procedures in ways that research suggests will minimize errors. Psychologists compare the accuracy of different types of lineups, and argue that the highest accuracy identifications occur when a particular set of conditions exists. Pristine lineups meet the following conditions: Prior to the lineup, the victim is cautioned that the suspect may not be present. The lineup itself has one suspect and fillers who are similar to the suspect (Wells et al., 2015). If at any point the victim expresses doubts, the lineup stops and the doubts are recorded, since persisting after doubts has been indicated is associated with high error rates in identifications. At the conclusion of the lineup, the victim or witness immediately rates their confidence in their identification, since only at this point is confidence related to accuracy.

A further approach, proposed by Sauer et al. (2019), is to have witnesses rate their confidence in an identification for everyone in the lineup, rather than simply saying yes or no (a culprit likelihood rating). Comparisons could then be made among the confidence ratings.

Sequential lineups have also been extensively compared to the current, widely used, simultaneous lineup. In a sequential lineup the suspects/fillers are presented one at a time, with the eyewitness indicating "yes" or "no" for each person. At this time, the research literature does not clearly establish that one approach is superior. In fact, neither procedure produces very impressive accuracy rates (Brewer & Palmer, 2010).

One alternative procedure that should clearly be avoided is the show-up, which Wells (2005) points to as a source of error. In a show-up the witness is presented with the suspect alone, often on the street or in a picture. This is an error-prone way of obtaining an identification but is in use, particularly where limited resources make it difficult to hold pristine lineups.

All of the suggestions for improvements in the identification process can be challenging for law enforcement. As an example, using informal initial procedures like pointing out someone on the street or showing photos of possible suspects are valuable to officers involved in immediately responding to a crime, but may contaminate later identifications. Later in the process having a double-blind lineup requires a department to have an officer besides those involved in the investigation available to conduct that lineup.

3.5   Suggestibility

Another issue that can affect eyewitness evidence, apart from general unreliability, is suggestibility, where witnesses accept and act on the suggestions of others. In this case, improper behavior by legal authorities may shape the statement of a suggestible witness, leading to an identification error. Suggestibility errors may be triggered by cues of which a police officer is unaware or by deliberate efforts to shape the outcome of a lineup. In either case, the behavior has the effect of providing a second source of information about the "correct" answer, which reflects the beliefs of the officers, not the memory of the eyewitness.

An important finding of psychological studies is that, while some law enforcement personnel may deliberately make suggestions there are also many well-intentioned officers who may unwittingly give cues to eyewitnesses. Those officers can honestly feel that they are being neutral in their conduct, while observers detect subtle, often nonverbal, cues given to witnesses. For example, studies demonstrate that if a witness receives post-identification positive feedback from an officer, their confidence in their memory increases in future identifications (Semmler et al., 2004). One reform to address the suggestibility issue is the double-blind lineup. In that procedure, the administrator does not know which person is the suspect or even if there is a suspect in the lineup.

It is possible to get the courts to exclude an identification based upon evidence of inappropriate suggestion, regardless of whether it was deliberate or accidental. The *Simmons v. United States* (1968) decision says that exclusion should occur if there is a "very substantial likelihood of irreparable misidentification" (p. 384). The judge must determine whether the identification was "impermissibly suggestive," and if so, whether the identification has information value regardless of these errors (*Manson v. Brathwaite*, 1977). This rule is consistent with psychological studies showing that intentional and accidental suggestions can both impair eyewitness accuracy (Berkowitz & Javaid, 2013). The key legal issue is not why the suggestion occurred, but whether it introduces a substantial possibility of error.

The Supreme Court addressed police misconduct via suggestibility in eyewitness identification in *Perry v. New Hampshire* (2012). Justice Ginsburg indicated that, absent evidence of police misconduct through inappropriate suggestion, the jury should be entrusted with evaluating the reliability of eyewitness testimony, consistent with the general view that juries can account for error and that there are mechanisms to correct for imperfect evidence in a trial (cross-examination, expert testimony, pattern instructions).

To understand the Court's decision, it is important to focus on the due process framework of the *Perry* case. The Court suggests that the Constitution only requires that evidence not be used in a fundamentally unfair way by State actors. It is designed to protect citizens against misconduct by legal authorities. Beyond that, the Court suggests that the system currently has mechanisms for managing the possibility of error in the evidence (even if psychologists suggest they are inadequate).

A dissent by Justice Sotomayor argues that concern with eyewitnesses should be not only be with deterring improper police conduct. She argues that it is the likelihood of misidentification that violates a defendant's right to due process. She points to issues beyond suggestibility, and notes that the general unreliability of eyewitnesses, their powerful impact upon juries, and the inability of ordinary tests to correct these problems all suggest the need for better procedures for managing eyewitness testimony.

Sotomayor notes:

> It would be one thing if the passage of time had cast doubt on the empirical premises of our precedents. But just the opposite has happened. A vast body of scientific literature has reinforced every concern our precedents articulated nearly a half-century ago, though it merits barely a parenthetical mention in the majority opinion. ... Over the past three decades, more than two thousand studies related to eyewitness identification [and its malleability] have been published. (p. 738, *Perry v. New Hampshire*, 2012)

3.6   Modern technology as information for an eyewitness

Modern technologies such as closed circuit television, body cameras, and various handheld devices that record videos have raised additional questions for psychological research and challenges for the legal system. Can people recognize faces from video? Reviewing studies of identifications from surveillance video, Wixted and Wells (2017) conclude that "people are quite poor at being able to accurately match a stranger to a surveillance image, even for high-quality images" (p. 16; also see Davis & Valentine, 2009).

Nonetheless, in recent years, as video recordings have become a ubiquitous source of information on news and social media sites, the legal system has also begun using them more routinely to identify suspects, supplement traditional reports from eyewitnesses, and monitor interactions between police officers and citizens.

It would seem as if a video recording is the ideal eyewitness. The event is preserved and can be watched repeatedly under perfect conditions by multiple people. Yet, unique individual viewers are involved in perceiving the images with videotaped events, just like real-world events, so the psychology of perception is also relevant.

Psychological models predict that as people acquire, consolidate, store, and retrieve video images, each individual's memories will be influenced by their prior beliefs, stereotypes, and attitudes. Consequently, the perceived images will diverge from the common video material as they are recreated in the minds of observers. People watching the same videotape will not create a single perceived event, but rather a set of similar, but not identical, psychological representations of that one event.

This pessimistic view of video contrasts with an optimism based on the general misperception, already discussed, that memory is analogous to photography. An example of this belief is a suggestion by the Supreme Court in *Scott v. Harris* (2007). That case is concerned with police actions during a car chase that was captured on videotape. The majority of justices thought that their conclusions were self-evident (despite there being dissenting views among the justices about what the video showed), and uploaded the video itself, inviting the public to view it and see for themselves.

Which view of video-based identifications is correct? On one level both are correct. In a video recording some aspects of an event are so salient that most viewers will agree about their content, just as eyewitness accuracy is high under ideal conditions. On the other hand, studies make clear that different people can view a videotape of the same event and "see" different things. What they "see" reflects not only the objective event, but also the viewer's psychological makeup.

These findings replicate those of classic studies in perception. In an early study, Hastorf and Cantril (1954) asked students from two Ivy League colleges to evaluate a series of controversial officiating calls made during a football game between their schools. They found that students viewing the same game on film were more likely to perceive errors in officiating when the penalty assessments were imposed on their own team. This type of error illustrates the idea of motivated cognition, because it reflects the influence of the viewer's loyalties on how they view events. This situation is analogous to an adversary procedure because the people involved were aligned with one side.

It is similarly the case that prejudices shape perceptions. Vallone et al. (1985) showed that when people were asked factual questions about stimuli that they had been shown the facts they remembered were shaped by their level of racial prejudice. This classic finding has more recently been extended to studies of the shooter situation, in which officers must quickly decide if a person seen on a video or in a photo is holding a cell phone or a gun. Prejudiced officers are more likely to mistake the cell phone as a gun if the person pictured is Black (Correll et al., 2007). The bottom line is that psychological theory predicts that different people will perceive the same viewed event differently, and research supports that prediction. Importantly this same area of research suggests that well-designed training can reduce or eliminate the influence of prejudice on police shooting behavior, suggesting that there are ways to address biased perceptions.

Kahan et al. (2009) showed the video of the car chase from the *Scott* case, discussed above, to 1,350 Americans and found sharp differences of opinion about whether the driver "posed a deadly risk to the public." This is an opinion, not a judgment about facts. A factual judgment would be how many miles per hour the car was traveling.

Studies also show that prior beliefs also shape people's perceptions of the facts viewed in videotape form. Kahan et al. (2012) designed an experimental study in which the same videotape of a public protest was presented as being staged by liberal or conservative protestors. This framing shaped how viewers "saw" the events depicted.

Studies examining visual fixation help by providing an understanding of how people's prior level of positive identification with the police shapes what they focus on when viewing videotapes of citizen–police interactions, as well as their subsequent decisions about responsibility and punishment (Granot et al., 2014, 2018). In these studies, people looking at the same video literally did not see the same thing, because their prior views caused them to focus their attention on different aspects of the encounters.

It is also possible to shape how people perceive events through inadvertent or deliberate camera placement. Studies show that observers perceive the same interrogation differently depending upon whether the camera is focused on the defendant or on the interrogator (Lassiter et al., 2009). This means that the way that videotaped images are initially captured has important downstream consequences in terms of how events are later perceived and understood.

These findings point to similarities with the issues already outlined for traditional eyewitness evidence (Granot et al., 2018). People over-believe the veridicality of their memories of video, failing to recognize how their interpretation of such evidence leads to inaccuracy. And, again, people are unaware of the ways in which they are reshaping events that they witness.

One interesting way that videotapes are different from eyewitnesses is that, with a videotape, multiple people can view the same event. Consistent with the logic of a jury, a deliberation among those people may cancel out the influences of prejudice on the group consensus about what the videotape depicts. With an eyewitness only one person's memory is considered.

A rapidly expanding area of law enforcement involves the use of machines as eyewitnesses through facial recognition programs. At this time it is an open question whether these mechanical algorithmic approaches can avoid the problems of inaccuracy and bias that are found with human eyewitnesses. Conceptually the issue is the same: ability to pattern match.

3.7   Remedies in the legal system

Psychological research has made clear that there is a general discrepancy between the probative value of eyewitness identifications and the weight they have in the minds of jurors (Berkowitz & Javaid, 2013). At this point the legal system has not developed a response to this problem that psychologists find satisfying. However, psychological research has played an important role in bringing the problem to prominence within law, leading to incremental improvements over many decades: permitting expert testimony on eyewitness identification, excluding identifications tainted through improper suggestion by legal authorities, and improving investigatory procedures such as lineups.

In recent years, several states have made efforts to address the general issue of error in eyewitness testimony. New Jersey asked a special master to review evidence on this issue in the context of *New Jersey v. Henderson* (2011). Based on its review, the New Jersey Supreme Court concluded that before eyewitness identifications are admitted as evidence, their probative value should be carefully scrutinized by judges in all cases. Oregon went further when its Supreme Court decided to put the burden on the state to establish that such evidence should be admissible (*Oregon v. Lawson*, 2012). Overall, there is great variation in state standards, but there is a general trend toward increased scrutiny of eyewitnesses, some of it directly linked to psychological research findings.

Wells (2020) argues that psychology has had a strong impact on the design of lineups. This has occurred through state level legislative changes that impact lineup procedures. He notes that 29 states, affecting 65 percent of the American population, have passed such legislation. Wells further argues that clear evidence of injustices is important in driving reform. As he puts it, the problem has to reach "tragic proportions" (p. 1324), something exposed in this case by evidence from the Innocence Project showing obviously wrongful convictions and the faces of the people influenced by these errors.

In the United Kingdom concerns about the unreliability of eyewitnesses have led to the imposition of rules through which a person cannot be convicted solely on the basis of testimony by an eyewitness (Devlin Committee, 1976). So, it is also possible to imagine solutions to the problems noted based upon changing legal standards.

Instituting such a safeguard in the United States is hindered by a number of institutional factors already touched on: Legal authorities face public pressure to identify and convict suspects, while often lacking resources and manpower. Legal authority in America is distributed across thousands of local communities, which have inconsistent standards and procedures. The adversary system motivates police and prosecutors to strive for convictions in addition to seeking accurate verdicts.

The culture of plea bargaining leads to eyewitness identifications rarely receiving formal vetting, and keeps the actual impact of eyewitness error out of the public eye. That, in turn, means that the system faces very little pressure to improve because the tragic proportions of harm Wells talks about are never salient. Many well-intentioned legal decision-makers accept this system because the lack of appropriate data obscures systematic error of the type revealed in psychological studies and because participation in the adversary culture leads to unconscious mental blinders that justify existing practices. Given the desire to resolve cases and the high perceived barriers to obtaining convictions, legal authorities would be expected to resist imposing new hurdles in the system.

3.8   Building upon research findings

Managing eyewitness identification evidence highlights the challenges of changing a system that is based largely upon "commonsense" intuitions. Accepting the premise of research findings, the legal system could raise the standards for conviction and require greater supporting evidence. This would pressure police officers and state forensic experts to raise their standards for investigation and require greater funding to do that or it might lead to fewer convictions. Either way, it would lead to outcomes that might be politically unpopular. Creating momentum for such changes requires building support for the idea that the system ought to be based upon evidence-informed policies. And, it involves providing the resources to make that possible.

The ideal reform is one that will increase the likelihood of identifying the guilty but lower the likelihood of misaccusing the innocent. This meets the goal of justice but does not undermine the crime control mandate of legal authorities. Psychologists often focus primarily, or exclusively, upon the misaccusation of the innocent (convicting the innocent) without addressing the legal system's concern with identifying and convicting the guilty.

My goal in this book is to promote the value of a legal culture based upon the findings of empirical research. Such an effort encounters several issues highlighted by eyewitness identification. First, a case-based system focuses attention on individual problems and people and obscures recurring systematic errors. Those errors are best identified when data is considered across people and over cases. Second, the informal resolution of most cases means that much of what goes on in the system is loosely documented. Third, the adversary culture has a high level of public support in the United States. However, as noted, it is a culture that is not well suited to managing scientific evidence. Finally, building an evidence-informed legal system requires a society that values and accepts the results of research. There are areas of American life, such as public health, where the ideas around research validity are well established, but the legal system lags behind those areas in its commitment to evidence-informed policies and practices.

None of this is to suggest that research-informed change is not possible. Evidence of eyewitness reform, as least around that aspect of the issue which is centered around creating better lineups, is clear (Wells, 2020). In this case psychology has driven reform. It has done so because psychologists have adapted their approach based upon their understanding of law. As it has proved challenging to introduce evidence of eyewitness error into trials in effective ways, the field has shifted to trying to prevent errors in the first place. This structural approach has been more successful.

4 Credibility assessment: lie detection, interrogation and confession

Another area of psychological research relevant to the legal system involves studying the ability of people, whether laypersons or experts, to detect lying. Credibility assessment plays an important role in the judgments ultimately made about a defendant's guilt or innocence, and also affects the earlier decisions of police officers and prosecutors, shaping whether a person is viewed as a suspect, and is subsequently arrested or prosecuted. The lie detection literature is thus particularly applicable to investigatory procedures. Credibility assessment is closely linked to the psychology of person perception, which examines how people make inferences about another person's character and motives.

Once the police view someone as a suspect, they engage in interrogation procedures designed to elicit a confession. Interrogation processes are also the subject of psychological research, not only because there is interest on the part of legal authorities in improving their effectiveness, but also because they have been found to lead to false confessions. Interrogation is a procedure involving at least two people and its study draws upon the psychological literature on interpersonal dynamics.

4.1   Detecting deception

In their contacts with the legal system, people often have reasons to lie, either by giving false statements or by omitting information. During police investigations, pretrial meetings, and plea bargaining sessions, legal authorities make decisions about whether and how to move forward, based on their assessments of the credibility of parties in the case. If a case goes to trial, judges and juries do the same. Knowing when people are lying is part of being able to accurately weight evidence and is central to judging their credibility in both civil and criminal procedures.

Because almost all cases are settled via plea bargaining, the initial credibility assessments of legal authorities are central to what happens to most people entering the criminal justice funnel. These impressions matter because they set in motion a process that becomes increasingly shaped by confirmation, rather than investigation. Initial judgments start a process of "tunnel vision" that moves toward supporting those early impressions (Findley & Scott, 2006). Thus it is crucial that accurate judgments be made about whether a person is lying during the early phases of a case. People also need to have a realistic conception of how able they are to assess the truthfulness of a witness, so that they can appropriately discount for error and intentional falsehoods in their decision-making processes. As already discussed, the existence of error in evidence does not preclude using it, so long as people weight that evidence accurately, taking into account the degree of error associated with it.

A key question at all stages of a case is how well people can read others. There are two bodies of lie detection research. One is concerned with people's everyday ability to discern when someone else is lying. The second focuses on using technology to detect lying. The prototypical technology is the lie detector or polygraph test (Alder, 2007; Lykken, 1981) although in the era of brain science a number of different approaches have been suggested, including various measures of electrical activity or blood flow in the brain.

Detecting deception in others requires people to make an uncertain inference, and how well people do this is an empirical issue. Do they accurately estimate their degree of error when trying to detect lying in others, or do they have too much confidence in their ability? Do they know the indicators of lying, so that they can reliably use the presence or absence of those indicators to make judgments?

There is a large volume of research on lie detection and the first overall conclusion of that literature is that people are not very good at detecting lying. Bond and DePaulo (2006) suggest that when people seek to make credibility judgments they are accurate 54 percent of the time (50 percent would be the rate for pure chance). This overall rate combines 61 percent success in correctly detecting that people are being honest and 47 percent in correctly detecting that people are lying. In discussing this literature Gunderson and ten Brinke (2019, p. 80) point to "dismal" accuracy rates.

The literature identifies several possible types of information that can be useful in detecting deception. Those include independent evidence that could confirm or undercut a person's statement, people's verbal behavior, nonverbal cues, mechanical lie detection and particular techniques of interview or interrogation.

One way to tell if people are lying is to compare what they say about facts of a case to independent evidence about the facts. This is not a psychological issue. Investigators can gather information and compare it to the statement given by a suspect. An example is confirming an alibi using cellphone location data, which might suggest that a person was not in their office when a crime occurred, but rather at the location of the crime. In many cases the first stage in evaluating credibility is gathering this type of confirmatory evidence.

This is the proverbial "circumstantial" evidence and is often not enough within itself to make final inferences about lying. However, it can rule people out of contention, making it necessary to look elsewhere for a plausible suspect. Alternatively it can focus the interest of law enforcement officials on a particular suspect and lead them to adopt interrogation methods designed to elicit confessions. Ruling people out of contention at an early stage is particularly important because this encourages the police to look more broadly for the likely criminal, instead of focusing upon an initial suspect.

4.2 Verbal signs of deception

If objective facts do not clearly demonstrate whether a person is telling the truth, it is necessary to rely on psychological tools of credibility assessment. One approach is analyzing what a person says and the way they say it, i.e., their verbal behavior. The psychological research in this area yields a mixed verdict. Reviews of research on this technique generally suggest that methods of lie detection that rely on analysis of verbal behavior make too many errors to be admitted into courts (Steller & Koehnken,

1989). For example, using verbal behavior DePaulo and DePaulo (1989) were unable to find a single significant difference between trustful and deceptive students.

On the other hand, some more recent studies point to a number of promising leads for future efforts to detect lying using verbal behavior. An extensive review by DePaulo et al. (2003) identified several verbal signs that research suggests might be helpful. Liars spend less time talking, tend to provide fewer details, are less likely to include spatial and temporal information, provide equal detail for recent and older events, have longer speech latency, engage in more silent pauses, and have more speech hesitations. Lies are also less logical and plausible. In other words, there is evidence of some behaviors related to speech that might help someone differentiate the truth from a lie. Similarly, Vrij (2008) suggests that verbal cues associated with lying are clearer than are nonverbal cues, so investigators are better off paying attention to speech than they are to nonverbal behavior.

Does this mean that focusing on speech produces evidence of sufficient accuracy to be used by legal authorities? As noted, researchers suggest that this is not the case. Consider Statement Validity Assessment (SVA), which is the most popular technique for coding speech. Despite the positive findings noted above, studies of this approach suggest a mixed conclusion. Vrij (2000) suggests "Although I believe that at present SVA evaluations should not be allowed in court as a substantial piece of evidence, SVA evaluators appear to be able to detect truths and lies more accurately than would be expected by chance (p. 153)."

Verbal detection approaches to assessing truthfulness also include experiments using cognitive manipulations. An example is causing an increase in the amount of thinking that people have to engage in (their cognitive load) when talking to investigators. The assumption is that it is harder for liars to manage manufacturing stories than it is to remember the truth, and that their ability to make up a story about events is undermined by having to do other complex tasks at the same time. For example, an investigator can ask for a story to be told in reverse order, tell speakers to maintain eye contact while talking, and ask unanticipated questions. This cognitive model has been found to be superior to traditional interviewing, with lie detection rates of 67 percent vs. 47 percent for the traditional method.

In general, progress in detecting deception has been made with superior methods of eliciting and coding verbal responses, although researchers argue that error rates remain high (Gunderson & ten Brinke, 2019). Research on verbal strategies also informs the use of particular questioning approaches during interrogation (DePaulo, 1992), which will be discussed later.

4.3   Nonverbal signs of deceit

Nonverbal signs of lying have been of particular interest because of the belief that people may be unaware of their physical "tells" or, even if aware of them, may be unable to control them. One set of theories suggests that the mental activity needed to produce deception shapes a person physically, and that these changes can be detected. There might, for example, be emotional leakage reflected in facial activity (Ekman, 1985). Lying is also mentally taxing, which may be discernable through signs of stress.

Regardless of which signs are used, the core question is whether there is reliable nonverbal evidence about the occurrence of deception. In a review, DePaulo and Morris (2004) conclude that the relationship between nonverbal cues and deception is faint and unreliable. Further, it is not clear whether particular interview protocols can enhance this relationship (Vrij et al., 2019). Conventional wisdom aside, scientists believe that nonverbal cues are not clearly and consistently linked to whether someone is lying.

The scientific conclusion differs from the popular literature which has many discussions of nonverbal cues. The ability to detect people's deception through "tells" is central to many novels and movies in which the protagonist has the ability to accurately read other people. These intuitions and lay theories about them generally lack compelling empirical evidence. For example, Ekman's (1985) well-known model which uses small changes in people's face to determine truth lacks empirical support. Vrij (2008) concludes: "It is a lamentable state of affairs that professionals are taught all sorts of techniques with no evidence that they actually work" (p. 303).

4.4   Physiological/neurological methods for detecting deceit

A number of new approaches have recently been suggested for assessing the credibility of a suspect, including various measures of electrical activity or blood flow in the brain. However, the prototypical technology in this area is the "lie detector" or polygraph test (Alder, 2007; Lykken, 1981).

The polygraph has a long history with the popular literature on law (Lykken, 1981). As an aspect of the general sensationalizing of law enforcement's effort to solve crime, the media has dramatized the idea that the police can use the polygraph to detect lying. This is reflected in the label "lie detector" instead of the more neutral term polygraph. Lykken's book is titled "A tremor in the blood", while Alder subtitles his book "The history of an American obsession".

In contrast to being able to detect lies, the police have often used the mistaken belief among suspects that the lie detector works as a manipulative way of eliciting confessions, as opposed to definitively being able to discern truth using polygraph readings. Nonetheless, the image of being able to reach into people's brains and discern truth has powerful appeal, and the lie detector has allure as an instrument perceived to enable that goal.

The polygraph measures physiological changes. People have one system of emotional arousal, which is equally triggered by romantic attraction, fear of lie detection, and other dangers, such as the fear of being wrongly accused of a crime. Impact on that arousal system can be detected through changes in factors such as blood pressure, breathing rate and galvanic skin response. All of the various indicators measured by the lie detector are aimed at assessing the degree of general arousal.

A frequently used approach to lie detecting via machine is the control question approach. In that approach, possible suspects are asked about two types of questions. One set establish baseline arousal when telling the truth. Suspects can honestly agree with questions about what their name is or what city they live in. Another set are intended to provoke lying: Have you ever stolen anything in your life? Have you ever had impure thoughts? The responses show an emotional profile for arousal associated with deception, because it is believed that people will lie by denying such behavior. Suspects are then asked whether they committed the crime and their arousal is noted. A comparison of these target responses to the other arousal profiles is used to assess guilt.

A variant of the control question approach is the guilty knowledge test, where knowledge of true facts is used to elicit a response (Lykken, 1981). A suspect is asked, for example, whether the victim's dress was blue, green, or red, knowing that a guilty suspect would know red is the correct response, triggering an involuntary reaction. This test is more accurate, but requires possessing facts about a crime that only the perpetrator would know.

There have been a vast number of research efforts to evaluate the accuracy of polygraph tests. As one example, Granhag and Hartwig (2008) concluded that lying people are correctly identified as lying 86% of the time (while 14% of the time they are inaccurately labelled as telling the truth), while people telling the truth are said to be lying 34% of the time (while 66% of the time they are correctly labeled as telling the truth). This illustrates the general finding of asymmetry in this literature. The test is reasonably good at identifying those who are lying (a true positive), but also has a high rate of falsely saying that truth tellers are lying (a false positive).

It is clear why use of this technology is appealing to law enforcement authorities, who are under considerable pressure not to let the guilty escape. However, the benefits must be traded off against the cost of innocent people being accused of lying. The same romance with technology that has made the polygraph an American obsession has led the courts to be concerned that allowing its results into a court would have "prejudicial impact."

It is inevitable that at least some false accusations and false exonerations will occur in any legal system. With this technology, while there will be cases where the polygraph clearly indicates that some people are lying and others are not, the challenge is in interpreting results between these two extremes, where evidence is more ambiguous. The tester identifies a number of signs that might indicate deception. They have to decide how strong this evidence needs to be before they infer that the person is lying. From an accuracy perspective, it would be better to present lie detector results as a probability estimate, rather than as a lying/not lying assertion.

However, those doing the assessments are pressured to make to make dichotomous decisions, since it is more difficult for the legal system to process a finding that a person is possibly lying. This parallels the earlier point that eyewitness confidence is more nuanced than the simple yes or no answer that the legal framework often seeks. Pressure to make a simple judgment notwithstanding, polygraph operators do sometimes say a test is inconclusive.

More recently, there has been a proliferation of different types of neuroscience-related tests of lie detection. A review of these technologies for the Department of Defense concluded that despite the polygraph's shortcomings, there is currently no viable technological alternative to polygraphy testing (Heckman & Happel, 2007). Monteleone et al. (2009) similarly state that: "Although brain imaging is a more direct index of cognition than the traditional polygraph, it is subject to many of the same caveats and thus neuroimaging does not appear to reveal processes that are necessarily unique to deception" (p. 528). The common problem with detecting changes in physiological arousal, blood flow in the brain or changes in electrical activity is identifying a unique signature associated with deception.

Summarizing this research Simpson (2008) concludes that "the present state of the science in this area is unlikely to meet legal standards for admissibility in court proceedings" (p. 494). There is some recent evidence that fMRI technology can potentially be more accurate than polygraph results, suggesting that in the future these techniques may meet legal standards for accuracy (Langleben et al., 2016).

Even if brain scanning technologies are found to be capable of greater accuracy, there are still reasons that they may not be useful in legal settings. Researchers point out that brain scans require a willing subject. An unwilling subject can easily destroy data via countermeasures as simple as refusing to remain still in the machine. Ganis et al. (2011) demonstrate that in an experimental situation with 100 percent accuracy, accuracy dropped to 33 percent when the subject actively employed countermeasures. Similarly, studies suggest that polygraphs can be undermined by active countermeasures, such as randomly curling one's toes or counting backwards from a high number by successively subtracting seven, a task that produces stress (Office of Technical Assistance, 1983). These findings suggest that the legal authorities are unlikely to be able to extract truth from unwilling suspects using these technologies.

On the other hand, defendants can willingly participate in these efforts and use the results to support their claims of innocence. There may be a role for these technologies in eliminating suspects who are willing to be tested. However, in that role the question remains whether a suspect wants to take the risk of being falsely labelled as being deceptive. In defense situations lawyers can hide the results of a test if they do not obtain the exoneration they seek.

Polygraphs are widely used in investigations and suspects are often asked to consent to take a polygraph "to clear themselves." If they refuse such a refusal will also be known by prosecutors and may be considered in plea bargaining. Quality controls through excluding suspect evidence from decision making are not in place during this pretrial stage.

In addition, polygraphs are also used in screening for jobs in law enforcement or for federal jobs requiring a security clearance. In addition, the use of polygraphs for screening potential employees is widespread for private industry jobs. These situations share the feature that the validity of the polygraph is unlikely to be subjected to scrutiny. A person labelled as lying may not know that they failed a polygraph or, if they do know, may lack any way of raising questions about the test's validity. They are simply told that they failed a security check or that they have not been hired for a job.

4.5   Perceived accuracy of credibility assessment

The general finding is that people are not good at detecting lies. More recent evidence suggests that this rate can be improved by particular interviewing protocols, supplemented by better analysis of speech content (Vrij, Fisher, & Blank, 2017; Vrij, Meissner et al., 2017). There are also new models that improve people's accuracy in assessing credibility by using a variety of verbal and other cues in combination. Hartwig and Bond (2014) suggest that a multiple cue model is accurate 67 percent of the time, whereas their best single cue model is accurate 43 percent of the time.

An additional issue is that people are not only bad at detecting lies, but also that people generally overestimate their ability to perform well on this task. Gunderson and ten Brinke (2019) point to persistent overconfidence. In other words, "we are not as good as we think we are" at detecting lying (Vrij et al., 2019, p. 296). People similarly overestimate the accuracy of mechanical approaches such as a polygraph.

Further, people have poor awareness of when their judgments about someone's credibility may be in error, because they do not have a clear sense of which indicators have a strong or a weak relationship to lying (Vrij et al., 2006). Gunderson and ten Brinke (2019) suggest that both laypeople and professionals rely on non-diagnostic indicators, putting greater weight on folk wisdom than on empirically validated findings.

Finally, as would be expected if people do not know what indicators to consider, people's confidence is unrelated to their accuracy. DePaulo et al. (1997) found in a meta-analysis that the confidence–accuracy relationship was not significantly different than zero. A meta-analysis is a study that considers a number of studies at the same time, weights each by its validity, and reaches an overall conclusion about the correct conclusion of the literature. This allowed the authors to consider the entire literature and end up with one overall estimate of the true relationship between confidence and accuracy.

These findings suggest that the same argument can be made for having expert psychologists testify in cases involving credibility assessment as in cases involving eyewitness identification. However, there has been little effort to have psychologists play this role, because the ability to evaluate deception is considered part of common knowledge. This is not necessarily a permanent barrier, since eyewitness testimony has also been considered a part of common knowledge, and the courts have nonetheless increasingly allowed expert testimony on that issue. At this time, however, no effort has been made to make an argument that experts should testify.

One might assume that law enforcement professionals are more accurate in assessing credibility than the general public. Although there is a belief among police and judges that as experienced professionals their abilities to detect deception are greater than those of laypeople, research does not support this belief. It shows that experts are more confident (Kassin et al., 2005; Meissner & Kassin, 2002; Vrij, 2008), but that in general their greater confidence is not justified. For example, more experienced parole officers are more confident in their ability to detect deception, but are not more accurate (Porter et al., 2000).

4.6   Interviewing techniques

The ability to detect lying can be improved through training in more effective interview methods. However, many training programs today teach incorrect information, so a beneficial first step would be eliminating those programs. For example, the widely used Reid technique (Lykken, 1981) uses three components: factual analysis; the behavioral analysis interview; and interrogation. Factual analysis eliminates suspects based upon independently confirmed facts (e.g., alibis). This is followed by a behavioral analysis interview, which is a structured interview conducted with the suspect. This interview is similar to that already outlined for polygraphs. The interrogator uses the features of baseline verbal and nonverbal behavior associated with truthful and false statements and compares them to investigation related questions. Unlike the polygraph information about the features of truthful and false statements is drawn from the Reid training, manual which presents overall results, not findings established uniquely for each suspect. The Reid technique teaches that liars will appear less comfortable, avert their gazes, shift more in their chairs, engage in more grooming behavior, and seem less helpful. The Reid technique manual aside, all of these are signs that research suggests are not actually related to lying. The third stage of the Reid technique occurs once the suspect is judged to be likely lying and is an interrogation seeking a confession.

There is evidence that Reid-trained officers are less accurate in determining whether a suspect is lying (Kassin & Fong, 1999). Gunderson and ten Brinke (2019) note that "Popular police training about indicators of deception—if not grounded in empirical research—can exacerbate inaccuracy and foster overconfidence" (p. 82). Based on their (mistaken) belief that they have a identified a reasonable suspect through their ability to detect deception, police officers shift from truth-finding to using various persuasion techniques to elicit a confession. They engage in tactics such as lying to the suspect, justified by the belief that there is a compelling reason to think that the person is "truly" guilty.

There are alternative techniques for conducting interviews, which have become more widely used in recent years. One model is to strategically withhold information, rather than presenting all information to suspects up front as in the Reid technique. Research suggests that this strategic approach improves the interviewer's ability to detect lies because the investigator can better compare suspect statements to other information (Hartwig et al., 2005). In addition, this approach does not rely on lying or manipulating suspects. It is based upon a rapport-based information-gathering interview process.

4.7   Interrogation and confession

It might seem that interviewing suspects to discern the truth is the same thing as interrogation, but that is not the case. Interrogation is worthy of separate attention because of its distinct social dynamics, which are not only about determining truth, but also about obtaining an admission of guilt. Vrij, Fisher, and Blank (2017) refer to such confession-seeking social dynamics as involving accusatorial approaches. Such approaches, the most common example of which is the Reid technique, emphasize psychological manipulation (Leo, 2008).

The Reid technique often involves the use of deception, which officers are legally allowed to engage in. They might tell someone that their accomplice has confessed, or that a polygraph has revealed that they are lying. They utilize social pressure through isolation and intimidation. Officers manipulate beliefs about the consequences of confessing and try to diminish feelings of guilt and responsibility to encourage people to confess. From an accuracy perspective, studies show that the tactics in the accusatorial model result in high levels of false confessions (Meissner et al., 2014). The benefit from a law enforcement perspective is that it leads to a relatively large number of confessions, allowing crimes to be solved.

A second problem with confessions arises from the fundamental attribution error. A person who has confessed in a highly pressured social situation often later says that their confession was false. But judges and jurors are disinclined to believe them. Why? As in other settings, people do not fully understand the influence of social dynamics in the interrogation on suspect behavior. They underestimate how much people's actions reflect the pressures of their surroundings, and wonder why someone would confess unless they were guilty. Therefore, people tend to believe confessions, even when they are induced by the manipulation of situational pressures. An especially damaging situation is one in which suspects, unable to recognize the pressure that led them to confess, come to believe in their own false confessions (Kassin, 2015).

An important contribution by psychologists to the criminal justice process is identifying and showing the value of the new approaches to interrogation, which do not rely on social pressures. These new approaches focus on revealing truth as an interrogation goal, not on creating social pressures to confess. One reason for advances in identifying better methods of interrogation is that the military has provided substantial funding for research in this area. While the military has a mixed history in its treatment of suspects, in this case the goal is to identify approaches that lead to accurate information being retrieved. Studies in terror interrogation found that accusatory approaches involving coercion, in addition to being viewed by many as unethical, were not effective in gathering information.

Recent empirical studies support the virtues of rapport-based, information-gathering models. One of the most common is referred to as the PEACE approach (Preparation and Planning, Engage and Explain, Account, Closure, and Evaluate). It was developed in the United Kingdom and has been studied by an international set of psychologists. In the PEACE approach, stage one is preparation and information gathering. Stage two is engaging and explaining to build rapport. Stage three is the interview itself. This is a cognitive interview for cooperative people (Memon et al., 2010). Conversation management through the strategic use of information is the approach for non-cooperative people (Bull & Milne, 2004). Fact-finding is emphasized; deception is not used. The goal is to gather a detailed narrative and then look for contradictions within it as a sign of possible deception.

Using the PEACE model reduces the likelihood of false confessions and increases the elicitation of accurate information, because it is experienced as non-adversarial by suspects who are more highly motivated to volunteer accurate information (Meissner et al., 2014). Central to the success of this method is the development of rapport, a positive and productive affect between people. Rapport is developed through active listening, positive communication, expressing empathy and respect, humanization, affirmations of the suspect's self-image, expressions of interest, and projecting calm (Abbe & Brandon, 2014).

The PEACE model is particularly desirable because while it is equally likely to obtain confessions from the guilty, it reduces the likelihood of false confessions from the innocent (Meissner et al., 2014). Thus, its introduction does not hinder efforts to identify the guilty. For this reason, many police departments have been open to using the PEACE model in their questioning of suspects. Overall, this area of research is an example of a productive collaboration between psychology and law enforcement. The PEACE model is an example of the positive results when the goals of law enforcement align with research findings.

4.8   Managing error in law

The literature on credibility assessment points to several issues of error management that have broader implications in law and psychology. One is the question of level of accuracy. How often are estimates correct and how often are they wrong? It is striking to say that people are generally no better than chance, but there are also suggestions that newer approaches may improve accuracy. How good do decision makers need to be for their judgments to be allowed in legal proceedings? Further, error is typically manifested as an error tradeoff. For example, the polygraph is suggested to be better at detecting lying than detecting truth telling. How much weight does the system think should be placed on each type of error? And, what should govern whether evidence that has flaws is admitted into legal proceedings? Currently it is considered important to decide whether something is a "scientific finding", although it is clear that level of accuracy is not necessarily linked to this determination. It is assumed that people can manage uncertainty with nonscientific information more effectively than they can with scientific findings and this assumption needs to be subjected to study by psychologists.

5   Prejudice, bias and discrimination

American society has a long history of discrimination toward a variety of groups based on race, ethnicity, gender, sexual orientation, age, and other factors—discrimination that at times has been reflected in and supported by the legal system. A particularly egregious example is America's record of oppression and injustice in dealing with Black Americans, but a variety of groups viewed as marginal or "other" have also been the focus of social control efforts through the legal system.

The field of psychology has made many contributions to understanding group-based prejudice and racism, and psychologists have engaged in efforts to address the negative impact of these social dynamics on law and on the practices of legal authorities (Jones et al., 2013). This chapter reviews how research in law and psychology has helped to change the legal system on issues related to prejudice, bias, and discrimination, including the effort to desegregate schools, abolish the death penalty and address discrimination in the workplace. We examine how psychological research has been used as evidence, as a tool for advocacy, and in identifying ways to eliminate implicit bias from the legal system.

5.1   Stereotyping and prejudice

In an ideal world, people evaluate others from a neutral perspective, making decisions about each person as an individual, based on their statements and behavior in a particular setting. The reality of social perception is more complex. As previously discussed, people make many decisions in a satisficing way, using casual attributions to evaluate others, and putting little mental effort into tasks they regard as less important. Thus, in many social settings, people react to others in terms of their group membership rather than their personal characteristics. That approach, called stereo-typing, is a strategy that relies upon using superficial features (race, age, gender, weight) to make inferences about a person's character, motives, and likely future behavior.

If the only information we have about a person is that they belong to a particular group, we form our initial opinion of them based on our stereotype of that group. As we get to know an individual that superficial opinion is typically replaced by a more nuanced view that is based upon person-specific information. Stereotyping can seem to be a useful strategy when no other information is available, but is clearly suboptimal, since individuals do not simply reflect the average features of the groups to which they belong. Research suggests, in fact, that variance in behavior within groups is greater than variance in the average behavior across dif-ferent groups. In other words, there are more differences among men than between men and women on traits such as intelligence and sociability.

Group-based stereotyping is especially suboptimal and even harmful when defined around a set of presumed negative features, reflecting group-based prejudice. Prejudice is an example of a motivated cognition strategy that supports goals other than understanding the world accu-rately. It can be activated when people want to have high self-esteem. People can enhance their sense of self-worth by the perception that they belong to a high-status group. Social psychologists have shown that one way that such groups can elevate their status is via positive distinctiveness (Hewstone et al., 2002; Tajfel, 1974), viewing their own group members as better than those in some other group.

Social psychologists study psychological processes that counter positive distinctiveness. A particularly important one is emphasizing superordi-nate identity. This is the shared identity that the members of different subgroups have in common. Although people in our society are loyal to different racial or ethnic groups, everyone is united through being an American. Appeals to this higher shared identity lessen the impact of subgroup loyalties on behavior.

The use of group membership to promote individual feelings of high status and self-worth is a universal human tendency. However, not every-one is equally strongly motivated by this desire. An aspect of a liberal world view is regarding equality as an important social policy goal, lessening the desirability of a system based on group hierarchy or status. While liberalism supports the idea of equality within and across groups, other sets of social values, like social dominance orientation, emphasize status differences among groups (Sidanius & Pratto, 1999).

The role of ideology and social values such as social dominance orientation highlights the point that there are a variety of factors that can promote or undermine group based prejudice. Another is called realistic group conflict. People and groups compete for resources and opportunities and people recognize that in some situations they are adversaries. In those settings demeaning and dehumanizing opponents facilitates excluding them from access to resources and opportunities.

Psychological theories promote intergroup contact as a mechanism for reducing prejudice, emphasizing contacts that are cooperative, rather than adversarial, to minimize perceived conflict. When people object to immigration for fear that immigrants will take their jobs or use of collective resources, they are acting based upon perceived group conflict, which may or may not reflect a real threat. A jigsaw classroom, on the other hand, presents students from different groups in a classroom with problems that can only be solved (to the benefit of all) if the class draws upon the contributions of all of their members. An important research finding in organizational settings is that diversity can lead to more creativity, but only if the workplace culture allows diverse perspectives to be included in decision making.

5.2   Inferring biased motives

A key issue in law is whether some authority is acting motivated by prejudice. The problem of inferring someone's motive for doing something is complex because the motives underlying an action are not directly observable. They have to be inferred. If a police officer stops a person the question that person will ask is "Why did the police stop them?", which is a motive inference. The person might infer that the officer is prejudiced and stopped them due to their race or age, or they might infer that their behavior, the time and location, or other factors led the officer to believe they were breaking the law. People infer officer motives from what the officer says and does, as well as from what they are doing and the nature of the situation, filtered through prior stereotypes and prejudices about the police.

Inferences about prejudiced motivations are important in legal terms because the actions of legal authorities are illegal if they are motivated by group-based prejudice. The challenge is to go from the perception that someone is being prejudiced to the type of objective evidence of prejudiced motivation that would be acceptable evidence in a legal setting. The fact that a person might infer that a police officer is motivated by bias does not in and of itself show that bias is actually occurring.

In the past, efforts to identify prejudice were made easier by a generally greater level of willingness to openly express attitudes that show racism, sexism, xenophobia, homophobia, and a variety of other types of group-based bias. Reading novels or watching films from the 19th and early 20th centuries makes clear that demeaning stereotypes were part of the everyday culture of the time and were more openly expressed. America has changed and people increasingly recognize that it is not appropriate to make such biased comments around others. Today people in legal roles, whether judges or jurors, are directly warned not to act on any prejudice they might hold. Even those people who harbor prejudice typically realize that they should not express it openly. This makes detecting the existence of such prejudice challenging. This is highlighted by movements like the one which stigmatizes people for using the n-word.

While it would be great to imagine that America has moved forward into a post-racial society, many people in America today would dispute that suggestion and argue that, rather, prejudice has become more subtle. The most direct manifestation of this argument is the development of the idea of subtle or implicit bias. Evidence suggests that such prejudice continues to influence people's actions. Bias is a pattern of negative statements or behaviors toward members of a particular group that is based upon prejudice. Evidence suggests that bias continues to influence people's actions.

A particularly important argument is that such implicit bias is something that people are generally not aware of having or acting on. That is why it is labelled implicit. If asked, people sincerely state that they do not have any biases. The existence of bias of which they are unaware is manifested in subtle ways, such as "micro-aggressions" when dealing with people from different groups. These can include statements, such as disparaging people's culture or they can be behaviors such as sitting further away from minority group members at meetings or interrupting them more when they are talking. Hence, psychologists suggest that group-based discrimination has gone underground, not disappeared.

As people have increasingly recognized the existence of implicit bias, there has been the suggestion that we need to act in response to signs of disparate impact, an aggregate pattern of difference that is linked to a group characteristic. We need to use aggregate indicators of differential or disparate treatment because it is no longer possible to rely on overt expressions of prejudice. When people were more open in expressing prejudice it might have been reasonable for the law to rely upon such statements during a trial process to indicate the presence of bias. Today, because people do not express bias openly, this traditional approach is no longer reasonable and a new way of determining whether actions are the result of bias needs to be utilized. Legal authorities have in the past rejected looking at differences in the outcomes for different groups as evidence of bias, but it seems necessary to reconsider that approach.

An example of the use of disparate impact is inferring bias from the finding that, even if we account for the likelihood of a person of a particular race being a criminal or of differences in the crime rate in some neighborhoods, the police stop minorities disproportionately often. An examination of the policing literature indicates that the use of disparate impact metrics carries its own set of methodological challenges (Neil & Winship, 2019). As an example, people from different ethnic groups often do commit crimes with different frequency and that has to be taken into account when determining whether different rates of police stops might reflect bias on the part of police officers.

5.3   Psychological research and desegregation

Throughout the 20th century, America struggled to deal with the legacy of its mistreatment of Black people and the general lingering prejudice and discrimination in its society and institutions. This subject has been an important area of research in the field of social psychology, and has had a key role in the evolution of law and psychology. The classic early volume on this issue by a psychologist is Gordon Allport's *The Nature of Prejudice*

(1954). That book details initial efforts by psychologists to define and address issues of prejudice.

Around the same time, the historic Supreme Court decision in *Brown v. Board of Education* (1954) used psychological research to justify confronting the legacy of segregation in the schools. In that decision the Court ruled that segregated schools were by definition unequal, and ordered that they be integrated, explicitly citing psychological research to support the decision. In the *Brown* case the NAACP integrated social science evidence into their courtroom arguments and appellate briefs (Kluger, 1975), building on an early memo by Pauli Murray (1987). This research suggested that Black children had low self-esteem, linked to segregation, which undermined their academic performance.

In footnote 11 in the *Brown* decision, the Court makes the argument that segregation is inherently damaging to minorities, citing psychological studies. The Court's justification of one of its most famous decisions using an explicit reference to psychological research gave psychology a status in policy studies it did not have prior to this case. What is particularly important is not that advocates put forward psychological evidence in seeking a change in the law, but that the Court acknowledged that evidence and implied it used it as a basis for its decision.

Two types of evidence were cited by the Court in *Brown*. One type was a survey which showed that the consensus among social scientists was that segregation hurts minority achievement. The second type of evidence was the "doll" study (Clark & Clark, 1947), in which minority children said they "preferred" White dolls, suggesting low self-esteem. While psychologists were pleased that the study was cited by the Court as evidence, subsequent research by psychologists has raised many questions about the quality of that study and the validity of its argument.

Supporters and opponents alike rapidly focused on the psychological issues the Court addressed, with many opponents seeking to undermine the decision by undermining the research. This resulted in a large area of research on desegregation, self-esteem, and minority academic achievement, research both supporting and attacking the Court's reasoning. The Court responded by taking an unusual step. It decided that the arguments made were to be considered facts of law, not empirical findings. As a result, they could not be overturned by new empirical facts that contradicted those cited by the Court. This helped to settle a legal issue, but is clearly in conflict with the norms of social science. No research finding is ever regarded as definitive and the field is constantly moving forward with new findings. Legal authorities want settled law, while social scientists generally argue that "further research is needed." Interestingly, the Court could have made the same decision on doctrinal grounds, without any reference to research, in which case it would have clearly been a fact of law.

What is especially relevant to law and psychology is the explicit reference to empirical research in psychology and the linkage of equal treatment to studies of student self-esteem. This explicit reference can be contrasted to the ruling that was overturned in the *Brown* case, *Plessy v. Ferguson* (1896), which legalized segregation in public settings. That decision did not cite behavioral science research, but did rely on an intuitive understanding of human nature, as it was viewed at that time. It argued that integration was pointless, because people's characteristics were defined by their biology, an assumption of the prevailing social theory of the day. That theory, social Darwinism, argued that abilities are biologically determined and therefore largely unchangeable by different social climates. There would be no point to creating a melting pot if change were not possible.

The Warren Court of the 1950s accepted a different social science model: that integrated educational settings (a melting pot) would shape the psychology of minority students for the better. Later research has also cast doubt on the underlying psychological model of self-esteem referenced by the Court (Schofield & Hausmann, 2004). It is interesting to note that studies of the dynamics of the Warren Court suggest that footnote 11 was added at the last minute (Kluger, 1975). It can most reasonably be seen as a post hoc effort at legitimating the decision, rather than as a determining factor during deliberations. On the other hand, presenting this social science evidence was central to the strategy of the NAACP and Kenneth Clark testified at the initial trial in the *Brown* case.

The *Brown* decision was historic and led to a new era of race relations, but its impact on the field of law and psychology was mixed. On the one hand, it provided heightened visibility to psychological research. However, it also associated psychology with progressive action on civil rights, including controversial policies such as school busing, undermining the idea that social science is politically neutral. For decades after this decision the *Brown* decision was cited by politicians in discussions about whether the government should fund social science research, labelled by some as "advocacy."

It is also important to note that the Supreme Court ignored a brief by psychologists about how to implement the decision (i.e., outlining remedies). Psychologists called for requiring an immediate and unequivocal change to lessen public resistance to the remedies imposed. In a follow-up case to *Brown*, often called *Brown v. Board of Education II* the Court told states to move forward with all deliberate speed (*Brown v. Board of Education II*, 1955). This framing of implementation provided cover for efforts to delay change and led to decades of efforts to undermine desegregation and to widespread social conflict in both the South and in northern cities. When psychologists are criticized for the social conflict resulting from *Brown*, they point out that their suggestions for how to avoid that conflict were ignored by the Court.

5.4   Bias and capital punishment

During the latter half of the 20th century, racial prejudice, law, and psychology intersected in a series of decisions on capital punishment. This is relevant to prejudice because those being executed were disproportionately non-White. There had long been majority popular support for the death penalty in the United States, but in the 1960s that support declined to a minority position, leading to the possibility that the death penalty would be abandoned. At that time the Supreme Court considered the constitutionality of executions in *Furman v. Georgia* (1972).

In the *Furman* decision Justice Marshall suggested that the justification for capital punishment was to deter crime, and so turned debate over the death penalty into a discussion among psychologists and other social scientists about whether empirical research evidence demonstrates that the death penalty deters crime. After decades of research and several National Academy of Science panels, the consensus of social scientists is that there is no evidence to suggest that the death penalty has a deterrent effect. However, social science cannot definitively show that the death penalty does not act as a deterrent, only that there is no evidence of a causal relationship. The repeated failure to find an association does not prove that no association exists. From the perspective of legal authorities, the unwillingness of social scientists to say conclusively that the death penalty has no deterrent effect has hindered efforts to abolish the death penalty. Those supporting the death penalty have thus continued to raise the argument that it acts as a deterrent to murder, in the ongoing absence of evidence to support that position (Weisberg, 2005).

As the debate on research methods and findings continued, public support for capital punishment rose as high as 80 percent in the 1980s and '90s. It has since declined again to 56 percent in a recent Gallup poll (2019). Psychological research has been important in helping to understand why the public supports capital punishment. While often presented as being a response to fear of crime, psychological research shows that support for punitive public policies like the death penalty is primarily driven by social values (Tyler & Boeckmann, 1997). The public views criminals as outsiders who are not members of their community and do not respect and share mainstream values. Consequently they view criminals as only controllable through the use of threats linked to the fear of punishment.

Racial prejudice in death penalty cases was also directly addressed in *McCleskey v. Kemp* (1987). In that case the application of the death penalty was contested based upon the argument that it was applied in a racially unequal way. This case led to an argument about the type of evidence that the law would accept to show bias. As has already been noted, the social science position is that differences in the impact of punishments on people from different groups (disparate impact) are possible evidence of racially motivated bias. The traditional legal evidence of racially motivated bias in contrast is a "smoking gun," in the form of a clearly prejudiced statement. In an earlier era, explicit appeals to racial prejudice and stereotypes were common in trials. In the *McCleskey v. Kemp* case there was no evidence of expressions of bias against the individual on trial. However, there was statistical evidence that if controls are made for the nature of the crime, Black defendants were more likely to receive a death sentence. In addition, people accused of killing White victims were more likely to be sentenced to death than those accused of killing Black victims (Baldus et al., 1990).

The Court rejected the use of statistical evidence and decided that it was necessary to show conscious, deliberate individualized bias on the part of decision-makers in this specific case to establish racial bias. *McCleskey* is important because it created a high bar for judicial scrutiny concerning racial bias. It has been virtually impossible to challenge any aspect of the criminal justice process for racial bias in the absence of proof of purposeful discrimination on the individual level. The fact that Black defendants might generally be more likely to receive the death penalty does not show discrimination, and the courts will only accept evidence that the particular defendant on trial was disadvantaged through prejudice-based actions. As in other areas discussed social framework evidence of overall disparities does not demonstrate that any particular defendant experienced biased treatment.

While social scientists have long made the argument that disparate impact is important as an indicator of bias, its importance has been amplified by the increasing evidence noted suggesting that prejudice has gone underground, but not disappeared. Further, in line with the role of social science in many of the areas discussed in this book, the role that evidence can best play is to highlight general findings, not make comments about the case of any particular defendant. Those general findings, of course, have implications for individual cases and those can be drawn out by the legal authorities involved in those cases.

5.5   Implicit bias

The task of identifying prejudice was easier in the past, because many majority group members of our society, especially White men, held and openly expressed bias toward minorities and women (e.g., stating that minorities are lazy and dishonest, women are weak and passive, etc.). Old-fashioned racism was supported by the perception of exaggerated, negative traits within minority groups. For example, in 1933, 84 percent of White respondents labelled Black Americans as superstitious, and 75 percent labelled them as lazy (Devine & Elliot, 1995). Racism is also reflected in agreement with items such as, "Black people are generally not as smart as White people." And "It is a bad idea for Black and White people to marry one another." These open expressions of racism decreased over the decades. In a 1982 study, only 12 percent of White respondents still called Black people lazy (Devine & Elliot, 1995); today, almost none call them superstitious.

Social psychologists argue that new forms of racial attitude have replaced the openly expressed bias of the past. One is modern racism (Henry & Sears, 2002), one element of which is the denial that ongoing discrimination exists through support for statements such as, "Discrimination against Black people is no longer a problem." Another element is antagonism toward minority demands, e.g., "Black people are getting too demanding in their push for equal rights." Finally, there is resentment about "special favors" for minorities, reflected in survey items such as, "Over the past few years, Black people have gotten more economically than they deserve." Agreement with these statements reflects a continued form of prejudice, but one linked to issue positions, rather than overt stereotypes.

Modern racism is also supported by inaccurate beliefs. For example, Kraus et al. (2019) found that White Americans significantly overestimated the wealth of Black families, relative to White families. Strikingly, people's overestimates increased in magnitude as they were asked about more recent historical periods. They believed that greater progress was being made than was actually the case. Such misperceptions are not confined to the lay public. In *Shelby County v. Holder* (2013), Chief Justice Roberts argued that America has proved immensely successful at redressing racial discrimination and integrating the voting process. So much so that he argued further enhanced protections were not needed (*Shelby County v. Holder*, 570 U.S. 529, 2013). These misperceptions are an example of motivated cognitions that justify the status quo.

As noted, the problem of identifying actions that flow directly from prejudice has become even more complex as racism has become more subtle and implicit. Legal authorities have been forced to confront questions about racial bias affecting policies and practices, even when it is not openly expressed, leading to a reexamination of the potential relevance of disparate impact. If two groups appear to receive different treatment, does this reflect bias? Consider the already noted case of policing (Glaser, 2014). If police officers stop minority motorists more frequently than they do White motorists, are they displaying bias? The police often justify their actions as simply reflecting reality, i.e., saying minority group members commit more crimes. Even when evidence disputes this, which it does not always do, it is still possible that police officers believe it. So, are they acting on incorrect facts, rather than on prejudice?

The challenge of the law is to determine when to infer bias from evidence of disparate impact in such situations. This is even more complex when there is some correlation between race and propensity to commit crime, but a correlation that does not fully account for differences in police action. The most obvious argument is that if there is no disparate impact bias is not occurring.

Perhaps the most important recent advance in psychological research on bias has been the articulation of the new concept of and demonstration of the existence of "implicit" bias. As previously noted, these are unconsciously-held beliefs about a social group that shape attitudes, feelings, and behavior. Psychologists have shown that people can sincerely believe that they are unbiased, yet still harbor and act upon implicit biases (Jones et al., 2013). These include the association of Black Americans with aggressive and criminal behavior, as well as many dehumanizing attributes (Eberhardt et al., 2006; Goff et al., 2008). These associations also lead to biased behavior. When White people are presented with pictures of Black criminals that vary in the degree to which they reflect prototypically African American features, they display more punitive attitudes toward those who are more prototypically Black, even when controls are placed on what crimes the person has committed.

Addressing the issue of the legal importance of implicit bias is especially challenging for law, because it has become necessary to look for less obvious signs of bias, for example, those signs which are revealed in implicit attitude tests. An implicit attitude test draws upon psychological theories about memory as a network of associations. When people deal with a person, that person's race, gender, or other characteristics trigger associations with general group-based features that have been learned through experience or communicated as cultural knowledge. People might, for example, immediately associate a White male with the characteristics of coldness, emotional distance, competence, etc. The argument is that such associations occur automatically and rapidly, and guide how people respond to others.

These associations are relevant whenever a legal authority is deciding what action to take toward a particular person. If a police officer regards a person as suspicious and stops them, is it because of something that particular person is doing or does their appearance trigger general associations connected to the person's group memberships that leads to the officer's decision to stop them? When a prosecutor, judge, or jury makes a decision about the fate of a defendant, are they judging the nature of their crime or do they make associations with general characteristics that they connect to that person's race, gender, or age? Acting toward a person based upon features of the groups they belong to is illegal, but how can that influence be assessed in a particular case?

Psychologists have helped to change legal culture, gradually gaining widespread acceptance among legal actors for the idea that implicit bias exists and needs to be addressed in some way by legal authorities (Redfield, 2017). In recent years many court systems and police departments have developed training programs to combat its effects.

In an earlier chapter remedies for eyewitness and credibility detection errors were discussed. The same two approaches outlined in those cases are relevant here. One approach is to change the structure of legal procedures to minimize the likelihood that bias will be involved. A structural change often suggested is blinding (Robertson & Kesselheim, 2016). In a blind procedure race is omitted from the available information. A case record, for example, could be evaluated without information about the suspect's racial group membership. These procedures are widely used in employment applications and with student admissions.

A second approach is to educate people about their biases and ask them to put them aside so that they do not influence their decisions. This approach is widely used in implicit bias training programs for police officers, prosecutors, judges and in many private sector corporations for managers. They are also used with jurors. The assumption of such programs is that once people understand the idea of bias they will be more aware of its possible role in their decisions and better able to factor out such influences when making decisions.

Consider first the idea of making people aware of the need not to act upon their biases. An important use of the implicit bias literature is to encourage the development of legal procedures for managing bias by making their existence manifest and encouraging people to put them aside. Under the current system a judge asks prospective jurors to put aside their prejudices, both as a general admonition in all cases to decide based upon the evidence, and whenever pretrial jury selection questioning (voir dire) suggests the possibility that a particular juror might have a bias relevant to the case in question. Jurors are also asked to ignore anything they learned through prior publicity, and to disregard prejudicial remarks made during the trial. This presumes an awareness that one has biases or is aware of extra-judicial information, and a willingness and an ability to put them aside.

As at many points in this discussion, with biases the key legal issue is not whether people have biases or know extra-evidentiary information about a case. The issue is whether people can and/or will effectively separate those biases or that information from their decision-making. The evidence raises serious questions about whether jurors can, in fact, act in this way (Green & Hagiwara, 2020; Ruva & Coy, 2020; Steblay et al., 1999, 2006). Thus, psychology is raising a fundamental challenge to the way the legal system manages this type of extra-evidentiary impact upon legal decisions.

Jurors are not the only actors in the legal system who may harbor unconscious bias. The same may be true of judges, prosecutors, parole boards, and probation/parole officers. All of these actors are asked to put aside their biases, and the question of whether they can or will disregard them is central to whether the legal system provides fair and equal treatment. Our legal system is based upon the premise that people will be judged for their individual actions, not in terms of group characteristics which are outside their control such as their race, gender, or age.

If the legal system has a problem with implicit bias, what can be done about it? This issue was addressed in a recent volume from the American Bar Association (ABA), *Enhancing Justice: Reducing Bias* (Redfield, 2017). The volume draws heavily on the suggestions of psychologists about combating bias, emphasizing efforts at de-biasing. The de-biasing approach involves recognizing and suppressing implicit responses. People must first be made aware of their biases and then must be motivated to suppress them in their behavior. This puts responsibility on the individual actor, based on the assumption that a motivated decision-maker can recognize and control their biases, once they are made aware of them. The focus on individual actors taking responsibility for addressing bias fits well with key aspects of the legal system. Law and psychology here converge on a person-focused effort to combat bias.

An example of the effort to manage bias is provided by the already discussed shooter task. This is an experiment in which people have to decide whether to shoot at Black/White suspects who are holding a gun or a cell phone. Research finds that college student shooting decisions are shaped by bias. Through training, however, police officers are able to interrupt the impact of their stereotypes on their shooting decisions, exercising cognitive control (Correll et al., 2014). The important point is that this training does not try to eliminate stereotypes, but rather to break their connection to behaviors.

Other psychologists emphasize the psychological finding that people's actions are powerfully shaped by the situational forces they operate within. Payne et al. (2017) approach the problem of bias from the situational aspect of association, noting that implicit biases are highly contextual. They show that the degree to which behavior changes due to biases depends upon the situation. Rather than being a long-term, stable attitude that shapes how people act across circumstances, the manifestation of bias is dependent upon context.

These authors suggest that it would be more helpful to focus on the situations which lead to the heightened accessibility of undesirable associations, than on whether people have such biases. Researchers should try to identify situations in which implicit biases shape behavior and work on changing the situation, instead of trying to change people.

Consistent with this perspective, Swencionis and Goff (2017) identified circumstances in which police officers are particularly likely to make biased decisions. As an example, they point out that people are more likely to act on implicit bias in ambiguous situations. A solution is to change the situations in which people work to make them more structured, and to use checklists and requirements for accountability to remove ambiguity.

The ABA Commission on Women in the Legal Profession recently released a report, *You can't change what you can't see* (2018), which uses a situational approach in addressing bias. The report argues for a strategy based upon "bias interrupters." Metrics are used to identify situations where bias exists (via findings of disparate impact) and to assess the effectiveness of counter measures in those situations. Where bias occurs, interrupt it. If that interruption works, disparate impact should diminish or disappear. In other words, this report sees identifying and changing situations as the key to reducing bias and recommends using empirical findings to guide such efforts. The report offers a variety of suggestions about how to interrupt bias and combines situational analysis with other efforts to control bias-motivated behaviors.

5.6   Testing

Testing is another way to counteract both explicit and implicit bias, by providing neutral, fact-based mechanisms for making allocation and advancement decisions. Testing is widely used for that purpose in employment and educational settings (Dobbin, 2009; Stryker et al., 2012). Psychologists have long been involved in test design and development. The prototypical example is the IQ test, a test of intelligence, but psychologists have also developed other tests to assess a wide variety of types of aptitude. The field of psychometrics focuses on developing and validating tests (Michell, 1999).

Tests are viewed as an anti-bias remedy because they are objective. They have been used as a corrective measure in settings where old boy networks were the traditional method of hiring and promoting employees. In so doing they have helped to overcome institutional bias that restricted access to jobs for minorities and women. Their widespread adoption in work and educational settings is often seen as a bright spot in the application of psychology to law.

In the case *Griggs v. Duke Power Co.* (1971), the Supreme Court established the idea that firms whose hiring practices showed disparate impact could defend themselves by showing that their hiring was based on a valid employment test. A test must be validated through an empirical study showing a connection to job performance. It can then be legally used to screen prospective employees. This two-stage testing process is widely used today in employment settings, and is credited with having been important in the integration of workplaces (Stryker et al., 2012). The key to such a testing approach is requiring a demonstration of a connection between test scores and skills related to job performance (Shultz & Zedeck, 2009).

Many classic psychological tests are built not around job performance, but around intelligence, beginning with the IQ test. Most people have taken some form of merit test for admission or advancement in a school, or for admission into college, graduate school, law school, or medical school. Their development and use were part of an effort to counter the means by which White males dominated most American institutions in the 20th century: using their discretionary authority combined with their stereotypes to favor people from their own cultural and ethnic backgrounds for advancement. In this arena, replacing intuitions with quantitative indicators has been recognized as a progressive step for the law (Dobbin, 2009; Stryker et al., 2012).

However, the widespread use of tests is also controversial, because of criticism that they are culturally biased and penalize test takers who are not from the dominant culture. The IQ test has been presented as establishing "pure" intelligence, but has repeatedly been shown to be linked to cultural background. In some cases such "neutral" tests have also been used to undermine progress in eliminating bias. An important example is tracking in schools. When schools experienced pressure to desegregate, one approach they used was to integrate but also track students and put non-White students in vocational track classes, creating segregation within integration. Such tracking was legitimated through the use of tests like the IQ test. When used in this way, testing can be seen as a way to disguise the operation of prejudice behind a veneer of scientific objectivity.

An example of the way that prior assumptions guide test development is provided by the development of the widely utilized Wechsler and Stanford-Binet Intelligence tests. When those tests were constructed the psychologists involved removed any items that showed a gender difference because they believed such differences did not exist. Items showing any difference were therefore considered poor items and eliminated. Consequently, while the test would appear to show that men and women have equal "intelligence" in reality the test was implemented so as to confirm the presumptions of the people who created it.

The case of testing also highlights an ongoing issue in law and psychology. As noted, testing was developed with the cooperation of the NAACP as a counter to hiring and promotion based upon social network connections. Similarly, testing as a gateway into educational settings was created to counter inclusion based upon social ties and monetary contributions.

Tests have helped to create a perceived culture of merit. While they can be tools of social progress, meritocratic arguments also legitimate a particular view of equal opportunity in America. Tests promote advancement on merit, but they also define merit, as well as providing legitimation for the existing degree of social mobility.

The idea of advancement based upon individual effort and merit draws attention away from the role of social structures in shaping access to opportunities for skill acquisition and motivation. Children growing up in better-off families have many opportunities to develop the skills that enable them to succeed at "merit assessing" tests (Coleman, 1964). Wealthy families can further tilt the scales by paying for tutoring and preparatory courses, in addition to supporting a broad range of enrichment opportunities for their children. The myth that testing measures pure merit creates opportunities for traditionally disadvantaged group members, by countering stereotypes, but makes social allocation seem more neutral and unbiased than it really is.

Testing has received less attention among those seeking social change than more high visibility efforts that involve desegregating schools or abolishing the death penalty. But it was also part of the effort of the NAACP to promote racial equality. The use of testing has been a tool of advancement away from an era in which a highly segregated work force was maintained through a combination of informal hiring practices and union rules favoring White workers. Requiring the empirical demonstration of a connection between hiring practices and job performance has motivated employers to avoid disparate impact in their hiring practices, both to avoid litigation and to prevail when it occurs. This is also a novel area of law because in this setting the courts have granted an important role to findings of disparate impact. Disparate impact creates a presumption of unfairness that an employer has to provide empirical findings to refute. While government agencies do not face similar legal threats, the use of employment tests has also led to advances in the diversity of government agencies ranging from local police and fire departments to national agencies such as the Post Office.

5.7 Discrimination in organizations

Psychological research on the impact of expressions of bias is also important in other areas of law related to discrimination. Traditionally, American society was highly segregated in most areas of life, including where people lived and worked. In recent years, people have become increasingly likely to work in settings that are diverse, exposing traditionally dominant groups to opportunities to lessen their prejudices, but also putting women and members of marginalized groups into situations in which they are a numerical minority and can become subject to prejudice in a variety of ways.

In *Price Waterhouse v. Hopkins* (1989), the Supreme Court addressed a district court decision which accepted an argument of firm liability for sex discrimination in Hopkins's partnership decision. This case is important from a psychological perspective because it illustrates the use of information about stereotyping as evidence of sex discrimination. It is also important because the Court accepted the idea that discrimination could occur through the culture of a work organization, distinct from evidence of malicious intention on the part of a specific actor.

During the trial, Susan Fiske, a social psychologist, testified concerning the antecedent conditions in the firm, which encouraged stereotyping of Hopkins and other women. This position was supported by a brief from the American Psychological Association, and when the Supreme Court made a decision, it accepted the psychological evidence as relevant to their determination. The Court did not dismiss the expert testimony, but accepted it as general background information about the presence of an environment conducive to acting on prejudiced stereotypes.

The Court made a decision in *Price Waterhouse* that was consistent with the psychological argument about the impact of stereotyping. It also made a point of not dismissing the psychological evidence, something requested by Price Waterhouse. On the other hand, the Court described sex stereotyping as something that was obvious from comments of overt bias made in the firm, e.g., "Hopkins should take a course at charm school" (*Price Waterhouse v. Hopkins*, 1989; see Fiske et al., 1991, p. 1054). The justices further suggested that expertise in psychology to testify about a hostile work environment was not needed to see that bias was occurring since there was evidence of overt bias. Hence, while the position advocated by psychologists prevailed, the Court was clear that psychological evidence was not the basis of their decision, but rather "icing on Hopkins's cake" (see Fiske et al., 1991, p. 1054).

5.8 Micro-aggressions

A second workplace-related development flows from the change to more subtle forms of bias. An important concept that has emerged along with the idea of implicit bias is that of micro-aggressions (Sue, 2010; Williams, 2020). Micro-aggressions are subtle expressions of prejudice through snubs, slights, and verbal remarks, both intentional and unintentional. They include micro-insults, such as interrupting women when they speak or sitting further away from a minority group member in an interaction, and micro-invalidations, a denial of a person's distinct identity, or unique ideas and experiences. A particularly important characteristic of such micro-aggressions is that they are often unconscious manifestations from the perspective of the harm-doer. While they are found to cause psychological distress to those who experience them, they are not necessarily based on an intentional desire to hurt others.

Irrespective of the intention of the actor, studies show that micro-aggressions do cause psychological harm to their victims. Demonstrating behavioral harm, for example, leading a victim to commit suicide or quit their job, has been more difficult in many contexts, but some studies do point to such harm, for example, through the impact of anxiety and stress upon victims' health outcomes (Lee & Hicken, 2016; Thurston et al., 2019). Research findings demonstrate that micro-aggression can even lead to an impact on victims that is as strong as are traditional experiences of overt discrimination (Liu & Quezada, 2019). That impact can occur through both a person's own personal experiences, or via group or institutional level policies and practices.

Despite the evidence of harm, studies of court decisions in discrimination cases suggest that plaintiffs in such cases are unlikely to prevail unless they make a claim of overt prejudice (King et al., 2011). Eyer (2012) argues that juries and judges continue to apply the type of smoking-gun test found in traditional law, looking not at whether the plaintiff suffered damages (psychological or behavioral), but at whether they believe the behavior on the part of the defendant was motivated by biased intentions.

Eyer argues that the reason that people have trouble winning discrimination cases is that their argument runs counter to the widespread belief among Americans that advancement in our society is based on merit. This belief is called contest mobility by sociologists (Parkin, 1971) and it reflects the important role that the belief in opportunity plays in Americans' views about the nature of American society. Sometimes called the Horatio Alger myth, it plays a role in legitimating markets, and reassures people by promoting the idea that opportunities for advancement are open within American society. It also supports legal and political stability, because when people are not successful, they hold themselves responsible, rather than blaming society for failing to provide them with fair opportunities (Tyler & McGraw, 1986). When a person challenges this ideology by arguing that they suffered because of discrimination, it is psychologically threatening to others. It undermines the argument that mobility is based on merit and, therefore, raises questions in their minds about whether they can advance if they work hard. It suggests that there are barriers to advancement that are linked to ascribed features (gender, race), rather than what people do (achieved characteristics).

Leaving aside whether mobility in America is actually based on merit, Eyer (2012) suggests that jurors and judges alike are resistant to accepting claims of discrimination by individuals or groups because they evaluate them through their lens of "meritocratic" cultural beliefs. Eyer further suggests that one solution is to frame legal claims in terms of individual harm, rather than making a discrimination argument, so as not to trigger this set of cultural values.

6 Criminal responsibility

In earlier chapters we discussed the role of psychology in shaping the search for truth. A separate issue is the search for an appropriate, just response to criminal wrongdoing (Slobogin, 2007). Once a judge or jury has established their view on the facts of a case, they must decide whether the person is criminally responsible for the crime before deciding how much and in what way to punish a wrongdoer. An evaluation of a person's "culpability/responsibility" for criminal conduct occurs prior to whether and how severely people decide to punish the defendant for their crimes.

From a legal perspective criminal responsibility requires the presence of a harmful act, committed voluntarily (actus reus), indicating a guilty mind (mens rea) (Beattey & Fondacaro, 2017; Gordon & Fondacaro, 2017). People look back at an action and infer what the defendant was or was not thinking at the time. It is typically presumed that their action was voluntary, except in circumstances that will be outlined here.

Psychologists study a variety of issues related to perceptions of responsibility (Slobogin, 2006, 2007). The key initial point is that, while an important factual question in a criminal case is determining what the defendant did and the circumstances around their crime, the fact that someone broke a law does not mean that they will be viewed as legally responsible for their conduct and punished by society. People who are intellectually disabled or insane may not be viewed as able to form the level of criminal intent needed to be seen as legally responsible. Only when a person is viewed as having a certain level of culpability/responsibility can they be held legally responsible for their conduct and sanctioned. Even under these conditions a defendant may be held to be less than fully responsible for their actions because their capacities are diminished in some way. Their conduct may be excused or justified in some way and their punishment mitigated.

One defense is acknowledging committing the crime, but denying being criminally responsible for the act. This involves giving an explanation that might mitigate a judgment of legal responsibility, and thus reduce punishment. It is important to distinguish between an argument that denies criminal responsibility entirely by denying capacity, such as insanity, and an argument that acknowledges capacity and, hence, possible responsibility, while providing reasons not to hold a person fully criminally responsible for the crime.

6.1   Mental illness as a defense

The classic case of denying responsibility is pleading insanity. Insanity means that a person is not criminally responsible for their conduct because they lack the cognitive and motivational elements that a person needs for legal culpability. Insanity is a retrospective judgment about functioning at the time of the crime. It differs from competence, which is an evaluation made at the time of trial (Poythress et al., 2002). A person who is not competent is not tried. This assessment focuses on whether the person understands the nature of the charges against them and whether they can assist in their own defense.

The legal system is interested in a clear-cut determination of insanity. Psychology recognizes that many people exhibit some symptoms associated with poor mental health and that those may or may not lead to a lack of culpability. Mental health/disorder is only a predicate requirement for criminal culpability. You can be seriously mentally ill with schizophrenia but if you know right from wrong and knew what you were doing an insanity defense would not succeed. Plenty of mentally ill people are convicted. Insanity is a legal construct not a psychological one. Insanity is judged by the jury or judge in a trial and not by the psychological expert.

The number and type of symptoms occur on a multidimensional continuum, making it hard to decide when a person reaches some threshold of "insanity." Studies estimate that around 20 percent of the general American population has symptoms of at least one diagnosable mental disorder, while around 4 percent exhibits serious symptoms of mental illness (National Alliance on Mental Illness, 2020). The challenge for the legal system is to define a threshold above which a person meets a criterion of legal insanity, when in the real world, the number and intensity of the symptoms people exhibit vary widely.

One way to diagnose mental illness is by using tests such as the Minnesota Multiphasic Personality Inventory. These tests compare a target person to the features of known groups, usually involving comparison to prisoners or people in mental hospitals. Another approach is to use the *Diagnostic and Statistical Manual of Mental Disorders* (DSM), a manual of symptoms maintained by the American Psychological Association. This manual emphasizes behavioral and verbal symptoms that define psychological syndromes (i.e., constellations of symptoms joined together by connection to a common root cause). These signs of a syndrome are independently developed out of theories about a particular mental illness. This diagnostic approach also recognizes that people who exhibit symptoms may not feel that they have a problem, so acknowledgment of being mentally ill is not a key factor in whether experts label a person mentally ill.

A syndrome has two central features: (1) definable symptoms which are specified in advance and linked to psychological theories; and (2) evidence that these symptoms are exhibited in multiple situations and over time. The DSM also emphasizes the importance of behavioral indicators of disorder.

Some of the major diagnoses of mental disorder include schizophrenia, depression, mania/bipolar disorder, and antisocial personality disorder. An example of antisocial personality disorder is being a sociopath. This diagnosis has a set of common recognizable symptoms developing out of psychological theory, and the existence of this form of disorder is supported by evidence that these symptoms have been seen across situations and over time.

Antisocial personality disorder is of particular concern to the legal system, because it is associated with repeated violence and criminal behavior. A high proportion of lifelong criminals display this particular syndrome, which includes psychopathy and sociopathy. Psychopathy is hard to cure, because it is linked to inherited factors. Sociopathy is more strongly connected to early childhood social experience, and is more treatable.

The MacArthur Violence Risk Assessment Study found that the lifetime frequency of violence among those ranked as not mentally ill using the

DSM criteria is around 2 percent. The lifetime frequency of violence among those ranked as mentally ill is around 11–13 percent. This rate is similar among those with different forms of mental illness. In comparison, the rate of lifetime violence among alcoholics is 25 percent and drug abusers around 35 percent. These studies emphasize that, while mental illness is linked to higher levels of violence, it is not the best predictor. Situational factors, such as the presence of alcohol or drug use are the best predictors of violence in a particular set of circumstances (Monahan, 2007, 2013). Demographic factors such as age and gender are also important.

These findings highlight an important and recurrent point in this examination of law and psychology: situational factors matter (Hanson & Yosifon, 2004–05). It is not only or sometimes even primarily people's character and motives that shape what they do. As in other areas we have discussed, situational forces matter but people are generally unaware of the role of situations in shaping their behavior. A highly visible example of the underestimated impact of situational forces is provided by the classic Milgram experiment (1974). In this study an authority told participants to take actions that they believed harmed another person. In many cases people followed these instructions. Later both the participants and observers held the participant responsible for the harm. Neither the participants nor observers were sufficiently aware of the power of social pressure, so both groups assigned responsibility for engaging in the behavior to the decisions of the actor. Even the actor held themselves responsible.

6.2   Legal insanity

As a legal rather than psychological concept, insanity means a person is not legally responsible for crimes they commit because, due to mental illness, they are not aware of what they are doing or are unable to understand that their actions are wrong. Exact legal definitions of criminal insanity and the tests for it vary by jurisdiction.

The classic test of insanity is the M'Naghten rule (1843), which considers whether the person is "laboring under such a defect of reason, from disease of the mind, as not to know the nature and quality of the act he was doing, or, if he did know it, that he did not know he was doing what was wrong" (FindLaw, criminal/criminal-procedure/the-m-naghten-rule. html). This is cognitive impairment.

Today the law generally acknowledges that there are the two possible reasons that a law might define conduct as due to insanity, including the classic test of cognitive impairment. In practice there is wide variation if whether particular states actually do define insanity in each way. Supreme Court has recently allowed restricting insanity to the narrow grounds of cognitive incapacity (*Kahler v. Kansas*, 2020), which is only one of these possible reasons.

The first possible standard is the earlier test of cognitive incapacity, or in lay terms, "not knowing right from wrong." The second is motivational/ volitional impairment, which is having an "irresistible impulse." This involves knowing a behavior is wrong, but being unable to stop one's actions. Examples of irresistible impulse include pedophilia (sex involving children), kleptomania (stealing), and pyromania (fire setting). The 1962 American Law Institute standards of insanity used these two concepts: lacking the ability to appreciate wrongness (cognitive impairment) or being unable to conform one's conduct to the requirements of law (volitional impairment).

The criteria for volitional impairment have been criticized as being easily feigned, since it is hard to know if an impulse is irresistible. This is the principle under which the defendant John Hinkley was acquitted in 1981, after attempting to shoot President Reagan. Outrage over this verdict led many states to alter their laws to make them more restrictive. In 1984, Congress passed the Insanity Defense Reform Act, which eliminated the volitional prong of the insanity defense in federal courts. This is one of a variety of attempts in recent years to make insanity defenses more difficult to implement and less likely to succeed.

The verdict in the Reagan assassination case helped to foster the impression that there is widespread abuse of insanity pleas. Silver et al. (1994) found that, while in their study less than 1 percent of felony indictments led to an insanity plea, the public estimated the percentage at 37 percent. Further, only 26 percent of such pleas led to a favorable verdict, but the public estimated the rate of success at 44 percent. Overall, the public thought the likelihood of "getting off" via a successful insanity defense was much greater than is actually the case.

It is important to distinguish the public's misperception about abuse of the insanity defense from its support for the idea of recognizing mental illness as a factor in sentencing. A national survey conducted in 2012 found that 87 percent of Americans thought that fairness required taking mental illness into account during sentencing for a crime (Tyler, 2012). This is in comparison to 92 percent who thought that the nature of the crime that a person committed should be considered when deciding upon an appropriate sentence.

Because it is the original excusing condition, insanity defenses have a storied history in the law and there has long been a fascination with mental illness in popular culture. However, it is clear that in the current legal system the opportunities to plead insanity are restricted and the likelihood of success is low. This does not mean, however, that a person who admits committing a criminal action is without options in seeking to mitigate the punishment they receive. At the same time that the possibilities for a successful insanity defense have diminished, a variety of types of excusing condition defenses have developed, each with some success. While an insanity defense denies criminal responsibility due to mental defect, mitigation defenses usually acknowledge some responsibility for the crime, but suggest it is diminished by particular factors in a case.

6.3   General damage

One type of mitigation is a general damage approach. In this case the defendant argues that some events earlier in their life have caused damage, which makes them unable to function like a normal "reasonable" person.

The early discussions of general damage focused on biology and on XYY or XXY syndrome. These are chromosomal conditions associated with developmental and behavioral disorders. Some suggest they are related to criminal behavior, although research raises questions about this argument (Stochholm et al., 2012; Witkin et al., 1976).

6.4   Neurological capacity of juveniles

More recent discussions of biological/neurological capacity are informed by developments in brain science. These are noteworthy for showing that, during early life and extending through adolescence, a person's brain has not yet developed to adult levels. Unlike the biological defense noted above, this defense is linked to a specific period of time, after which capacity reaches adult levels. Research suggests that adolescent brain development renders young offenders incapable of forming adult responsibility judgments. Bolstered by hard scientific evidence, this work has gained considerable traction in legal decisions and has had a powerful impact upon the concept of adolescent responsibility.

Psychological research has articulated cognitive and developmental differences between adolescents and adults, with a particular eye toward deficits in adolescent capacities (Slobogin & Fondacaro, 2011; Tyler & Trinkner, 2018). These limits suggest that prior to a particular age those who commit crimes might be treated as having diminished capacity and might be sanctioned less severely.

Research has highlighted how, relative to adults, adolescents have lower self-control, higher impulsivity, and engage in greater risk-taking behavior (Steinberg, 2007). Adolescents are more sensitive to immediate rewards than adults (Galvan et al., 2006), a distinction which has been used to explain potentially harmful reward-seeking behavior among adolescents, such as drug and alcohol use, risky sexual behavior, and committing crimes (Bonnie & Scott, 2013). Further, adolescents are especially susceptible to peer influence (Chein et al., 2011). Taken together these results have the legal implication that the drastic increase in criminal behavior found during adolescence is due in part to the still developing adolescent brain (Scott & Steinberg, 2010; Slobogin & Fondacaro, 2011; Steinberg, 2014).

Policy-makers and lawyers use this cognitive and neurological evidence to argue that adolescents should not face the same legal penalties as adults, even when committing "adult" crimes (see Cohen et al., 2016, for a review). The most prominent of these policy advances are court cases that preclude the death penalty for crimes committed under the age of 18 (*Roper v. Simmons*, 2005). The same evidence has also been used in the growing movement to raise the age of criminal prosecution in adult courts in some states. The challenge has been that the crimes committed by adolescents, while potentially due to underdevelopment, for this very reason sometimes represent examples of extreme and senseless violence toward others.

Neurology also provides an explanation for why diversion away from criminal punishment makes sense for juveniles. Rehabilitation is particularly likely to be successful with juveniles because they are still developing (Cullen, 2013; Lipsey & Cullen, 2007). So, psychologists suggest that the best solution for most juvenile offenders is to divert juveniles out of the juvenile justice system and focus upon rehabilitation, not criminalization and punishment.

This arena is one in which psychology has evidence that legal authorities view as compelling, so it has had a powerful impact on law. The results of research on adolescent biological, cognitive, and social capacities have been very persuasive to judges and other legal authorities. In that process the details of such findings have sometimes been lost to policy-makers (Aronson, 2007). An example is the complaint by Justice Scalia that the Court considered neuroscience and decided that juveniles are capable of making abortion decisions but not capable of taking adult responsibility for their criminal conduct. He argued that a double standard was at play. In fact, neuroscience evidence suggests that adolescents reach adult levels of decision-making capacity at a relatively early age, but struggle into their twenties with the issues of impulse control, susceptibility to peer influence and short-term/long-term risk balance issues which are key to whether people commit crimes.

It is important to recognize that this is a time-limited argument, since adolescents evolve into adults. The question of when they have the capabilities of adults is still open. While legal authorities have responded to psychological evidence by raising the age at which a person becomes a legal adult, almost none have considered moving that age of adulthood to 25–26, the time when psychologists typically say that brain development reaches adult levels. It is not clear how to use brain science to decide when a person is an adult. The research has not systematically mapped key signs of adult capacity—and, therefore, adult criminal responsibility—to either chronological age or indicators of brain size or brain functioning. We know how the different systems develop across time, but connecting those developments to some estimate of "adult-like" judgment capacity is a project not yet completed.

6.5   Rotten social background

Another general defense argues not for a particular developmental period, but for a life-long disability flowing from growing up in a toxic environment (Robinson, 2011). Delgado (1985) refers to this as a social adversity defense, or the impact of a "rotten social background." Variations on this general model include urban psychosis (the impact of poverty and violence), Black rage (the impact of racism), and television intoxication (Falk, 1996). The general factor uniting these defenses is that they are not linked to a specific event, but rather to general exposure to a particular set of toxic environmental conditions. Robinson (2011) refers to this exposure as a form of coercive indoctrination. Delgado (1985) suggests that these defenses should be considered to mitigate punishment. To date they have not yet been acknowledged very often by the law.

Monterosso et al. (2005) compared the weight of testimony about childhood abuse to that of evidence of physiological impairment (chemical imbalance) as factors mitigating perceived culpability among lay decision-makers. They found that physiological factors were more likely to exonerate actors of criminal responsibility. On the other hand, Schweitzer et al. (2011) found that showing fMRI pictures was not more influential in mitigating perceived responsibility than was simple verbal testimony about neuroscience. They further found that neuroscientific testimony had no greater impact on jurors than did clinical evidence about a defendant's earlier life.

Finally, in addition to general arguments of environmental damage there are situation-specific examples of diminished capacity. One clear example is the impact of drugs or alcohol upon violence. As has been noted, studies on violence show that in a particular situation the risk of violence is multiplied by the presence of either drugs or alcohol (Monahan, 2013). As has been noted, recognizing situational pressures upon individual behavior poses particular challenges for the law. The law focuses on the idea of holding people responsible for their actions. Within that framework, acknowledging the role of situational forces in motivating people's actions raises fundamental questions about how to allocate responsibility when those forces are shaping behavior.

A more complex case arises where diminished capacity due to situational forces can be viewed as self-inflicted (Yaffe, 2012). A person chooses to drink or use drugs, so their subsequent diminished capacity is different from the case of an adolescent whose brain has not fully developed no matter what behaviors they do or do not engage in. In reality of course, these issues are seldom unrelated, since a history of living in poor environments is a typical antecedent to adult drug and alcohol abuse.

A problem with responding to crimes from a situational perspective is the disconnect between the fact that a person is typically on trial for some set of actions, and the suggestion that their actions flow from situational forces. If situational forces were consistently held responsible, legal actors would have to reconceptualize how they respond to harm. So, for example, if alcohol or drugs cause violence, the solution could be legislative, i.e., to change the law to restrict availability. But in the immediate moment a judge or jury would likely not find this a satisfying response to a crime committed by a person. A particular person is on trial, not a particular situation. Decision-makers want to respond to crimes by taking some action that seeks to restore moral balance in social relations, and that traditionally means holding the perpetrator responsible and sanctioning that person (Darley & Pittman, 2003). Blaming a situation does not address the psychological desire for closure following a crime, something that happens when people feel that the criminal has been punished (Bandes, 2009; Murphy, 2003).

However, the question of what leads to closure remains very much open. As Fondacaro & O'Toole (2015, p. 498) note:

> More research on this topic is clearly needed to identify the extent to which public perceptions based on common sense about closure is supported by empirical evidence. However, just as the criminal justice system is a narrow tool for preventing crime, it is likely to be a narrow tool for bringing about the complex cognitive and emotional integration involved in obtaining closure after a threatening and traumatic event (Kanwar, 2002).

An important distinction among these general causes of diminished capacity is whether there is reason to believe that the person can change. A rotten social background argument could suggest that diminished capacity is permanent, while a situational defense suggests the possibility of change by changing the situation. The adolescent development argument suggests simply leaving teenagers alone to mature. Whether there is the possibility of change may lead to different views about how to respond to a general damage defense.

Presenting diminished capacity as a permanent condition suggests that multiple similar criminal behaviors may occur in the future. No matter how a criminal has acquired damaged capacities, and regardless of whether it is their "fault," they pose a long-term danger to others. A diagnosis of psychopathy reflects this dilemma. Due to its strong roots in biology and genetics, it is hard to treat psychopaths, and the prognosis for improvement is limited. On the other hand, can a person be held responsible for genetic defects? Given a choice, people would likely choose not to have genetic defects, but the decision is not theirs to make. So, can legal authorities hold them "responsible" for their condition? Responding in the affirmative seems much more reasonable when outcomes besides punishment are possible. The case for rehabilitation, however, is weaker when a condition is hard to change.

6.6   Distinct values

A modified version of the general damages defense is the cultural-values-based argument for diminished responsibility. Here the reasoning is that, because a person was socialized in a different culture, they have different values and react to events differently. Larcom (2015) gives the example of revenge killings, which a person is expected to engage in when someone from their group has been killed. Monahan and Walker (2018) give other examples. These include an Iraqi father kissing his son's penis as a sign of love, a Laotian man killing his wife for talking to an unattached man on the telephone, a Cambodian eating a dog, and people from various societies practicing female genital mutilation.

The issue is when, to what degree, and for how long the reasonable person standard can be modified to reflect the standards of another culture. Cultural defenses are challenging to law because the way society reacts to deviations from the reasonable person standard depends upon people's moral or emotional response to the behavior in question. Practices can be common and acceptable in other societies, but unacceptable in our own. People who are perfectly comfortable eating a cow or a chicken may find eating a dog to be repulsive and inhumane. Other people view eating meat from all of these sources as acceptable. Still others find eating any type of meat to be repulsive and inhumane.

Allowing distinct standards in judging conduct is also an issue when designing local courts. Should these courts give communities some degree of leeway to impose their own distinct norms on their members? The contrasting view is that laws reflect rights to which everyone in our society is entitled, such as the right not to be physically harmed by another, and that the courts should provide a venue for vulnerable people when they need to secure such rights, regardless of cultural background. This may lead to a judicial decision at variance with community norms, under the expectation that the legal system should seek to enforce society-wide norms within that community.

A statewide commission grappled with the issue of multiculturalism and varying local standards in California. In their report, *Justice in the Balance 2020* (Commission on the Future of the California Courts, 1993), the commissioners noted the state's future multicultural projections. They did not endorse mitigation of responsibility, but suggested that: "While the commission is adamant that different legal standards and different legal norms for different cultures are unacceptable, in matching a resolution process to a dispute in a justice facility every effort should be made to find a process appropriate to both the disputes and the disputants" (p. 78). They argue, in other words, for a process-based accommodation to diversity.

Beyond the legal system, the issue of universal standards has also arisen in recent years in the context of social media communication. Companies such as Facebook claim to enforce a common set of standards for content, including nudity and hate speech. But whose standards should apply? With a worldwide, multicultural audience, the issue is even more complex, because there is not necessarily a primary culture to define what a reasonable person considers acceptable. Aside from the historical fact that social media companies developed in the United States, it is not clear whether American standards should govern communications across the globe.

The issue of whether people should be pressured to change their values to be congruent with those of a dominant culture is a distinct challenge for the legal system in any mosaic or pluralist society. Which aspects of people's unique culture are they entitled to preserve and which should be changed? Is society only willing to be lenient during a grace period while the person learns dominant norms, or are people entitled to continue to engage in their own cultural practices throughout their lives? This is hardly a new issue, since societies have been dealing with conflicts between religious practices, cultural differences and the law for centuries. Whether it is an issue of sacrificing animals or refusing to fight in wars, religious values and legal rules can conflict. Equally important, but less dramatic, are issues like learning to speak English.

6.7 Specific damage due to past events

A defense of specific damage due to past events can arise when the victim had previously inflicted trauma on the defendant, or even when a situation brings up trauma that has nothing to do with the victim. This occurs when the perpetrator experiences post-traumatic stress disorder (PTSD) (Berwin, 2003, Chapter 2). PTSD is triggered when memories of a past traumatic event evoke the emotions of that earlier event, for example feelings of threat. This condition is often found among combat veterans. In such a case, the actions the person takes are often directed toward unrelated victims who are simply present in the new situation. In several cases (*State of Louisiana v. Heads*, 1980; *State of New Jersey v. Cocuzza*, 1981), war-like conditions triggered Vietnam War memories in veterans, who began shooting at those around them. Their defense was that their actions were a reasonable reaction to the perceived (though in reality, nonexistent) threat they felt, and that they were therefore acting in self-defense.

The PTSD defense was not recognized prior to the 1970s. PTSD is today recognized in the DSM as a distinct syndrome, but has the particular property of not just being coded by observing symptoms displayed at the time of the crime. There must be an historical event that involves directly experiencing or witnessing a trauma with the threat of death or serious injury. Further, there should be evidence of persistent symptoms following the event, for example, reexperiencing the trauma in nightmares or flashbacks, sleeplessness, irritability, detachment from others, and numbing of feelings. In addition, symptoms include heightened arousal in response to cues similar to the original event, avoidance of similar situations, and hypervigilance.

Although PTSD, also known as combat stress disorder, was once associated with veterans and the stress of combat, many types of events are now recognized as potentially traumatic. For example, 11 percent of the residents of New York City were assessed as having symptoms of PTSD in the wake of the September 11, 2001 attack on the World Trade Center (Galea et al., 2002). Events that have been linked to PTSD include experiences in war, hurricanes, accidents, and victimizations such as rape. For example, among people who have been assaulted, 76 percent report PTSD symptoms two weeks later and such symptoms are also found among 94 percent of rape victims. While PTSD symptoms fade over time, severe traumas can lead to symptoms persisting for decades.

Another type of diminished capacity due to prior trauma can happen when someone reacts against a specific person who has abused them in the past. Here there is typically a pattern of abuse over time. In this case the victim responds not against a stranger, but against their abuser. The most well-known example of this is battered woman syndrome.

Battered woman syndrome as a defense has high public visibility due to the efforts of proponents such as Lenore Walker (1979), but a battered child or any person who has experienced repeated abuse at the hands of another could be involved. The key element in this defense is that the repeated pattern of abuse leads the abused person to lose the ability to act in ways that meet the everyday standard of a reasonable person. Essentially, they become a person who is only reasonable from the point of view of their atypical past.

Psychologists have a role in this defense, because in order to understand the victim's mental state, an expert needs to testify about facts that are beyond the common knowledge of the jury. The expert explains why people stay within an abusive relationship even if they have chances to leave ("learned helplessness") and why they feel a different level of fear than a non-abused person would feel in a particular situation. In one case, for example, a child waited outside his home with a shotgun and killed his abusive father when he returned in the evening. Why did the child not run away? This is something a jury might not understand.

The battered person defense became more widespread following the publication of *The Battered Woman* (Walker, 1979). That book argues both that unusually high levels of fear and excessive sensitivity to violence cues (hypervigilance) can be reasonable in the absence of an immediate threat following a history of battering, and that learned helplessness or a fear of physical violence in response to trying to leave can prevent a person from fleeing even when they have the opportunity. Walker proposes a three-phase cycle: tension-building, where the abuser expresses emotion and the victim tries to diffuse it; battering; and then loving contrition, when the man shows remorse and kindness, and promises not to repeat the behavior. Subsequent researchers have amended this initial model in many ways and raised questions about its use (Slobogin, 2010). The key is "whether a reasonable woman who has been subjected to the battering and abuses to which the defendant was subjected would have believed that the killing was necessary" (Slobogin, 2010, p. 112).

Psychologists have looked at the areas where jurors lack common knowledge about situations involving repeated abuse. Schuller and Vidmar (1992) studied mock juries and suggest that jurors lack knowledge about a variety of aspects of this situation. They do not understand why a person does not flee, or why they might attack an abuser who was sleeping. This work also demonstrated that having an expert instruct jurors does educate the jury about these features of the situation, and that this new knowledge leads to different verdicts in studies using mock juries. They found that expert testimony reduced the likelihood of a verdict of murder by over 50 percent in their college student samples considering hypothetical cases.

Identification with the harm-doer is a different form of battering defense. It is possible that a victim can have diminished capacity due to trauma and lose the ability to act reasonably, but respond to that by acting in ways that favor their abuser. The classic example of this is Stockholm syndrome (Robinson, 2011). In this situation, a kidnap victim acts in ways consistent with the motives of their abuser, not trying to escape and even actively assisting the abuser. Patty Hearst, for example, was defended in court by the argument that she had taken on the goals of the Symbionese Liberation Army after being abused by kidnappers from that group. Again, expert testimony would be required in this type of defense to educate jurors about the defendant's mental state following abuse.

6.8 Profiles

We need to distinguish between syndromes and profiles. Syndromes are constellations of symptoms, i.e., particular patterns of behavior, defining a particular condition. They are connected by a theoretical statement of the nature of the syndrome. For example, sociopathy is associated with a constellation of behaviors that can be specified in advance. Psychologists focus upon whether the person displays a set of symptoms defined in advance by experts as characteristic of a disorder. They also ask whether the person displays these symptoms beyond the crime situation, i.e., whether they have behaved similarly repeatedly over time, and across different settings.

In contrast, a profile is a description of a set of characteristics empirically associated with a type of person. If a group of rapists are studied, for example, the typical characteristics of rapists can be determined and an accused rapist can be compared to this set of typical features. This is a fit to a profile. The characteristics are evaluated not by their fit to some prior theory about the characteristics of an illness, but by whether people labelled as members of the target group have those same features.

Several types of legal strategy, used by both the prosecution and defense, can employ the language of profiles. The rape trauma profile is a set of behaviors associated with someone who has been the victim of a rape. When a defendant accused of rape claims that sex was consensual, the prosecutor can counter by showing that the victim displayed a typical pattern of symptoms that is characteristic of rape victims. In other words, the person acts like a typical victim and not a typical fabricator of accusations. Symptoms associated with rape trauma include reimagining the event, having nightmares, sleeplessness, denial, shock, confusion, dazed/numb feelings, guilt/hostility, self-blame, depression, fear, shaking, racing heart, and distrust (Wrightsman, 2001, Chapter 12). An expert can testify about those symptoms and explain behaviors such as delays in reporting the event, lack of memory about details, etc.

Most studies show that rape victims usually have PTSD. PTSD is a syndrome, not a profile, so these two ideas are intertwined. The question is the origin of the list of symptoms associated with a diagnosis. If they are theoretically derived and linked to a common theory of why the symptoms are occurring, then they reflect a syndrome. If they are derived empirically by looking at the signs found among a sample of target people (in this case rape victims) then they reflect a profile. Syndrome features are deduced from a theory while profile cues are induced from the features of a target group.

One of the issues that has led to critiques of using profile data, rather than syndromes, is that profiles are not theoretically based. Profiles reflect the average finding on how a sample of a particular type of person behaves. However, people are not all average, so someone who reacts differently can have their behavior misinterpreted. An example is a stoic rape victim. Economou (1991) argues that, "Existing medical data indicate that there is no typical reaction to rape. Although researchers contend that all victims experience rape trauma syndrome, symptoms begin at different times and occur in varying sequence" (p. 1172). To the degree that there is variation among victims, using a profile to infer consent is less diagnostic for people who are not typical. From a legal perspective the question is whether it is reasonable to say that to fit a profile is evidence that a person was raped, but failure to fit a profile is evidence that a person is feigning injury.

6.9 Critiques of diminished responsibility defenses

Key to a credible defense of diminished responsibility is that the defendant needs to exhibit defined symptoms that characterize a particular syndrome based on a psychological theory. These symptoms should have been seen prior to the event in question and should have occurred repeatedly.

A critique of defenses that acknowledge wrongdoing but provide some form of excuse for that conduct is that lawyers create arguments using whatever evidence supports the particular circumstances of their client, so that factors that fit their client's case such as fear of being alone, fear of being in crowds, fear of the outdoors, and fear of the indoors are described in different rape trauma arguments (Frazier & Borgida, 1992). Without safeguards, this type of testimony can lack scientific rigor and be worthy of Faigman et al.'s (2020) comment on battered woman syndrome, that it "remains little more than an unsubstantiated hypothesis that, despite being extant for more than 25 years, has yet to be tested adequately or has failed to be corroborated when adequately tested" (Faigman, 2005, p. 234).

These problems highlight the question of whether psychologists should be allowed to testify in cases involving excuse defenses. There is clearly information that is beyond the common knowledge of jurors, and the social framework perspective of the expert testimony that psychologists provide can educate them. Slobogin (2010) suggests that, in the case of syndrome evidence, most courts have abdicated the *Daubert* role of evaluating the scientific evidence and do not assess whether the evidence has probative value. Consequently, "new types of syndrome testimony will undoubtedly continue to be proffered, limited only by the imagination of attorneys and the willingness of mental health professionals to testify" (p. 124). Since almost no cases reach trial, it is also important to ask how informal decision-making by prosecutors and judges is shaped by the probative value they place upon this type of evidence when dealing with defendants.

The general lack of scientific rigor in this area suggests the need for three types of psychological research. One area of interest is the current strength of the scientific case for different types of syndromes and profiles. As Aronson (2007) notes, scientists may see weaknesses that are not recognized by legal authorities. One empirical issue that can be studied is the degree of variation in the constellation of symptoms that a particular syndrome or profile displays. For example, what are the symptoms that manifest themselves following rape? Do they fit the predicted rape trauma profile? Are they consistent across instances?

A second area in which research is lacking is the type of scientific evidence about profiles and syndromes which is currently allowed into legal proceedings. Do courts accept the more strongly validated syndromes and profiles? How are such decisions made by judges? Prior chapters have shown that the courts vary in their effectiveness in vetting scientific technologies.

The final question is what type of evidence persuades decision-makers, particularly juries. As noted, defense lawyers have shown great creativity in finding ways to suggest that their clients should have their punishments mitigated because they acted under the influence of a syndrome. When is that an effective strategy? The use of defenses such as battered wife syndrome combines scientific evidence with often highly emotional and graphic testimony about abuse.

7 Sentencing, punishment and rehabilitation

After it makes a determination that a person is criminally responsible, the legal system sanctions misconduct in a variety of ways. These include imposing fines, community service, probation, or incarceration. This chapter reviews the literature on approaches to sentencing, punishment, and rehabilitation, with a particular focus on how psychology has contributed to efforts to understand and reform the legal system's response to wrongdoing.

7.1 Approaches to sentencing

Within the traditional legal system, the framework for dealing with wrongdoing is reactive. People are convicted and sentenced for their past actions, and punishment is determined by the nature of those actions, and what they reflect about the perpetrator's character and motives. A major part of the traditional response to serious crime has been imprisonment.

Punishment through imprisonment is hardly new. Classic scholars like Bentham (1748–1832) designed prisons and advocated for their use (Schofield, 2013). In his writings Bentham discussed a criminal law system based upon the detection and punishment of wrongdoing. His perspective was not unique. From this period of classic writing in criminology to the present, the deterrence model has been central to many efforts to design viable legal systems. And, a key to deterrence is having the capacity to punish those who break rules, leading to the construction and use of prisons.

Of course there are many reasons for sentencing, and lowering the crime rate is only one of them. Traditional legal models seek a just sentence based upon the nature of the crime and the character of the offender. They operate under the assumption that punishment deters future behavior. Even if punishment is not a deterrent to an offender's future conduct (specific deterrence) or an effective message to others (general deterrence), it is still justifiable on other moral grounds.

Recent discussions about sentencing draw upon three legal models for factors that might shape punishment and sentencing (Robinson, 2017). One is derived from philosophy and focuses on conceptions of philosophically derived fair punishments, i.e., "just deserts." This involves giving every person the appropriate punishment for the crime they have committed. This is a moral judgment.

A second approach is the criminological approach which is a utility model in which punishments are determined through studies of what punishment best deters future crime. Under this approach, many psychologists are involved in making forensic assessments that provide risk information to judicial decision-makers. The focus here can be on repeat offending (recidivism), or on the general deterrent effect on others of punishing one person. The underlying assumption is that punishment does deter future crime. The role of psychologists in making risk assessments will be discussed in a later chapter.

7.2 Empirical just deserts

The last model is empirically derived "just deserts," in which people are punished fairly, but the standards of fairness are drawn from public views, and reflect public perceptions of moral wrong. This model is articulated by the legal scholar Paul Robinson and the psychologist John Darley (Robinson & Darley, 1995).

The advantage of empirical just deserts, at least in theory, is that using this model builds public support for the legal system and the acceptance of legal authority. While the state claims primary authority to use force to manage social order, the reality is that people always have and often use the option of resolving their conflicts privately or enforcing rules outside the legal system. The highly visible problem of cyclical gang violence highlights the reality that, in some groups, acts of violence are not brought to the attention of legal authorities. Rather the offended parties seek private revenge through retaliation. One of the costs of violent retaliation is that the wrong person may be targeted, and that innocent bystanders may be caught in the crossfire.

Less dramatically, people may feel that they need to resolve disputes through private negotiation or mediation (Robbennolt & Sternlight, 2012). In these forums, differences in power and resources can sometimes lead to resolutions that seem lacking when evaluated against principles of rights or substantive justice. The empirical just deserts approach contends that, if the legal system makes decisions that accord with public views, people will be more willing to bring problems to the public courts and to abide by court decisions. It is important that the public courts be forums through which people feel that they can obtain justice.

In *Justice, Liability and Blame,* Robinson and Darley (1995) use an empirical research approach to determine what the community thinks is an appropriate punishment for a variety of crimes. For example, they consider what people think should be criminalized, when conduct is justified, and when people should be blamed and punished for particular actions. In each case they compare people's responses to formal legal codes. The findings suggest a general correspondence between the law and public views, with some clear differences. An example of a difference is the level of force which can be appropriately used for defense of property. People believe that more force is acceptable than is allowed in law.

Robinson argues that there are advantages to creating rules of criminal liability and punishment according to principles that track the community's shared intuitions about justice (Bowers & Robinson, 2012; Robinson, 2017). This argument builds on the suggestion that moral values shape the willingness to bring grievances to the court and to abide by court decisions.

While Robinson directs his comments to sentencing, the argument he makes has a broader application to the legal system. It is possible to consider the virtue of using public morality assessed through empirical research as a general model of legal rules. If the law brings itself into alignment with people's moral values, then the motivation to be moral will lead people to follow the law. Research shows that moral values are often the strongest force shaping compliance with the law, and also play an important role in shaping cooperation and engagement (Tyler, 2006a, 2006b; Tyler & Jackson, 2014). Empirically speaking, moral values have weight.

While commonly shared conceptions about morality are one important factor in public acceptance of court decisions, retributive justice research also illustrates the value of having a disinterested authority responsible for making decisions about punishment. Such a neutral authority can exercise discretion and interpret rules in light of the particular circumstances of the crime. Abstract rules of justice are typically not enough to define appropriate punishment in any particular case, and interpretation of the situation is required to establish moral accountability (Carlsmith & Darley, 2008; Darley & Pittman, 2003). So, some degree of discretionary authority is needed to interpret and apply rules.

A focus on moral values fits the legal approach of a backward-focused procedure designed to look at a past crime and assess the moral character (or lack of character) associated with the criminal. Moral defects are seen as deserving of punishment, leading to a retributivist approach to sentencing. Whatever the virtues of this model, it is fundamentally at odds with a rehabilitative model. A perfect example is the success of the Risk-Need-Responsivity model in offender treatment. That model views the most at risk offenders as in need of the most social support and treatment. In contrast, a model focused on moral character is likely to view the same offenders as the most deserving of harsh punishments. And, at a general level, the idea that corrections institutions should punish undermines arguments for jobs training and other forms of treatment that focus on helping offenders.

An example of the conflict between punishment and helping is illustrated by drug policies. Is drug use a sign of moral depravity or is it a form of illness? In the past drug use has been associated with moral turpitude and punishments have been harsh. More recently the negative stigma of drug use has become lower both as marihuana use has become more normalized and as the drugs which are problematic have become more likely to be the pain killers taken by mainstream Americans. However, proposals to move away from an effort to punish drug use to a "harm reduction" model which accepts such use but seeks to minimize harm to the user and society have continued to encounter moral outrage at the idea of suggesting that drug use is in some way acceptable behavior (MacCoun, 2013).

7.3 Aligning sentencing with public views

Judicial decision-makers have more information and potentially more expertise than laypeople, and their decisions reflect greater awareness of prior cases and legal rules. This means that inevitably their decisions will diverge from popular will at times, and the authorities will have to justify their actions. According to research they can best do this by reference to the fairness of their procedures (Rottman & Tyler, 2014; Tyler & Huo, 2002).

In the case of sentencing, it is important that all parties—victim, offender, observers—feel that justice is done. Although the victim's satisfaction with the punishment is often the focus, the offender's view is also important. If the offender does not feel fairly treated, their respect for the law will be undermined, leading to a greater likelihood of recidivism in the future. And the feelings of the public, the jurors, and family members of those involved in a case all matter, because the system needs broad legitimacy.

If all the parties feel that there has been an appropriate response to the initial wrong, this provides a basis for possible reconciliation and cooperation in the future. As an example, research on restorative justice conferences shows that when the victim can participate in deciding what to do in response to wrongdoing, and the offender apologizes, victims often become the strongest advocates of non-punitive (reparative) sanctions, such as community service, and take an active and ongoing interest in efforts to help the offender become a law-abiding and productive member of the group.

Psychological research supports the general value of apologies by harm doers and forgiveness by victims (Wenzel & Okimoto, 2010; Wenzel, Okimoto, Feather & Platow, 2008; Okimoto, Wenzel & Feather, 2012) and its usefulness specifically in criminal cases (Petrucci, 2002). Similar findings concerning apologies in civil cases will be discussed in a later chapter.

How do authorities gain acceptance for complex sentencing decisions among all the parties to an interaction? Decisions that depart from commonsense justice, even if they are more complex and reflect expertise and experience, are initially likely to be viewed as unfair by the parties. Studies suggest that the parties defer to such decisions when they perceive that the authority is acting with the intention of achieving justice—e.g., a relational concern (Tyler, 1988; Tyler & Huo, 2002). In other words, the key to effectiveness is that people have trust in the motives and sincerity of the authority. Authorities can depart from commonly understood principles of justice if people support them for relational reasons.

This leads to a further question: How do authorities communicate trustworthiness and create trust? Trust can be established by explaining the procedures the authorities are using and the reasons for their decisions and by acknowledging people's needs and concerns in their explanations. In order to do this, it is important to first give people the opportunity present their concerns and to provide evidence they feel is relevant, so that these can both be used in making a decision and in justifying it. An example of such a procedure is one allowing for victim impact statements. While it is arguable whether the suffering of victims is legally relevant to sentencing, victims want and value a chance to address the court and present evidence about that suffering, as well as about what punishment they believe is appropriate.

Victims often feel shut out of the criminal process, which is largely controlled by the state. This legal procedure has replaced an earlier system of "justice" in which the victim exacted private revenge by retaliating against the harm doer. The formalization of legal procedures can leave victims unsatisfied. As noted above, this feeling has been accommodated by allowing victims to make a statement before a victim is sentenced. Paternoster and Deise (2011) studied the impact of victim statements on death penalty decisions and found that there was an influence, mediated by more sympathy for the victim's relatives and less favorable perceptions of the criminal.

7.4   Rule breaking and social cohesion

The retributive justice literature supports the argument that an important part of people's justice concerns is about maintaining societal institutions. Reactions to wrongdoing are not just about how those immediately affected, i.e., the victim, their family or neighbors, etc., react to what the legal system does. Legal system actions are about the broader maintenance of society and social rules. Rule-breaking is viewed as a threat to social cohesion, and appropriate punishment restores the stature of group values (Carlsmith et al., 2002). Evidence suggests that people are motivated to punish when they view wrongdoing as undercutting a group's moral and social values, and that they choose the type and severity of punishment to restore an appropriate moral balance. A consequence is that those people whose actions and demeanor show a defiance of or disrespect for society, social values, and/or the social status of their victims are more likely to be convicted in courts and more likely to be severely punished once convicted.

The importance of punishment for society is illustrated in two ways. First, the entire community is motivated to be sure that justice is done. When rules are violated, people feel the need to punish rule violators, even when they are not personally harmed by wrongdoing and are at no risk of future harm from the offender. Second, symbolic harm to social status and community values is punished more severely than material harm. For example, Boeckmann (1997) compared people's reactions to scenarios describing varying types of behavior. He found that people believe that collective symbolic harm (e.g., burning the flag) should be punished the most severely. Punishment, in other words, is about restoring the status of the group and group rules, in addition to restoring the status of the victim.

7.5 Prisons in America today

The United States has a long history of punishment through imprisonment. However, American society today is distinctive in terms of the large size of its prison population. For example, as of 2015, the United States had 5 percent of the world's population, but 25 percent of the total number of people in prison, representing 716 per 100,000 people (Lee, 2015). This is three and a half times the rate of imprisonment in Europe. Focusing on minorities in the American system makes the comparison even more disproportionate. In 2018 Black Americans were 33 percent of the prison population, but only 12 percent of the general population (Pew, 2020). The numbers of Americans sentenced to prison are both historically unprecedented and internationally striking.

Why did this rapid growth in prisons happen? A large increase in the prison population began in the 1980s, during a period when there was a punitive political climate, a rising crime rate, and rapid social change. Two changes in the legal system's emphasis on punishment combined to drive this trend. First, was an increased number of convictions for crimes, in particular drug-related crimes, leading to more prisoners entering the system. Second, the development of mandatory minimum sentencing laws and guidelines, including California's "three strikes" law which requires life-time imprisonment following three criminal convictions, led to the imposition of longer sentences, greatly expanding the prison population.

Scholars estimate that the growth in incarceration led to a decrease in the rate of crime. However, the magnitude of this decrease was small, with an estimated decline of only 5 percent of violent crime (Kleiman, 2009). While this evidence supports the value of prisons as a tool in fighting crime, it also suggests that the drop-off in effectiveness is rapid, and that it was reached long before the American prison population stopped growing.

In addition, there is a great deal of evidence that lengthy sentences are ineffective in reducing crime. Studies of individual perceptions show that people are more strongly influenced by the swiftness and certainty of punishment, than by its severity (Kleiman, 2009). Consistent with this finding, as we have noted, the most severe punishment, the death penalty, is not found to deter crime.

Criminological studies further indicate that people age out of crime, so that keeping older offenders incarcerated has little deterrent value. From a deterrence perspective, prison reform advocates are currently focusing on reducing long sentences, ending mandatory minimums, and changing the drug laws which lead to the need for the first two reforms.

Why does America respond to crime by emphasizing the type of draconian punishments that have led to the high prison population? Despite the link to a perceived crime wave, Fondararo & O'Toole (2015) argue that it is still important to address the idea of retribution as justice that is deeply engrained in American culture. Crimes are viewed as moral wrongs, provoking the belief that criminals need to be punished. They argue that a cultural change is needed in which rehabilitation is regarded as the most morally appropriate response to wrongdoing. This argument aside, the current discussion about rehabilitation is built around the belief that it can effectively shape future offender behavior and is therefore an effective alternative to incapacitation and punishment.

7.6   Rehabilitation

In recent decades, psychologists have joined researchers in criminology in exploring alternatives to long-term incarceration. As noted, there is a long history of the use of imprisonment as a punishment. Alongside it there has been disagreement about the purpose of imprisonment. The term "penitentiary" reflects the early idea that a prison is an opportunity for criminals to reflect upon their crimes and be rehabilitated. On the other hand, the idea of deterrence has long been a stated reason for jails and prisons, along with suggestions that prison conditions should be harsh to better deter.

The debate around whether to give long-term sentences has revolved around the beliefs that prisoners either can or cannot be rehabilitated. The belief that rehabilitation was not possible became common before the era during which changes in sentencing led to the rapid growth of prison populations. The argument is summarized by Francis Allen in the classic volume, *The Decline of the Rehabilitative Ideal* (1981). Consistent with this argument, Martinson (1974) conducted a meta-analysis and concluded that there was no evidence that rehabilitation lowered recidivism.

At present, rehabilitation is making a comeback (Lipsey & Cullen, 2007). One important reason is the argument that rehabilitation is more moral and humane. Another is the finding of research that, whatever might have been true in the 1980s, today there is ample evidence that programs of rehabilitation can be effective. In addition, research findings make clear that long-term imprisonment has at best limited effectiveness in lowering the crime rate (Chalfin & McCrary, 2014; Kleiman, 2009; Paternoster, 2010).

Programs that work can be centered either in the community or in prisons. While the prison environment is not ideal for rehabilitation, studies nonetheless show that such programs can be effective. Lipsey and Cullen (2007) conducted a meta-analysis, the implications of which were optimistic, concluding that, "Every meta-analysis of large samples of studies comparing offenders who receive rehabilitation treatment with those who do not has found lower mean recidivism for those in the treatment conditions" (p. 314). Further, studies typically find that rehabilitation program have a stronger influence than the threat of new sanctions in shaping the likelihood of recidivism.

What type of treatment works? The review by Lipsey and Cullen (2007) suggests that a variety of treatments can be effective. What shapes success is whether programs are robust, and are constructed in ways that are consistent with the theories underlying their design. They emphasize that research shows that impact is "attainable" (p. 315) with well-designed and funded programs.

More recent research based on neuroscience both supports and refines the psychological literature on rehabilitation (Baskin-Sommers & Fonteneau, 2016). This work emphasizes that a "one-model-fits-all" approach is not effective, since offenders differ in terms of whether they suffer from mental illness, what type of personality they have, and whether they have substance abuse issues. In general, "two treatments ... mindfulness, and cognitive remediation provide alternatives that may be ... effective at targeting underlying mechanisms in the brain that tend to be maladaptive or dysfunctional in criminal offenders" (p. 433).

Another important finding of research on rehabilitation is that the public supports efforts to rehabilitate. This is particularly true for juvenile offenders, but a study of the public also found that people were generally more likely to support spending money on early intervention programs than on prison construction (Cullen, 2013). A national survey of Americans conducted in 2018 (Goff & Tyler, 2018) found considerable support for various programs linked to rehabilitation. When asked how to best prevent crime 58 percent thought that drug treatment programs would be effective, while 43 percent thought prisons were effective. It is interesting to note that in the same study, 21 percent thought that police use of force could be effective in preventing crime, while 65 percent thought that the police building trust in the community could achieve that goal.

7.7   Restorative justice

There are additional alternatives to incarceration in which offenders are diverted to other processes for managing their transgressions. Many alternatives to punishment begin with a focus on those offenders who are willing to acknowledge that they have done something wrong, and are interested in making an apology or providing reparations. Restorative justice conferences are an example (Johnstone, 2011). They are premised upon the acceptance of responsibility by the offender. Absent that, their potency is diminished and they are less acceptable to victims or to society. In cases where offenders are unwilling to acknowledge wrongdoing, punitive sanctions can still be imposed.

One of the most well-developed theoretical frameworks for rehabilitation is the restorative justice model (Braithwaite, 1989, 2002). This model suggests that it is beneficial to build around the idea of a good person who committed a bad act. The focus is on connecting the person to a favorable self-identity, so that they will not engage in bad actions in the future, because they will feel that such actions are inconsistent with their positive identity. (The key concept is to criticize actions, not people.)

When dealing with people who have broken social rules, restorative justice has the goal of heightening future motivation for psychological and behavioral engagement with society. In other words, one important goal when rehabilitating people who have committed a crime is to create better future community members.

Restorative justice conferences rely on reintegrative shaming (Braithwaite, 2002), which encourages repentance by the offender, and forgiveness by the victim and others, to restore social connections that offenders have with their family, friends, and community. These parties are present at restorative justice hearings, along with the victim, and their family and friends. All of those present are involved in reconnecting the offender to their community, granting acceptance but requiring responsibility. Restorative justice procedures strengthen the influence of social values on people's law-related behavior, motivating them to follow their moral principles.

A considerable amount of research has been conducted on the impact of restorative justice. It supports the claims that restorative justice: (1)

is seen by victims and offenders as a more humane and respectful way to process crimes than conventional justice; and (2) promotes desirable goals—less reoffending, more repair of harm to victims, fewer crimes of vengeance by victims, and more reconciliation of family and friends with the offender (Sherman & Strang, 2007). A recent review of face-to-face conferences (Sherman et al., 2015) supported the finding that restorative justice conferences reduce crime relative to standard criminal justice proceedings. This effect was found to be stronger for violent crimes than for property crimes. Such conferences also led to high levels of victim satisfaction.

The original restorative justice model is based both upon traditional Maori practices and on sociological models of shame management (Scheff, 1990, 1994; Scheff & Retzinger, 1991). However, it resonates with similar psychological ideas about the benefits of building people's commitment to following social norms out of the desire to gain and/or the fear of losing approval from others of significance in their lives. Social psychologists also recognize the importance of social norms.

A review of restorative-justice-based drug courts (Gottfredson et al., 2007) suggests that this alternative procedure "directly reduces drug use and indirectly reduces crime by increasing perceptions of procedural justice" (p. 3). In commenting on restorative justice, Braithwaite (2002) suggests, "The key questions are whether citizens feel they are treated more fairly in restorative justice processes than in courts and whether they are more likely to understand what is going on. The answer seems to be yes" (p. 48).

Restorative justice makes the point that people or groups can reconcile in the aftermath of harm. This point is also central to a number of psychological theories, and is supported by research. In particular, studies suggest that groups or communities can rebuild trust in much the same manner that restorative justice conferences build trust among the parties involved in a crime (Pettigrew & Tropp, 2011). Recent studies demonstrate that trust can be built within communities that have a history of perceived and real grievances against the police through gestures of reconciliation such as an apology (O'Brien & Tyler, 2020; O'Brien et al., 2020; Pettigrew & Tropp, 2011). This is relevant both within communities where legal authorities are mistrusted, and in post-conflict societies such as South Africa. Psychologists refer to these efforts as collective apologies (Wenzel et al., 2017).

7.8 Solitary confinement

Psychological research has contributed to the adoption of rehabilitation programs, both as a means of diverting offenders from prison, and as a way of benefitting them even if they are incarcerated. In prison environments that emphasize punishments when inmates break rules the use of coercive policies undermines intrinsic motivations to follow the rules, lowers trust in the authorities, and produces angry and uncooperative prisoners. This inevitably leads to efforts to manage inmates using mechanisms that do not require willing cooperation.

One end result of a punishment-based prison climate is the use of solitary confinement. The use of solitary confinement is widespread within American prisons since it is the ultimate form of social control. By confining inmates to single rooms, and eliminating virtually all contact with others, authorities reduce not only the potential for interpersonal conflict, but also reduce the need to deal with difficult issues related to creating and maintaining a legitimate structure of prison authority.

Psychologists have had an important role in demonstrating the negative impact of prison policies such as solitary confinement. Studies by psychologists have shown that the collateral damage of solitary confinement can be broad and long-lasting. Haney (2018) reviews this literature. Research by psychologists emphasizes that human beings have a basic need to establish and maintain connection to others, and that there are both physical and mental health consequences when they cannot do so. Drawing upon neuroscience research, Baskin-Sommers and Fonteneau (2016) detail some of these consequences. They include persistent emotional trauma and distress, affective disturbances, depression, apathy, impulse control issues, chronic anger, rage, and many other similar symptoms.

Haney's work is an excellent example of combining psychology and policy advocacy. Haney and Lynch (1997) detail the psychological harms of solitary confinement, harms which have been even more strongly demonstrated in more recent studies. They then focus on the challenges of getting the legal system to view these practices as a constitutionally prohibited case of "cruel and unusual" punishment. Recently, Haney's testimony was important in leading the Canadian legal system to ban solitary confinement (McNulty, 2018). In the ruling, Justice Leask accepted psychological findings and indicated that solitary confinement poses a significant risk of serious psychological harm. This research has also had an impact in the United States in leading to arguments that solitary confinement should be used infrequently, and only for short periods of time (U.S. Department of Justice, 2016).

Research in this area highlights one challenge for the legal system: deciding which researchers to rely upon. In the case of solitary confinement, it is noteworthy that while there has been a psychological movement toward opposing solitary confinement, others have questioned this movement. Morgan et al. (2016) review the literature and argue that "results do not support the popular contention that administrative segregation is responsible for producing lasting emotional damage" (p. 439). This same review does suggest that the use of segregation is not an effective way to suppress antisocial or criminal behavior.

This clash shows how, as with eyewitness identification, it is important to look for broader evaluations of a field of research, beyond the conclusions of any particular researcher. It is thus important that professional organizations—in this case the American Psychological Association— reached the conclusion that solitary confinement is harmful, especially for juveniles. In 2017, the American Psychological Association Board of Trustees took the position that "Prolonged segregation of adult inmates with serious mental illness, with rare exceptions, should be avoided due to the potential for harm to such inmates" (American Psychological Association, 2017). Of course, this is not the blanket critique of solitary confinement advocated by some psychologists. It addresses impact on one subset of prisoners: those with serious mental illness.

7.9   Prison climate

Solitary confinement is a specific practice which occurs within the more general context of a prison environment. Psychology has also been important in demonstrating that the climate within a prison shapes behavior, often in undesirable ways. There are many aspects of organizational psychology that are potentially relevant to prisons, as to other legal institutions. Historically the design of prisons has drawn very infrequently upon that literature.

Two issues have been of concern to legal authorities: violence in prisons and recidivism upon release. First, within prisons: Order is an important goal of correctional administration. Prisoners' compliance and cooperation is vital to the manageability of correctional facilities.

Misconduct damages the effective operation of penitentiary institutions, creates an unsafe and fearful atmosphere for both staff and prisoners, and increases the costs of correctional facilities (Goetting & Howsen, 1986). It is therefore important to understand how to motivate compliance among prisoners (Beijersbergen et al., 2015).

Prisons are generally structured around a sanction-based model of deterrence. One alternative framework is based upon research, is procedural justice (Thibaut & Walker, 1975). Scholars demonstrate that understanding correctional staff perceptions of procedural justice and organizational legitimacy allows administrators to build and maintain a more effective workforce in prisons (Lambert, 2003; Lambert et al., 2007, 2010; Taxman & Gordon, 2009). When the corrections staff feel fairly treated, they are more likely to treat inmates fairly.

Studies also focus on incarcerated individuals, exploring the relationship between inmates' perceptions of procedural justice and their compliance with prison rules. Sparks and Bottoms (1995) presented one of the earliest studies to examine the concepts of procedural justice and legitimacy in prisons. Based on field work in two English maximum security prisons, the researchers found it possible to identify instances of perceived procedural fairness or unfairness, which lead incarcerated individuals to be more or less likely to view authorities as legitimate. They conclude:

> The combination of an inherent legitimacy deficit with an unusually great disparity of power places a peculiar onus on prison authorities to attend to the legitimacy of their actions. This underlines the necessity of acting legitimately in terms of formal rules at all times, and attending to those elements of shared moral beliefs existing between staff and prisoners (for example in terms of humane regimes, distributive and procedural fairness and supplying meaning-

ful rationales for the exercise of power) so as to maximize the residual sense in which prison authorities may be entitled to call upon prisoners to confer consent. (p. 60)

An extension of this study reaffirmed the authors' findings, concluding that the procedural justice experienced by prisoners influenced their perceptions of the law and their behavior (Sparks et al., 1996).

In the years since these initial investigations into legitimacy in prisons, a number of studies have been conducted in the United Kingdom and the Netherlands (see Beijersbergen et al., 2015), and findings have demonstrated the legitimacy model's importance in reducing misconduct and rule violations among inmates (Beijersbergen et al. 2015; Reisig and Mesko, 2009). Brunton-Smith and McCarthy (2016) suggest that "Prisoners that are held in prisons where there are clearer systems in place to respond to problems, and where these systems are followed in a systematic and fair manner, are more likely to perceive the prison as legitimate" (p. 1043).

Scholars have consistently called for further explorations into prison life through a procedural justice lens. As Jackson et al. (2010) note:

> social order in this sense … is vital for the smooth running of prisons as much as it is vital for any other social institution …. Without the active cooperation of most inmates, most of the time, prisons could not function effectively. Absent such cooperation, at the very least prisons would have to be far more oppressive and institutionally violent than is currently the case, with all the implications this would have in terms of the well-being of the inmates, staff safety, and probably cost. (p. 4)

The forenamed studies document some of the ways procedural justice has been found to have an impact on prisoners' perceptions of legitimacy and subsequent compliance while incarcerated. Beijersbergen et al. (2016) extended this exploration a step further, examining the relationship between perceived procedural justice in Dutch prisons and post-release reoffending. Inmates in a fairer prison were, as expected, less likely to recidivate.

7.10 Alternatives to prison: probation and parole

A particularly important aspect of the prison reform movement has been the movement toward probation as an alternative to prison, and toward earlier parole after some period of incarceration. This approach is in line with the general movement toward a view of the state's role as managerial. People of suspect character are identified, and then restricted and monitored for some period of time. However, they are not incarcerated.

Studies suggest that people typically prefer probation to prison, and consequently agree to abide by a broad set of conditions to avoid prison, under penalty of incarceration for failing to adhere to probation ground rules (Doherty, 2016). Those conditions are often challenging to meet—no association with other criminals, no entering bars, no drinking, no drug use, actively seeking employment, and meeting periodically with a probation officer. As might be expected, the conditions are often not met, and the people who violate them must then serve some period of incarceration. Such violations can be technical, for example, failing to meet with a probation officer, or they can involve further criminal activity.

As is true of many legal innovations, the use of probation has rapidly become an important part of the criminal justice system without much research on the impact it has on those people who experience that procedure. Given the highly toxic environment of many prisons, it might seem that an alternative is unlikely to be worse. Still, questions of whether particular policies and practices associated with probation undermine psychological well-being, or whether participants experience current decision-making procedures in the probation system as fair, have not been explored.

The system itself is built on giving discretionary authority to probation officers. Many revocations of probation do not involve the commission of crimes, but rather technical violations that can be applied in a highly discretionary way. Probationers may experience the decision-making process as opaque and arbitrary, and as limiting opportunities to explain actions or express views. Thus, it is not clear that the impact of probation on offenders will be more positive than incarceration, at least in terms of their views about the legitimacy of legal authority, their likelihood of recidivism, and their mental health and overall well-being. Raising these, as yet unanswered, questions highlights how a psychological perspective can help to shape the legal system's approach to evaluating and potentially changing its policies and procedures.

A second important area of prison research focuses on parole (Reitz & Rhine, 2020). Early in American history sentences were fixed based upon the nature of the crime. Over time reform movements increasingly emphasized rehabilitation, and provided inmates with training programs and other services designed to facilitate reentry. As belief in rehabilitation potentials declined prisons lessened inmate services and parole boards began to focus primarily upon retribution for the original crime committed, rather than rehabilitation potential (Hritz, in press).

Today there is a renewed effort to reform prisons by granting parole to larger numbers of prisoners. This movement draws upon many of the themes of this volume. One focus has been on predicting future risk of recidivism. This can be addressed by only releasing people in prison for nonviolent crimes, or it can involve the use of a risk prediction tool. If the question is retribution, the psychology of justice is implicated. A particular aspect of parole hearings is the possibility for statements by victims or their relatives. Hence, it is important to understand when those groups believe that justice has been served.

As in many areas in this book, social science research is important in several ways. First, because it shows that current policies do not reflect available evidence. In this case, lengthy sentences do not make society safer by deterring crime and releasing inmates serving long sentences is unlikely to impact on public safety. Second, evidence shows that there are alternatives that do work. Psychological research demonstrates that rehabilitation is possible, so resources supporting programs in prisons and support outside can be valuable.

As with research on interrogation the interests of various groups align in this arena. The public want to be safe. Policy-makers want to use public resources well. So there is the possibility of a solution that will gain broad popular support. Research facilitates such as solution by providing evidence that the status quo is not based upon facts, while there is an evidence informed alternative solution.

On the other hand, as Fondocaro and O'Toole (2015) note, reform requires an effort to address the fundamentally punitive mind set in

American culture. If the public and its leaders view criminal behavior as reflecting defective moral character and deserving punishment, then the fact based argument about whether punishment or incapacitation deters misses the mark (Tonry, 2014). A similar question has already been noted with the death penalty. Do we want to have a death penalty to deter crime, or because those who kill deserve to die? Psychologists cannot provide a "correct" answer to this normative question, but they can examine why American culture is distinctively punitive in comparison to other societies.

7.11 Positive psychology and prison reform

The topic of prison reform highlights differences in the motivating forces underlying law and psychology. In contrast to the regulatory focus of law, psychology focuses on creating the conditions under which people can live fulfilling lives with high self-esteem and feelings of value and self-worth. The argument can be made that the criminal justice system is missing an opportunity by failing to articulate a responsibility for legal authorities to promote people's psychological well-being. While some legal authorities may pursue the goal of helping people lead more fulfilling lives, for example, through the rehabilitation programs already discussed, such individual efforts are not formal goals of the American legal system. Some psychologists argue that positive, proactive goals should be more central to the design of legal institutions. The field of positive psychology, in particular, concentrates on the conditions that promote human growth and success, as well as resilience in the face of trauma.

Liebling (2004) talks about the "moral performance" of prisons and argues that they have a duty to enhance the lives of those within them. She argues that the psychological development of inmates should be one goal of prison sentences. A key to achieving that goal is that prisoners feel secure in the prison environment, and can focus on personal development. This involves respectful and decent treatment, reasonable and predictable rules and rule enforcement, and approachable staff. These features communicate that prisoners are seen as people, which is key to building trust. The central element in this work is framing prisons not in terms of the absence of violence, but in terms of the presence of opportunities for prisoners to move forward in their psychological development.

Liebling argues that the absence of the fear of harm should be seen as a beginning that creates a framework for prisoner development. The goal should be prisoners' psychological growth. In many American prisons the absence of harm is the end in itself and little additional attention is paid to the inmates' cognitive or social development.

A fundamental contribution that psychology and psychological research can make is to demonstrate that legal authorities, whether police officers, judges, or prison guards, can behave in ways that convey respect and caring, factors which are shown by research to enhance the self-esteem of those with whom they interact. The intrusions of legal authorities into people's lives, whether short- or long-term, and whether voluntary or mandated, do not need to undermine people's sense of self-respect, nor their perception of their status and standing in the community. Legal authorities can help to enhance those feelings, and have a positive impact on the vitality of communities and people within them.

Of course, as at many points in the legal system, it is important to acknowledge the challenging conditions in which many corrections systems operate. Overcrowding and inadequate resources make it hard to develop enrichment and educational opportunities. These combine with punitive attitudes that believe prison conditions should be harsh. Well-intentioned authorities have to struggle against such structural limitations. And they have to deal with their own ambivalence about treating people who have committed sometimes heinous crimes as worthy of respect and dignity. The idea of separting the good in a person from a bad behavior that is central to restorative justice is important, but moving from bad behavior to an inference that someone is a bad person is natural and intuitive.

8   Risk assessment

In an earlier chapter we discussed the challenges of determining whether someone is lying. Such credibility judgments are important at all stages of criminal and civil cases. They matter when police are questioning a suspect and when juries are deliberating to reach a verdict. Similarly, at many points in the legal process judgments have to be made about whether or not a person poses a future risk to themselves or others (their "future dangerousness"). Police officers have to make this judgment when they decide whether to detain a suspect and judges make this decision when they grant bail. It is an important consideration in plea bargaining, factors into decisions about how to sentence offenders, affects whether parole boards decide to release a prisoner, and influences probation or parole revocations.

As with decisions about whether someone is lying, at all of these points in the criminal justice funnel this estimation of likely future behavior is an inference based upon the information that actors have available. The functioning of the system depends upon such risk assessment decisions. One of the major recent developments in the legal system is the increasing use of risk analytics in reaching these decisions. A number of terms have been used to describe this process including the use of predictive analytics, risk assessment, prediction using statistical analysis, and actuarial assessment. While the approach is the same, the factors used in predictive models can vary widely. This chapter will review the development of such models and examine the role of psychologists in their creation and implementation.

8.1   Uncertainty in risk prediction

As pioneers in the arena of statistical prediction, psychologists might be expected to be happy about the increasing attention of legal actors to the risk predictions that psychologists make. Psychologists have assumed a larger role in a variety of legal decisions because they provide this type of information to legal authorities. However, within the field, taking on this role has been controversial. In earlier chapters the frustration of psychologists about their inability to shape the legal system was noted. In this case, the situation is reversed. Psychologists have been frustrated at being placed in a position in which their estimates of future behavior are being used in judicial decisions ranging from putting people in prison to executing them. In *Schall v. Martin* (1984) the Supreme Court suggested that there is "nothing inherently unattainable about a prediction of future criminal conduct (p. 278)." At that time, however, psychologists argued that their predictions are highly inaccurate. During this early period, studies suggested that of all those predicted to be violent, only about one-third would actually be violent. Thus, detention based upon predictions inevitably means that many innocent people will be detained.

Further, if a person is incapacitated based upon a prediction of dangerous behavior, they have no way to prove themselves non-dangerous. If given freedom, a person can show the error in the suspicion about their likely future criminal behavior by following the law. Someone given bail can show up at the trial, demonstrating their law-abidingness. With the managerial justice approach the person can avoid charges by showing up for several legal proceedings, i.e. by showing that they can and will follow instructions. However, preemptive incarceration denies them that opportunity. The best way to discern if a person is trustworthy is to give them the freedom to act, but that risks the possibility that they will use that freedom to commit further crimes.

Monahan (2007) notes that:

> Expert testimony predicting violence has been, and remains, an extraordinarily controverted use of science in the trial process. In fact, courts regularly remark that predicting future behavior is inherently difficult and most research indicates that psychiatrists and psychologists do not do it well. (pp. 75–76)

Monahan suggests that, paradoxically, judges take a lenient approach to evaluating this type of evidence and do not subject it to the type of standards for quality that the *Daubert* decision suggests could apply (also see Neal et al., 2019). This is the case because the psychological assessments that include assessments are not usually treated as being scientific evidence. Rather they are thought of as part of the traditional individual level assessments made by clinical and forensic psychologists.

8.2 Intuition vs. analytics

Traditionally those entrusted with making these decisions, whether laypeople or professionals, have relied on their common sense, information acquired from their experience and training, and their personal beliefs and attitudes to make inferences about future dangerousness. Psychologists refer to these as clinical judgments, because the prediction is derived from intuitive reasoning about a combination of inputs. Throughout the criminal justice funnel the legal system relies heavily upon such discretionary judgments about a person's likely future actions.

As noted in prior chapters, the legitimacy of the exercise of discretionary authority has been questioned in a variety of ways. Decision-makers have been viewed as acting upon heuristics and biases, and making judgments based upon extra-legal attitudes and prejudices. The neutrality of judges, the most visible legal authorities, has particularly been questioned (Simon, 2005). At the same time, there has been heightened public pressure on legal authorities to proactively prevent crimes. As Simon notes "During the 1980s incapacitating the dangerous came back to the fore as a justification for the massive increase in ordinary imprisonment" (p. 399). While in the past authorities were expected to solve crimes, today people believe that they can prevent them. One approach to preventing crime is proactive detention based upon anticipated risk. The combination of skepticism about intuitive risk judgments and a heightened desire to proactively prevent future violence has led to a search for alternative ways of anticipating future behavior.

One potentially more accurate and justifiable way of predicting the future is the use of objective indicators of likely dangerousness. The desire for such indicators has led legal authorities to draw on the existing psychological literature on predicting the future dangerousness of the mentally ill, in their search for empirical approaches that can be more widely applied within the context of the legal system. Today these approaches have been adopted in many contexts, and are used by police officers, TSA agents, and border patrol officers when deciding whom to stop and question, by judges when deciding about pretrial detention or sentencing, and by prosecutors when making plea bargaining offers.

Consider a concrete example. Someone has been arrested and is asking for release on bail. The judge making that decision has access to their court file, can see and talk to the defendant, and may have a police officer provide input about the circumstances of the arrest. It is increasingly common for the judge to also have as an additional input an assessment of the person's likely future behavior based on predictive analytic techniques.

How do predictive analytics work? They require a two-stage process. In the first stage, a group of people is studied. Information is gathered about those people and that information is used to predict some target behavior. This information includes criminal history, life history, demographic characteristics and sometimes psychological test results. Examples of future behavior include failure to meet with care management services personnel or a probation officer, failure to appear at a trial, or committing a new crime/violent act in the community. This analysis assigns a weight to every factor considered in the profile, which reflects the strength of its influence on one of these types of target behavior. It might be for example that the strongest predictor of appearing at a trial is age. Some of the information used in the model reflects things that the person has done, for example, their criminal history or prior instances of violent behavior, while other information is demographic (male, young). Some of the information is contemporary (demeanor, test scores) and other information is historical (demographics; grew up in public housing). This is the first stage.

In the second stage, a new person is considered. That person's score on each factor is determined and combined with the weight drawn from the prior sample. That leads to a prediction of the likelihood that the target person will engage in the target behavior. In this example the decision would be most heavily based upon the age of the new person asking for bail.

If we are considering whether to grant bail to Bill, who is a 26-year-old White man who grew up in foster care, we go to a data base that tells us how frequently other people who have the same features have in prior settings failed to appear when granted bail and derive a predictive score indicating the likelihood that this new person will skip bail. The weight we give to Bill's different attributes in creating a composite score for Bill is the weight that those attributes had in shaping the behavior in the prior sample. As noted, if the most important factor determining whether people have failed to appear in the past is their age, the model assumes that age will be the most important factor in determining what Bill will do.

Although risk analytics of the type described above are increasingly being used in the legal system, at this time there is still wide variation in how such techniques are applied by police departments, prosecutorial offices, and court systems. There is also variation in whether legal systems develop their own models to perform assessments, or rely upon tools developed by private companies, such as the Correctional Offender Management Profiling for Alternative Sanctions (COMPAS) tool.

8.3 Early use and development of predictive analytics

An emerging legal system goal is to estimate an offender's likely future behavior and make decisions based upon it. This is a proactive focus on potential harms, i.e., considering the person a "suspect" for future wrong-doing and trying to mitigate that anticipated future risk.

There is also an emerging managerial perspective, which defines the task of legal authorities as identifying suspect people and creating procedures for shaping their future actions through various forms of supervision or incapacitation. The initial entry into the system through an arrest "marks" a person as a potential future danger to others, and that predicted danger is proactively managed by legal authorities. The accused in this system often bargain away their freedom and agree to long-term supervision and restriction to avoid penalties such as imprisonment, typically before they have been convicted of any crime in a trial or even in advance of a plea bargaining agreement (Doherty, 2016). This system is not necessarily carceral in nature. It can also involve effects to get suspect people social services or employment opportunities. A diversion program can help a person by connecting them with a clinic at the same time that they are kept out of the formal criminal justice system.

Along with these trends there has been an increased use of quantitative indicators of likely future behavior. The legal system has varied in terms of whether such analytics constrain actors by establishing required sentences, or guide legal decision-making by providing recommended sentences. In either case predictive analytics provide a reference point which influences legal actors when they are making decisions. This quantification of future risk creates a role for psychologists.

The focus on predicting future behavior brings law into alignment with the long-term concerns of psychologists. The psychological literature on predicting future behavior, in particular "future dangerousness," has long been a part of the field of psychological studies of mental illness. Psychological assessments determine the nature of a person's mental illness and evaluate their possible future dangerousness to themselves and their community. There are a wide variety of ways to think about what makes someone dangerous, but the most common idea is committing a violent crime that hurts oneself or others.

Psychological studies of the mentally ill suggest that, contrary to cultural myths, mental illness is not generally associated with heightened levels of everyday violence. The mentally ill are more violent in specific circumstances, in particular when they are actively displaying symptoms of illness (hallucinations, etc.). On an everyday basis, rates of violence for the mentally ill are similar to those in the overall population. However, the cultural myths associated with mental illness have supported the creation of a robust field of prediction within clinical psychology.

The deinstitutionalization movement, which began in the 1960s, made the issue of violence among the mentally ill a particular concern. In a national shift away from incapacitation through long-term confinement, many people incarcerated in state-run psychiatric hospitals were released and the facilities shuttered, so that such settings were less available to house people. In addition, a prediction of future dangerousness became a requirement to justify a person's continued detention in psychiatric hospitals. As Monahan et al. (2001) suggest, the fear of such potential violence has been the ongoing driving force in mental health policy and law in the United States. When the mentally ill were widely returned to communities, fear of violence intensified, as did the need for a legitimate basis to justify involuntary commitment. To better understand this issue, the MacArthur Foundation funded studies to determine the risk of violence, studies that were a central support for early work on risk assessment tools.

The issue of justifying detention due to predicted future behavior has since broadened beyond a concern with those who have mental health issues. In *Schall v. Martin* (1981) the Supreme Court legitimated the detainment of juveniles who were predicted to be dangerous during the period between their arrest and their case disposition. The Court then extended this idea to all defendants in *United States v. Salerno* (1987). That case focused on bail, but led to a series of decisions to allow dangerousness to be considered in other situations, including parole conditions for sexual offenders (*Kansas v. Hendricks*, 1997), tort liability (*Tarasoff v. Regents of University of California*, 1976), and the death penalty (*Barefoot v. Estelle*, 1983). Taken together, these decisions have established the concept of future dangerousness as a legitimate justification for legal authorities to take proactive preventive actions against an individual. These judicial decisions were preceded by legislation. In the 1984 Bail Reform Act, Congress included the safety of others who might be victims if a defendant is released as a factor to be considered when making decisions about bail, alongside conditions that will reasonably assure the appearance of the person at trial.

Under this preventative approach, the legal system is increasingly relying on predictive analytics to justify depriving potentially violent offenders of their liberty based upon actions that they have not yet taken. Traditionally people are held to account after they break a rule (the reactive retributive model), although judges often reference their views about someone's likelihood of future crime when making sentencing decisions about past crimes. Formerly, judges relied on their common knowledge, not upon quantitative tools of risk assessment, to estimate likely future actions. In this respect judges and clinical psychologists have been similar. Clinicians have historically based their assessments and predictions on clinical interviews, through which they form overall intuitions about the person involved (sometimes supplemented with the results of tests). In both cases, the justification for relying on intuition is that it was formed through training, expertise, and experience. The current shift in focus from intuition to quantitative indicators reflects both the desire to make unbiased decisions, and to bring consistency and accuracy to prediction decisions.

8.4 Issues in profile creation

The use of predictions raises a number of issues, including who will make the prediction (e.g., psychologist or parole officer), how will it be made (with or without input from a risk profile), and what information should the profile contain if used in the prediction. Many types of information might be included in a profile: demographic information, history of past environments (public housing, schools), criminal justice history, and current elements of demeanor, attitude, and personality. Much of this information can be obtained from records, although some requires personal contact involving testing, observation, or clinical interviews. With archival predictions, authorities make use of data that is available from public records, for example, prior arrests.

Meehl (1954) distinguished clinical from statistical prediction, and outlined the features of each. Clinical prediction by either a psychologist or a judge is intuition, based upon expertise and experience. A clinical psychologist relies on clinical tools which may or may not be available to or used by a judge, while a judge relies on their legal background and experience, something not available to most clinical psychologists.

A statistical judgment relies on quantitative indicators based upon the past behavior of people who are similar to the person in question (Mamalian, 2011). This classic distinction is an oversimplification, and recently scholars have discussed a continuum from completely clinical to completely actuarial assessments (Skeem & Monahan, 2011).

Further uncertainty is introduced in risk predictions by the fact that most models do not include considerations of the situation into which a person might be moving in the future. In at least some cases it could be possible to anticipate the person's future environment, for example whether they will move into a toxic environment or a supportive family, and whether they have high-quality job opportunities. Further, the immediate impact of drugs and alcohol on the likelihood of violence is clear, but the degree to which the person will encounter such situational factors is often not included in predictive models. This is consistent with the general over-emphasis on the person, and under-emphasis on situational influences (long-term and immediate) found in the law (Sommers, 2011).

In theory, a decision-maker could balance these personal and situational forces, and make accurate decisions about someone's likely future behavior. However, as we have seen in other areas of the legal system, people systematically underweight situational influences across a variety of legal decisions, and have an over-belief in the role of personal factors. Identifying this error is a key type of information that psychologists can provide to both lay and expert decision-makers in legal settings, since it is typically beyond their common knowledge.

The risk profiles used in many legal settings are not usually based on a theory about why violent or criminal behavior occurs. They utilize the types of information that are available and that are found to be statistically associated with the target behavior of violence or crime. The key issue is strength of prediction, not the nature of the predictor variables. For legal reasons, models are usually not allowed to include race or ethnicity regardless of whether they are a strong predictor.

The atheoretical approach is what was earlier described as fitting people to a profile of known characteristics. In early psychological predictive tools like the Minnesota Multiphasic Personality Inventory (MMPI) people are compared to the characteristics of known violent offenders to determine their mental health status. The obvious advantage of this approach (which is often disparaged as "data dredging") is that the authorities do not need to have a theory about why crimes occur. If you share the features of a psychopath, then you are identified as a psychopath by this type of profile.

In assessing the accuracy of a predictive tool, psychologists look at predictive validity. If the target behavior is a new violent offense, the risk prediction tool is evaluated by how well it can determine who will engage in a new violent offense in the future. There are two types of mistakes that might be made by an assessment. One is predicting violence when none will occur (a false positive). The other is predicting non-violence when violence will occur (a false negative). Consistent with the origins of risk predictions in the arena of mental illness, much of the early research involved predicting violence in mental health settings like hospitals or following release into the community. As an example, Lidz et al. (1993) predicted future violence among people with mental illness in a community setting, using records, interviews with the patient, and interviews with the family. The Lidz study found that 53 percent of those predicted to be violent were violent, while 46 percent of those predicted to be nonviolent were not violent. Fazel et al. (2012) did a more recent and broader meta-analysis of 73 samples that included 24,827 people. They concluded that, when people are predicted to be dangerous, 41 percent will be violent and 59 percent will not be violent. When people are predicted not to be dangerous, 91 percent will not be violent and 9 percent will be violent. This supports the argument that predictions have high error rates. However, they are better at predicting who will be nonviolent.

Predictions are more differentiated when they involve a scale of likely dangerousness. An example is the pretrial risk assessment tool developed by the Arnold Foundation. In an initial development study for their tool defendants were scored on a scale of 1 to 6. Among those with the lowest score on the risk-of-new-violence scale (1), 1.3 percent commit new violent criminal activity while out on bail. Among those with the highest score (6), 11.1 percent commit a new violent act. For the target behavior of appearing for trial (the legal justification for bail) the percentage failing to appear was 10 percent for those with the lowest risk score of 1 on the fail-to-appear scale, and 40 percent for those with a score of 6 (Arnold Foundation, 2013). Testing and use of this prediction tool has subsequently been expanded to many jurisdictions. Along with this expansion there has been both support for and opposition to the use of this and other algorithms in the bail context.

8.5   Policy issues

As the use of risk profiles has become widespread, a number of policy issues have been raised. One issue is the use of private firms to develop and apply proprietary risk assessment tools (e.g., COMPAS). A key question is whether private companies disclose how their profiles function, how frequently there are updates, and the manner in which their profiles are validated by demonstrations of accuracy (Dressel & Farid, 2018). There is a temptation for cash-strapped governments to focus on cost savings through the use of private contractors, rather than creating their own government-managed profiles. The lack of transparency is troubling from a legal perspective, because people normally have the right to examine and ask questions about the evidence being used against them. Without transparency, there is no way of ensuring accuracy or disputing the factors that are being considered. A lack of transparency is also troubling in terms of the legitimacy of the state, because it is associated with judgments of procedural unfairness and undermines trust.

A separate issue is that of bias. In theory, profiles are unbiased by definition, because they are data-based and do not reflect the influence of non-neutral decisions by people with biased or prejudiced views. And, by law, they do not include race as a predictive factor. However, profiles can indirectly include potentially biased indicators which unfairly target a particular group without explicitly including race as a factor in a model. For example, they often include a person's arrest record. Research has shown that the police, either currently or in the past, have targeted certain neighborhoods and/or focused on people of a particular ethnicity or age for arrest. Thus, an indicator that seems objective may itself be a reflection of prior biased practices, with some people more likely to have an arrest record because of police actions where they live or due to who they are. Consequently, it is particularly important that the indicators used in a profile be transparent.

Another dilemma for decision-makers is the problem of balancing error trade-offs. This is an inherent issue with the use of predictions. In any situation there are some clearly dangerous people, some clearly safe people, and a large group of people in the middle. The likely future behavior of the people in the middle is more difficult to predict accurately. If the goal is to maximize taking violent people off the street, then the factors considered when predicting violence should be adjusted to identify more potentially dangerous people in this middle range. However, as the predictor is adjusted, a higher number of people in the middle group, who would not commit a future violent act, are flagged as dangerous. As noted, people denied bail or parole due to false positive errors in a profile have no mechanism for showing that they would be nonviolent. They are essentially presumed guilty of committing imagined future acts of violence. Once a profile exists and a person receives a high score, they will be preemptively detained.

It is also the case that the number of mistakes in which a person who would not be violent is (mistakenly) evaluated as being likely to be violent goes up when populations of mostly innocent people are considered. From a screening point of view, and with the goal of avoiding the mistake of mislabeling nonviolent people as being likely to be violent, the ideal population contains people almost all of whom are likely to be violent. A problematic population is one in which very few people will be violent. For example, juveniles have a low recidivism rate for violent offenses. In such groups there will be many mistaken predictions of likely future violence. In a population in which 90 percent will be violent, a test with 50 percent accuracy would misclassify only 5 percent of those studied as likely to be violent when they actually would not be violent. In a population in which 10 percent are likely to be violent, the same test would misclassify 45 percent as likely to be violent when they actually would not be violent. In other words, in a juvenile sample or a sample of the general population, a large number of those predicted to be violent would actually not be violent if left alone. This is an inevitable result of applying an imperfect test to a large group of people. For this reason, some psychologists argue that psychologists should not make predictions for groups that do not have high base rates of violence and, therefore, should refuse to test juveniles for potential future risk (Grisso & Tomkins, 1996), or use these types of profiles for general population screening, as currently occurs with employment testing.

8.6   Public perceptions of risk assessment

When clinical predictions are compared to statistical predictions, a paradox is revealed. Statistical predictions are more accurate. This conclusion was reached in the early Meehl review (1954) and has been supported by subsequent research. However, laypeople have more confidence in clinical judgments. As an example, in 2012 a national survey asked Americans whether sentences should be influenced by future risk assessments (Tyler, 2012). The study found that 77 percent thought it was fair to consider future risk in sentencing. When asked whether it was appropriate to use clinical judgments to make such estimates, 82 percent said yes. In contrast, only 62 percent thought it was appropriate to consider the results of a statistical model that predicted future behavior.

People want to use human intuition as the basis for predicting the future, rather than statistical models, and this view persists even when they have been told about the greater accuracy of statistical models. Research shows that if you present people with evidence that statistical models are more accurate, they continue to prefer to rely on intuition, even when making choices that impact on their own lives (Hastie & Dawes, 2001; Dawes, 1979; Scurich & Krauss, 2020). One way that legal authorities can make the use of models more acceptable is by presenting them as one input into a decision that is made by a human being.

Accuracy is only one of a number of goals in decision-making. People also prefer processes that help them feel secure. Sometimes these other motivations interfere with the goal of maximizing the pursuit of truth, or even with accepting truth when it is already known. In the case of judging, the preference for a person's involvement in the evaluation is not just about misunderstanding how best to find truth. It is also linked to the desire for a compassionate and caring decision-maker.

People are more focused on whether the authority has sincere "good intentions" and is trying to do best for people, than on whether they are competent and likely to make good decisions. And, it is not necessarily the case that this is irrational or suboptimal. People may have had the experience that the most serious problems occur when authorities are dishonest, corrupt, or self-dealing. Their focus may be upon recognizing and addressing these problems, because past experience labels them the greatest threat to a group. This highlights the risks that people associate with the absence of a person of good character controlling their fate and that of others. In the earlier discussion of eyewitness evidence it was noted that the law is particularly concerned with managing corrupt motives among legal authorities. This is distinct from managing the use of evidence which has various levels of accuracy. An authority can be honest and sincere and base their actions on poor quality intuitions.

Another example of the preference for human over impersonal decision-making is provided by the case of traffic cameras (Wells, 2012). In this case, people want the opportunity to manage their feelings of self-worth and to maintain their self-esteem in a situation that threatens it: being cited for breaking the law. Traffic cameras are the ultimate unbiased decision-maker, and are highly accurate. Nonetheless people do not like them. Why not? The Wells study shows that people view receiving a ticket as an interpersonal interaction, in which they are entitled to an opportunity for identity management. People want to explain that they are respectable and law-abiding members of the community, who should not be confused with deviants and criminals. Drivers often deflect away from the identity threat of receiving a ticket from police officers, whose actions communicate a moralized symbolic meaning. They do that by telling officers they should be focusing on real criminals and serious crimes, not bothering honest and generally (although not in this case) law-abiding citizens. All of these efforts are independent of the indisputable accuracy of the camera. Opportunities to achieve these other identity management goals are denied to people when they have no human legal authority with whom to engage in interpersonal dialogue. Ironically, the accuracy of the camera is a heightened identity threat since it is hard to argue that the police camera made a mistake, something commonly suggested of police officers.

8.7   Legitimating decision-making authority

The need for actors in the legal system to consider future risk when dealing with defendants has encouraged the use of evidence-informed predictive tools, either as a constraint on discretionary decision-making, or as one of many sources of information considered during decision-making. One reason for the use of statistical information is that it enhances accuracy. Another is that it promises neutrality and is "scientific," thus helping to legitimate a legal change restricting people's civil liberties.

The law traditionally had clear limits on the state's right to restrict people's freedom, and people who were not a known flight risk were long entitled to post bail and remain free until their case was settled. In 1984, the Supreme Court interpreted the Federal Bail Reform Act as permitting detention on the basis of possible future dangerousness. Criminologists already believed that judges were likely taking such estimates into account, since the seriousness of the charge against a person has been found to be a significant predictor of bail. This decision explicitly labelled such a practice as lawful.

Using actuarial prediction to assess the risk suggests that such decisions are made in an unbiased manner may help legitimate this extension of state authority. With this extension of state authority as a given fact, the use of risk profiles formalizes the effort to discern risk accurately, making it more uniform and less susceptible to influence through stereotypes and biases. An approach using evidence-informed predictive tools can thus be seen as delivering on the promise to be unbiased in an era when there is widespread controversy about the possibility of biased policing, judging, and criminal sentencing.

It is also possible to ask whether this form of decision-making legitimizes the law in the eyes of the defendants, whose fate is in the hands of a profile. There is very little research directly addressing this topic, but research generally suggests that people prefer systems where they have the opportunity to state their case to an authority, whom they believe is considering and taking into account their personal background and needs (Tyler, 2006a). Interviews with defendants appearing in court suggest that defendants react negatively to the perception that judges are simply checking the boxes (as they were required to do with the federal guidelines), and giving them a preordained score when deciding their fate. Individualized justice promotes perceived legitimacy and facilitates rehabilitation.

In an earlier chapter the factors that might lead decision-makers to mitigate punishment were discussed. One was a "rotten social background." Research suggests that introducing a risk assessment tool into sentencing lessens the degree to which these early deprivation factors influence sentencing. Skeem et al. (2020) examine the use of risk assessments by judges. They find that the use of risk assessments changes the way that judges view the defendant's background. Traditionally, judges have considered socio-economic disadvantage as a factor mitigating perceived blameworthiness, leading to lower sentences. With a risk analysis, judges are more likely to view socio-economic disadvantage as increasing the perceived risk of future criminal activity, leading to higher sentences. The use of the risk assessment, in this case, has the effect of weighting the scale against defendants from such backgrounds because it shifts attention to the likely future consequences of deprivation.

8.8   Profiles as an antidote to bias

Quantitative indicators limit discretion, and the way such limits are viewed depends on how the discretion of legal authorities is perceived to be influencing decisions. A key issue in sentencing reform has been the perception that judges are racially biased. To the degree that this is true, sentencing guidelines or risk profiles that limit the flexibility of judges can be viewed as managing the impact of prejudice. Similarly, if the police are perceived as acting on prejudice when deciding whom to stop and search, risk prediction tools that limit discretion could be viewed as a valuable reform.

Requiring a score on an evidence-informed checklist makes the actions of individual officers more consistent, hopefully less biased, and if it is an empirically validated profile, more justifiable. As an example, the skyjacker profile discussed in *United States v. Lopez* (1971) establishes factors that must be met by a target person for a screening system to divert them to a scan (in the pre-TSA era when passengers were not generally scanned). The essential component of this risk model is that it fits the model of a typical statistical algorithm. Using a sample of prior cases, a set of criteria that predicted a hit (a person carrying illegal items) was established, and a checklist created. This list was then used to assess passengers, and those who met the criteria were diverted for scanning. The key aspect of such models is that the officers cannot simply pick people based upon their intuitions. They must match them to a previously created checklist. And the criteria on that list must have been found in a prior empirical study to be linked to the predictive goal. Today all passengers are scanned, although the TSA still uses empirically derived checklists as supplementary tools to determine who might receive secondary screening.

There are other applications of profile-based law enforcement intrusions. The drug courier profile developed by the DEA is also used at airports. In *United States v. Sokolow* (1989) the Court accepted a profile as a basis for searching a potential passenger. That profile included buying a ticket with cash, using a false name, and appearing nervous. In some cases, the courts have ruled that at least one of the factors in a profile must involve the current actions of the person, for example, that they appear nervous. In addition, the courts usually do not allow race to be considered.

8.9 Alternative uses of risk assessment

In addition to the advantages noted above, the use of profiles legitimates taking actions against people based upon their predicted future behavior. However, it is equally possible to use risk profiles as a tool of social reform. Simon (2005) argues that they can counter retributivist feelings. This is possible because predictive analytics can also be used to identify those people whose likelihood of future violence is low (the undangerous). They can provide a justification for releasing people. The 2017 Model Penal Code endorses the use of such low scores on risk assessments, i.e., indicators of a lack of dangerousness, to support diversion toward reduced or alternative sentences.

One example of the potential value of predictions that a person is a low risk for dangerous future behavior is the case of sexual psychopath laws. People have an understandable revulsion against sexual predators, and laws have sought to require future registration and identification after a sentence is complete. Evidence from risk predictions suggests that, in many cases, the risk of recidivism is lower than both the public and many political leaders believe (Hanson & Morton-Bourgon, 2009). In such cases, presentation of a low recidivism risk prediction can be an argument to justify lessening the restrictions upon offenders after they have served their sentence.

At this time, the use of risk predictions in law is focused on those people who are within the legal system, moving through the criminal justice funnel. However, the concept of taking action based on projections of future risk could be applied more widely. The limits are ethical and legal, not empirical. In a classic paper, Moffitt (1993) argued that there is a small group of young people who continue into a life-long pattern of criminal behavior. Those people can be identified at an early age (with some degree of error) based upon early biological and cognitive damage, and early social neglect or abuse in their family or community. If the principle of incarceration in anticipation of future violence becomes normative, and likely future criminals can be distinguished with an acceptable level of accuracy, would a general strategy of proactive intervention be desirable?

It is equally important to ask how to best intervene. The identification process predicting risk for long-term criminality could be a prelude to additional efforts to help those at-risk individuals while they are still young. This would be a proactive risk-need-responsivity approach. Conversely, it could involve early labelling as a suspect person, and heightened surveillance or other forms of management.

If the only issue involved is accuracy, advances in neuroscience are rapidly improving the ability to identify at-risk individuals. The general underlying psychological argument is that early life lays down a pattern for later life that can be detected through various psychological tests, including brain scans. Factors shaping adult conduct include both in utero biological and cognitive deprivation, and early damage through poor parenting or environmental stresses. Predictions about a person's likely future life-course can be made when they are still a child.

Using predictive analytics changes the way legal decisions are made. The question is whether the changes that occur are desirable. From a psychological perspective there is nothing inherently difficult about using such predictive tools as long as their accuracy or lack of it is appropriately accounted for. Their use however presents legal authorities with a number of important ethical, political and legal questions, many of which have not yet been fully addressed. These issues have been raised from the beginning of the study of risk assessment in early discussions of possible justifications for institutionalizing the mentally ill. What makes this area particularly interesting from a psychology perspective is that in this arena legal authorities have been more willing to embrace psychologists than psychologists have been willing to be embraced.

9   Civil justice

The discussion in prior chapters concentrated on various aspects of the criminal justice system, which has been the primary focus of law and psychology research. Crime and criminal justice have also received the most attention from the public, through news reporting, books, movies, and television series. Less visible in popular culture, but of equal importance, is the civil justice system, which has jurisdiction over a wide variety of non-criminal matters. Law and psychology researchers have similarly engaged in research that contributes to our understanding of the civil justice system, and illuminates the effectiveness and perceived fairness of procedures used in settling civil disputes.

Civil law issues concern the private relationships among members of a community. The issues included within civil law are contract disputes, debt collection, evictions, bankruptcy, divorce, child custody, probate, personal injury, and property disputes. Most civil cases are handled at the state level, through a variety of processes administered by the state courts. These issues vary greatly in terms of how much they matter to the parties, how emotional the issues are, and the degree to which they involve questions of dishonesty and bad faith. A civil case can be a simple one involving a request for compensation for a faulty product, or it could be a highly emotional and contentious dispute over child custody.

9.1   The role of civil courts

Civil courts exist to respond to a "universal need present in every society for some method of resolving disputes among individuals" (Breyer, 2010, p. 138). This function is central to the power of the law to address grievances, and redistribute resources to restore justice. Because the civil justice system is more directly controlled by private parties, it is especially affected by issues of litigant psychology. People have higher levels of control in the civil system, and can shape their actions based on their personal goals. The state continues to have civil enforcement powers but does not "own" civil disputes, and does not decide whether and how they will move forward, to the same degree as is true in criminal cases.

And, although civil jury trials are as infrequent as criminal jury trials, civil disputes are settled in the shadow of what the parties believe would happen with a jury trial, so their impact is broad. Civil jury trials serve a number of functions (Hans, 2014). They inject community values into decisions about reasonable conduct and appropriate compensation. They act to balance government and corporate power. They enhance the popular legitimacy of the legal system by providing a transparent and neutral forum for the redress of injustice. And they educate jurors about law and government.

There are a number of reasons why the civil justice system is less visible to the public than the criminal justice system. People are, first of all, unlikely to come into contact with civil courts. A 2012 national survey indicated that 2.5 percent of the United States' population interacted with a civil court to resolve a conflict in the prior two years (Tyler, 2012). In addition, the outcomes of civil court cases are generally not dramatic, are often rooted in interpersonal conflict and are resolved via a small monetary settlement, and thus lack wider societal impact. There are occasional media discussions of civil cases, for example, instances where juries award multimillion-dollar compensation for harm from corporations to plaintiffs with questionable injuries. These flashy instances aside, however, the operations of the civil courts are normally not very visible to the general public.

This general lack of visibility means that the public is largely unaware of striking changes that have taken place in the nature of the civil justice system since the mid-1980s. There has been a steep decline in the percentage of cases reaching trial, due in part to limited resources, high costs and a concerted effort by business interests to remove litigation options through mandatory arbitration agreements. It is increasingly difficult for people who feel wronged to appear in a traditional courthouse. During this time there has been a corresponding increase in settlements and the use of alternate procedures. Some of these mechanisms are supported by the state, e.g., court-annexed mediation; others are in private hands, e.g., required arbitration to resolve commercial disputes (Talesh, 2009), or simply hiring a private mediator to settle a dispute instead of engaging with the state.

While they may function under the public's radar, civil courts are important from a societal perspective. Legal authorities have long suggested that the key to community vitality is having a mechanism that reassures people that they have recourse to a just mechanism for resolving conflicts and enforcing agreements (Hurst, 1956, 1964). Having such recourse is central to people's willingness to negotiate contracts based on trust, which, in turn, are a key to economic development. People who are entering contracts need to feel that there is a way to get justice if the other party fails to fulfill their obligations. People who are harmed by another person or organization need to believe that some neutral party will support their claim for compensation and even impose punitive damages when warranted. Written agreements that are enforced by the legal system lower the risk that people take when trusting others about whom they have limited information. In spite of the fact that civil courts are seldom involved in resolving broken contracts, the symbolic presence of court-based justice still shapes people's actions.

The courts deal with failures to adhere to agreements, but social scientists also ask why people honor such agreements in the first place. For example, what conditions create contracts to which all of the parties will adhere? Psychologists and other social scientists have studied which features of contracts lead people to honor them. They find that several factors shape willingness to adhere to consumer contracts, in particular. One factor is that the contracts are written in an easily understandable way, so that people will actually read them and feel committed to their terms (Plaut & Bartlett, 2011). Making a contract understandable, and putting the terms in the contract itself, rather than on a website, so people are more likely to read and know them, promotes adherence (Wilkinson-Ryan & Hoffman, 2015). Giving people choices about the terms when a contract is established also promotes adherence (Eigen, 2012).

Research on how people react when others break the terms of a contract reveals that laypeople have a distinctly different image of contracts than is reflected in the law.

From a legal perspective breaking a contract is not a "moral" wrong. It is acceptable to break a contract if you compensate the person who suffers harm. Laypeople view honoring a contract as a moral commitment, and breach as a moral wrong. Hence, they view the issue of contract breach as reflecting on the character of the person who breaches (Wilkinson-Ryan & Hoffman, 2010). Monetary compensation feels incomplete to many people, because it does not deal with the perceived moral failure of the offending party. People often want the courts to step in and require the person to fulfill the contract, while the more typical legal resolution is to assess damages.

This research highlights a question to be addressed later: How much do we care if disputants feel that the legal system has addressed a problem in a way that they view as appropriate or inappropriate? Is it important if there are people who feel that the civil remedy does not adequately address the harm they have experienced?

9.2   The dispute pyramid

The progress of cases and suspects through the criminal justice system is sometimes spoken of as the criminal justice funnel; in the civil justice system, the metaphor of the dispute pyramid is often used. Both models suggest that a large number of the cases that are initiated, few reach a formal trial. Most are disposed informally along the way (Albiston et al., 2014; Kritzer, 2010).

Studies in the civil justice arena are especially interesting because researchers have made an effort to step back and identify the problems that people have in their everyday lives for which a legal response might be appropriate. They refer to this as assessing the legal needs of the public (Curran, 1977). In other words, these researchers start not with the act of the person seeking recourse from the law, but with the person recognizing that they have a problem in their life they need to manage. The question is how they manage that problem and when they choose to involve the law. For example, if someone drops and breaks a cellphone, it creates a problem to be solved. They may not regard the problem as caused by a failure on the part of the manufacturer (defective glass), and if they do, they may or may not choose to pursue legal action seeking restitution from the manufacturer.

What are the legal needs of the public? According to Curran (1977), they include real estate transactions, property damage, writing a will, divorce, personal injury, a consumer dispute, and an estate allocation following a death. As is clear, these differ widely in their nature, their severity, and their likely emotionality.

The core finding from research is that people's normal response to everyday problems is to not involve law, i.e., to accept their losses and carry on. In the situations where people do take action, they tend to act informally. They may talk to the other party in a dispute, or go to a vendor to complain about a defective product. People seldom consult an attorney or pursue a case in the legal system. When civil claims are filed, they are typically resolved by informal settlement conferences that occur prior to a court appearance. Claims that do move forward may be heard in a small claims court before a judge (bench trial), and/or where a person can appear pro se (without an attorney). Overall, recourse to a full formal trial and/or working with an attorney are not the predominant ways that people respond to the problems in their lives.

There have been conflicting views expressed in the civil courts literature by scholars studying the legal system over whether or not Americans are a litigious people, who too frequently sue, assisted by juries that give civil plaintiffs excessive monetary awards for their injuries. This image has been promoted by the business community, which has sought to limit access to civil courts. An important contribution of social scientists has been to show that this image is unjustified from a variety of perspectives, including by comparison to the historical rate of the use of courts, and their rate of use in other societies (Galanter, 1983; Robbennolt & Hans, 2016). In fact, people in America do not often pursue legal recourse for many grievances where there is justification for doing so. Further, when they do pursue a legal case, they typically get modest settlements. Americans underclaim in relationship to their legal rights, rather than overusing the civil justice system.

9.3   Naming, blaming, claiming

Why do people pursue litigation? The classic effort to address this question is an article by Felstiner et al. (1980–81) who distinguish three stages: naming, blaming, and claiming. Naming involves recognizing that an injury has occurred. Blaming turns that injury into a grievance by viewing someone else as responsible for the problem. Finally, this leads to a legal claim. The underlying assumption of this model is that movement through these stages is motivated by an expected utility model of economic gain or loss. This economic view is widely shared by lawyers, who believe that people want damages and are motivated by the prospect of economic gain.

Evidence does not support the view that people pursue civil claims solely or even primarily for economic reasons. From a rational perspective, balancing the costs of litigation against the average expected gain, there is typically little expected economic benefit from moving forward with a civil case. Rational people should try to settle. However, this does not take into account the psychology of people's exaggerated views about the merits of their case or their negotiating ability, distortions which might lead perceived utility to differ from actual utility. There are also other reasons for moving forward.

Studies of civil plaintiffs suggest that they are motivated by many factors not linked to economic issues. People want financial compensation, but also may want an apology, an acknowledgement of wrongdoing, or an explanation of the circumstances and causes of the harm. They further want justice in the form of appropriate punishment for bad actions or malevolent actors. They may want to call attention to corporate or government action they believe highlights indifference or willingness to harm others. There are many reasons to sue, beyond compensation for damages.

When one person allegedly injures another, they will often make an effort to provide an account for the conduct that led to the injury. Specifically, they might attempt to disavow, explain, excuse, or justify the behavior that purportedly led to the injury. Alternately, they might offer an apology to the injured person. Apologies can be distinguished from other forms of accounting in that they acknowledge responsibility for the conduct that caused the harm. Accepting blame and expressing regret for one's behavior signals awareness of the norm or rule that was violated and of the harm caused to the other (Robbenholt, 2010). Like the excuses discussed in an earlier chapter the question is whether such efforts to account for conduct influence how the other parties react.

There are two issues. One is the legal consequences of apologizing. There is evidence that civil defendants, such as physicians in medical malpractice cases, may sometimes desire to offer apologies, but are concerned that disclosure or acceptance of responsibility would increase the possibility for legal liability. Apologies are potentially admissible in any future trial. Consequently, although the injured parties may want and expect explanations and apologies, many defendants avoid apologizing and are so counseled by their attorneys and insurers (Robbenholt, 2009).

Does it help if people apologize? Robbenholt (2008) suggests that the perceived benefits of an apology are leading some states to create a framework within which they are not a legal liability. Is that a good idea? Robbenholt notes that "Very little empirical research has examined the assumptions about whether, how, and under what circumstances apologies may influence decision making in civil litigation" (p. 197). Her review suggests that people do want apologies when they are injured. In the medical context whether a physician apologizes shapes whether a patient seeks alternative medical advice. Apologies also shape how injured parties view the offender, for example, whether they think they have good moral character. Finally, after an apology those injured are more likely to accept a settlement offer. All of these findings support the suggestion that apologies can play a constructive role in facilitating the settlement of legal disputes.

The view that people are pursuing more than money when they make a civil claim corresponds to the finding that people often seek a forum in which they can present their grievance to a neutral judicial authority, make their arguments, and receive a decision based upon the law (Barclay, 2004; Hadfield, 2008; Relis, 2006–07). People do not easily trade that opportunity for faster and cheaper procedures.

9.4   Perceptions of fairness in civil procedures

From the perspective of civil court authorities, it is important to provide people with a forum that they will experience as fair. Why? Because studies suggest that procedural fairness leads to both decision acceptance and court legitimacy. On the individual level, when parties experience the procedure as fair, the decision is more likely to heal the wounds caused by a conflict, promoting reconciliation and future cooperation. As an example, if a child custody hearing results in joint custody being awarded, it is desirable that all parties defer to the decision of the court and participate amicably in the raising of their children. This is more likely to happen when the parties feel that the procedures used by the court were fair. On the system level, it is important for courts to build and maintain their legitimacy so that people will bring their disputes into the legal system and accept their resolution there, rather than engaging in extra-legal retaliation—which may end productive relationships, and is unlikely to lead to a resolution acceptable to both parties. On the other hand, the courts offer the possibility of a resolution based upon legal rules, while informal procedures are often more affected by the parties' relative power and resources.

Tyler and Huo (2002) studied people in California who brought a variety of issues to the civil court system. They found that the primary factor shaping willingness to defer to the settlement achieved in a courtroom was perceived procedural justice, which mattered more than how much the party won or lost, and whether they received the outcome they felt they deserved.

In 2014, the California court system studied people's views about the legitimacy of and overall trust in the state courts by interviewing a random sample of residents, as well as a sample of attorneys (Rottman & Tyler, 2014). The primary factor affecting people's views of court legitimacy was whether they perceived the court's case management procedures as just, followed by the distributive fairness of verdicts, and then by performance issues such as cost and time to resolution.

Interestingly, much of the discussion about and reporting on the legal system has been from an instrumental perspective, on the assumption that issues of litigation cost, delay in case resolution, and outcome favorability drive litigant reactions to the legal system. Research findings suggest that laypeople are not primarily instrumentally oriented in their evaluations of the civil or criminal courts. Rather, procedural justice is consistently central to the evaluation of the civil courts, and it is the element of procedures least connected to outcomes that particularly matters: treatment with dignity, respect, and courtesy. A key contribution of psychological research has been to highlight the noneconomic concerns that influence people's interactions with and perceptions of the legal system.

The California study suggests that in commercial cases noneconomic concerns may be less important, with parties placing approximately equal weight on distributive and procedural fairness. On the other hand, a study of pretrial mediation of business disputes in federal court found that, even when substantial amounts of money were involved, the parties decided whether to accept the results of the mediation settlement conference primarily by assessing the procedural fairness of the conference, not the amount of money they would win or lose (Lind et al., 1993).

The California study further finds that, while lawyers care about procedural justice, they are generally more strongly impacted by outcome fairness than are members of the general public. The findings concerning lawyers in the California study are consistent with the finding of Heuer et al. (2007) that judges generally put less weight on issues such as respectful treatment of litigants than do litigants themselves. They found that judges put stronger weight on the societal costs and benefits of decisions, and less upon the procedural justice provided to the parties. This is not a unique feature of judges, but rather a general property of people in powerful positions (Keltner et al., 2003).

9.5 Damages

The civil court system allows the judge and the jury to price noneconomic harm at whatever level they consider to be appropriate compensation, allowing them to include issues of pain and suffering in their calculations. While lost wages and hospital bills are more straightforward there is no reason that human decision-makers cannot manage less overt and tangible loses.

A key factor driving the size of settlements through jury verdicts in civil cases is the extent of quantifiable harms, but that is only one factor that they can and often do consider in their calculations (Robbennolt & Hans, 2016).

A difficult question for jurors is how to translate harm into money. As the issues in a conflict move beyond fairly straightforward compensation for documented harms into economic questions like monetizing lost future income, and estimating the value of noneconomic issues like "diminished future quality of life" and "pain and suffering," civil juries are put into a challenging situation that psychologists have sought to understand (Reyna et al., 2015).

Studies make clear that jurors struggle with the task of estimating appropriate damages. They try to construct a coherent story that best represents the facts, and then apply existing legal rules to that story (Robbennolt et al., 2003). However, studies emphasize how difficult this is for lay jurors who lack the type of knowledge about other cases that lawyers and judges typically possess and use in settlement discussions.

One challenging aspect of understanding civil cases is the wide variety of goals that can shape case outcomes. As noted, in the simplest case, the goal is to compensate for objective damage. However, decision-makers also consider the needs of the victim and the offender, community values, the desire to express condemnation of conduct, the desire to deter future conduct, and punishment for moral wrongdoing (Robbennolt et al., 2003). Studies suggest that jurors try to balance these various objectives, putting different weight on different goals, depending upon the unique features of a case. They do so to establish an appropriate amount for a damage award.

While this is normally the jurors' only task, they are also sometimes asked to consider additional punitive damages to punish egregious wrongdoing, and to discourage others from such actions in the future. Extra-judicial opinions about corporations (Hans, 2000) and doctors (Vidmar, 1995) can also be important in interpretations of wrongdoing.

9.6   The disappearing civil court

The volume of civil cases has long posed a challenge for the limited resources of courts, and the system has thus sought ways to divert cases away from traditional trials. One national effort was the alternative dispute resolution (ADR) movement, which created mediation programs within court systems starting in the 1980s. Litigants were provided with the option, or even required, to attend mediation sessions prior to having the opportunity to appear in court.

Research supports the value of this approach, showing that when the parties can make an agreement in mediation they are more satisfied and more likely to adhere to that agreement over time than if they resolve their case in litigation (Pruitt et al., 1993). Interestingly, even when parties do not agree on a solution in mediation and move on to a court session, they end up more satisfied with the ultimate resolution of their dispute if there was mediation (Emery et al., 1994; McEwen & Maiman, 1981).

Studies of mediation link its success, at least in part, to perceptions by the parties that it is a fairer procedure. In particular, people feel that they have greater opportunities for voice when they can participate in a mediation session (Tyler, 1988, 1989). This is partly due to the training of media-tors, which emphasizes listening to the disputants and acknowledging their concerns. Because they lack authority to dictate a solution that the parties must accept, mediators need to be more sensitive to the views and concerns of the parties. In this way mediation is distinct from arbitration, which is more like the courts in that a third party dictates a solution, which the litigants are required to accept. Today the use of mediation and similar services is widespread, both within the court system and in private ADR forums that the parties pay to use.

As the pressures on the courts due to case volume have intensified and funding levels have declined in many states, the use of ADR models has increased. In addition, there has been increased use of private mediation services among people who are interested in a reasonably fast resolution of their problem.

More recently, a variety of other alternatives to the traditional courts have evolved. One rapidly emerging alternative is online dispute resolution (ODR). There are a variety of such forums, mainly similar in that people do not go to a brick-and-mortar courthouse to make their case before a judicial authority. Beyond that, the forums vary in many ways. They can exist outside the legal system, as is the case with online procedures used by companies such as PayPal. They can involve written correspondence or video links with legal or other authorities. Decisions can be made by algorithms or by human decision-makers. Those decisions may or may not then include detailed explanations for particular decisions, or opportunities to appeal.

ODR is being adopted by national or state court systems in the United Kingdom, Canada, New Zealand, the United States, and other countries. An example of a well-developed system is that of the Canadian province of British Columbia. Their civil resolution tribunal manages motor vehicle injury cases, small claims disputes, property disputes, and disputes within cooperative associations. The system puts disputes through a series of stages. First, people complete a solution explorer module to define their problem. They are then connected to the other party to negotiate virtually and try to reach a solution. If they cannot reach a solution, in the next stage a "case manager" works with them (online) to try to reach an agreement. Any agreement reached is turned into a court order, and enforced by the courts. Finally, if no agreement can be reached, an independent member of the court system will make a decision about the case. That decision can also be enforced like a court order.

Traditionally it has been viewed as important to have a public forum in which people can redress their grievances in open court, in a physical courthouse, before a judge. Hans (2014) outlines the values served by these traditional civic courts. From this perspective, the changes now occurring in the system would seem to be creating a lesser, "secondhand" form of justice. But it is important not to jump to this conclusion, at least from the psychological perspective of whether the parties feel that they have received justice.

Some of the most interesting research being done today by psychologists is concerned with the issue of how the parties experience online dispute resolution in civil cases (Mentovich & Rabinovich-Einy, 2019; Katsh & Rabinovich-Einy, 2017; Sela, 2018). This research considers what people need from a dispute resolution forum to believe that justice has been done and to abide by the outcome. Ideally, the solution will also restore productive interaction among the parties. As an example, Sela found that online forums in which the parties could send text messages to the judge and receive video messages back were viewed as the most procedurally fair. The study found that these led to lower feelings of frustration, anger, hopelessness, and stress compared to a two-way video procedure. As online forums proliferate, it is important for psychologists to more fully explore the role of structural variations on the experiences of disputants.

Another developing alternative to civil courts is private adjudication. This can occur when the parties contract with a private mediator outside the courts, often through agreements that require disputes to be submitted to arbitration (Telesh, 2009). This is the case with many website service agreements, where the terms and conditions specify that disputes will be resolved by a private arbitration service. Concerns have been expressed about whether these forums are viewed as neutral and rule-based by consumers and further research is needed in this area.

A final alternative is a class action. Although the civil justice system is organized around the idea of the individual grievant, it is also possible for litigants to join together as a group. This is labelled a class action and requires those involved to have similar claims against a common party. From the point of view of litigants, this combining of claims enables people to move forward in pursuing grievances which they might be unable to afford to pursue as individuals.

While the courts have recently erected higher barriers to certifying class actions, research by legal scholars shows that joining together as a class confers a number of psychological benefits on claimants (Burch, 2010, 2011, 2016). One key benefit is group solidarity. A general finding of collective efforts to rectify injustice, as is true of individual efforts, is that the probability of winning is low. As has been noted, this encourages individual parties to settle or drop their case when they think as rational actors.

When victims join together, they form a group with a collective identity. The dynamics of such groups provide mutual social support, which supplants economic considerations as a reason to continue. Just as individuals sue for many noneconomic reasons which sustain them in moving forward, groups reinforce the motivation of their members to continue forward with their case. Creating a class of similarly aggrieved people builds a community joined in solidarity against a common antagonist. This has positive in-group identity-linked benefits regardless of whether the parties win. Those benefits can sustain an effort that would be more likely to falter if undertaken by an individual. The group can also play an important role of helping others in the group deal with the psychological fallout of whatever injury led to the creation of the group.

It is important not to believe that the only issue in designing civil forums is how the parties feel. There is a public value to transparency in a public hearing about civil wrongs. This value is particularly salient in situations in which the offending party may have acted in ways that raise questions about ethical or moral responsibility. In such cases the interests of society are not served through a private settlement that is not disclosed. Even if the parties are satisfied, there are reasons to be concerned about the societal implications of such a closed system. These issues are less likely to be central in cases in which there are not questions of egregious or inappropriate conduct. Errors are made and mistakes do happen. Sometimes a simple solution between the parties is straightforward and there are no societal implications of the settlement beyond the demonstration that there are legal mechanisms for addressing injustices.

9.7   Reforming civil justice

As the role of traditional courts has declined and alternatives have arisen, the question of why we need the public adjudication of civil disputes has come into focus. Is there a problem if traditional judicial forums disappear? This question connects back to the argument about whether the availability of courts performs important functions for communities. If so, can those functions be performed in other ways?

Studies of the daily experiences of the public show that there are an enormous number of everyday civil justice problems in people's lives that are potentially actionable within the existing framework of the law (Sandefur, 2009; Sandefur & Albiston, 2013; Sandefur & Smyth, 2011). These problems involve issues like evictions, job insecurity, access to healthcare, etc., whose effective resolution shapes the quality of people's lives. For most of those problems, people—especially those living in poverty—do little or nothing, either in the legal system or in other ways.

The legal system defines the problem of people not pursuing civil cases as a lack of available legal services, and advocates more and better courts, and greater funding of legal aid. As an example, the civil Gideon movement promotes public funding of lawyers for indigent litigants in civil cases, similar to the current funding for criminal cases.

Sandefur (2009) suggests that the problem is a lack, not of access to law and legal services, but of access to justice. She notes that cost issues are not the primary reason that people do not contact lawyers. Rather, they do not consider many problems to be legal problems. She argues that the key is to define institutions like the courts and create policies and practices within them built around the concerns of users, not of legal authorities. This leads to a variety of institutional frameworks, some within the court system and some as alternatives. An example is a neighborhood dispute resolution center staffed by local volunteers.

How do lawyers fit into this picture? Her studies suggest that lawyers are useful in two ways: they help people navigate the current legal system when they enter into it, and they hold the courts accountable for following their own rules. To the degree that people can address their problems outside the courts, these functions become less valuable.

This perspective is a good one from which to ask what types of procedures for managing conflicts and regulating conduct lead people—disputants, offenders, victims, and the general public—to feel that there are appropriate mechanisms for the redress of injustice, and for the management of rule violations in their communities. And, by extension, what leads people to view the system as legitimate, and to willingly accept it and defer to its rules and decisions? A similar question is raised by Quintanilla, who studies different forums for pro se litigation in civil cases. He suggests that civil procedures should be built around research on what leads disputants to feel that they have received justice (Quintanilla, 2017; Quintanilla & Yontz, 2018).

Drawing on the institutional design literature, Brigham (2008) argues for justice institutions based upon the principle of delivering justice in ways that will engender the deference of both involved parties, and the belief that justice has been done among people in the community. The design of those institutions should be based upon empirical research evidence of the type psychologists have contributed. As she argues, "Without the capacity to undertake systematic, comparative institutional assessments, recommendations of reform may be based on naïve ideas about what kinds of institutions are good or bad and not on an analysis of performance" (p. 9).

9.8   The flexibility of the civil courts

Civil justice is a rapidly expanding arena of psychological research on law (Robbennolt & Hans, 2016). One important reason is that civil justice procedures are much more flexible than criminal justice procedures. This system has been more open to case management approaches other than trials, including settlement conferences, both state managed and private mediation and arbitration, and, more recently, online dispute management. In addition, because it is driven by litigants, civil justice procedures are a particularly good arena for understanding what people want from judicial authorities. This information is key to building a system of civil justice that promotes community vitality.

Civil justice is also deeply connected to core issues in psychology. It involves psychological theories regarding responsibility for one's actions, blame and moral wrong, models of causality, evaluations of harm, estimates of psychological pain and suffering, etc. Given these many interconnections the recent development of research in this area is important and should be expanded. It is striking how discussions of criminal justice often dominate law and psychology, while issues of civil justice are both equally important and equally addressed by psychological theories.

10 Legal decision-makers: judges and juries

Judges and juries have key roles in the legal system, listening to testimony, assessing the credibility of witnesses, weighing the evidence, and ultimately deciding on the guilt or innocence of defendants. The state empowers these legal actors to redress harms on behalf of the community through rational, rule-based processes that facilitate fact-finding and orderly judgments of guilt. In addition, juries ensure that the values of the community are brought into the system, legitimating it and helping to foster public acceptance. For all of these reasons, the decisions of judges and juries have been closely scrutinized for accuracy and fairness, and psychologists and other social scientists have long studied their decision-making processes. In this chapter we look at the research on how judges and juries reach decisions, how the characteristics of these decision-makers affect outcomes, and how the public perceives their role.

10.1 Historical perspective

Legal psychologists have produced a large volume of work on jury decision-making, the extent of which is illustrated in reviews of jury research by Devine (2012) and Devine et al. (2001), as well as by Hans and Vidmar (1986), and Vidmar and Hans (2007). Although the jury looms large in the research literature, it is more of a symbolic than a real presence in the everyday processing of cases. As previously discussed, most criminal cases (over 95 percent) are disposed via plea-bargain or dismissal, without a trial of any kind—bench or jury. Similarly, most civil cases (over 95 percent) are settled outside of a courtroom.

Because they are infrequent some social scientists argue that the heavy concentration of research on the jury is misplaced (Lempert, 1993). On the other hand, Valerie Hans and Neil Vidmar point out that, while infrequent, jury trials are most frequent with high-profile and important cases with societal implications. These cases also have a broad impact because many cases that do not reach trial are settled with an eye to what would happen if a jury were making the decision. Disputants bargain in the shadow of the jury.

Across cultures and time, there have been wide variations in the existence and role of juries (see Ivkovic et al., 2021). Some nations, such as the United Kingdom and the United States, have long traditions of jury involvement in legal decisions. Other nations have recently added or changed the role of juries in their legal systems, including South Korea, Mexico, Japan, Argentina, Spain, Kazakhstan, and Russia (Terrill, 2009). In contrast, there are recent cases where juries have been restricted or abolished, e.g., Singapore, Pakistan, India, and Malaysia. The juries that do exist also vary greatly in their composition and size, and in the rules that apply to their decision-making. In particular, some societies use mixed tribunals which include both lay and professional judges.

Before juries were formalized as they exist today, people acted more informally, as groups of neighbors passing judgment on wrongdoers and settling disputes in their community based on their own knowledge and values. One of the present-day motivations for creating and maintaining juries is to ensure continued public acceptance of a legal system that takes control over responses to rule violations out of community hands, and places that authority in the hands of a professional group of lawyers and judges. Juries are one way to ensure that the public continues to play some role in resolving conflicts and enforcing rules, preventing this elite group from departing too far from the values of the community. In spite of the role juries play in supporting the legitimacy of the system, there has also been pressure from legal authorities and others to reduce the use of juries, which are criticized by legal professionals for costing too much money, taking too much time, and making poor decisions.

It is important to note the limits of a psychological analysis when talking about the role of the public in shaping legal decisions. Although the jury is intended to reflect the views of the community, juries have historically excluded marginal members of that community through a variety of structural mechanisms. These have been designed to keep minority group members off jury rolls so that they cannot be available to be selected as jurors. This compounds the statistical reality that members of any group that is a minority of the population are at best going to have a minority voice in jury deliberations. But there have been long-term efforts by political and legal authorities to eliminate even this minority voice through exclusion. While outside the scope of a psychological analysis such structural forces influence whether the views of the entire community are reflected in those institutions that are intended to provide lay input into legal processes.

Like juries, judges differ over time and across societies. One difference is that judges may or may not have formal legal training. In addition, judges may be elected or appointed. Further, the structure of the trial can differ. Sometimes single judges are involved, and in other cases there is a panel of varying size and composition. Finally, judges differ in their role. They can be neutral umpires or they can be actively involved in managing aspects of the trial like questioning witnesses. And, they differ in their degree and type of involvement in plea bargaining and settlement conferences outside of formal trials.

10.2 Public views of juries

Although jury trials occur relatively infrequently in the United States, they have a prominent place in the public's view of the legal system, especially in matters of criminal law.

As is reflected in their role in popular culture, juries appeal to the public as a direct representation of American democracy and as a mechanism through which community values can influence legal decisions. There certainly are cases in which the jury has had an important role in checking the authority of the state. A recent example is a set of cases in which jurors refused to believe police testimony, because of the view in the community that the officers were "testilying" (Goldstein, 2018).

The grand jury, which prosecutors consult before filing criminal charges, is at least theoretically a check on the ability of state actors to indict defendants. In everyday practice, however, grand juries reliably rubber-stamp the recommendations of the prosecutor, rarely failing to find probable cause for an indictment. Prosecutors are able to use their expertise, their experience, and their control of the process to shape grand jury decisions.

Psychological research on the question of how people want decisions to be made in the legal system finds that the public values juries. We would therefore expect jury verdicts to be more acceptable to the public than those made by a judge. For example, MacCoun and Tyler (1988) found that among a sample of the public 66 percent thought that juries are more accurate than judges, and 69 percent that they are fairer. They further found that 68 percent preferred a 12-person, unanimous jury for a murder trial, in comparison to other types of trials. In a 2008 Harris poll of Americans, 58 percent said that defendants in a jury trial experience fairness "all or most" of the time; only 8 percent said that the jury was "rarely" or "never" fair. When contrasting a jury to a judge, 50 percent said they trust a jury to give a fair verdict, while only 23 percent trust a judge.

Support for the jury is strong in spite of the fact that people recognize that jurors make mistakes. In a study of college students, MacCoun and Tyler (1988) found that they believed that 22 percent of guilty defendants were acquitted, and 36 percent of innocent defendants were convicted. Nonetheless, the students generally viewed jury trials as fair, and preferred them to trials involving only a judge.

In the case of a murder trial, MacCoun and Tyler (1988) found that juries were preferred by the public for a variety of reasons, including minimizing bias, being thorough in their decisions, procedurally fair, and accurate. People who were interviewed in the study also recognized that juries were more costly; and viewed community representation, thoroughness of deliberation, probability of error, and cost as variables to balance against each other. As a result, they were less supportive of a jury trial for relatively minor crimes like shoplifting, where cost was viewed as a more important factor, and the quality of decision-making less important.

10.3 Juries and the adversary system

As discussed earlier, the structure of a legal system can be inquisitorial, where the judge focuses on a neutral investigation of facts, or adversarial.

In the adversary system, the prosecution and defense present two conflicting sides of a case, each trying to persuade the jury that their version of truth is correct. The drive to win a case encourages arousing emotions and building narratives based more on the power to persuade than on fidelity to the truth (Although it is illegal to knowingly lie.). The goal of an adversary trial attorney is to win over the jury, and this goal is achieved by focusing on a compelling narrative, and deemphasizing evidence that raises doubts or presents ambiguities.

An important question in cases involving scientific evidence, such as psychological research findings, is whether the adversary system is the best procedure for determining truth. Thibaut and Walker (1975) suggest that the inquisitorial model produces the best factual determinations. They argue that when facts are the key issue, there should be an inquisitorial trial, or perhaps a bifurcated trial: inquisitorial to determine facts, followed by an adversarial trial using those facts to obtain justice (see Sevier, 2014, 2019–2020).

Thibaut and Walker also looked more generally at how the adversarial and inquisitorial approaches incentivize attorneys in trials. They created an elaborate experimental analogue of trials, and presented attorneys with the opportunity to pay for facts in an environment in which those facts were either favorable or adverse to their client's interest. They show that inquisitorial attorneys purchase a similar number of facts regardless of the favorability of the facts, since their motivation is to know the truth. Adversary attorneys are motivated to win. In that situation lawyers buy more facts when the balance of facts is against them so that they have a bigger pool of facts that favor their side to present at the trial.

The Thibaut and Walker (1975) study then moved to a trial setting, and the authors examined the presentations by attorneys. Inquisitorial attorneys present all the facts as they exist. Adversarial attorneys select among the facts, skewing their presentation in situations where the facts are against their client. As a consequence a coding of the facts that are presented in an adversary trial shows that they no longer reflect the favorability/unfavorability of the underlying fact pool. The facts presented are more likely to support the weaker party than is true in the pool of facts. Thibaut and Walker present this as a virtue of adversary procedures: they favor the disadvantaged. But, favoring the disadvantaged comes at the cost of accuracy. Adversary trials create an incentive to win, not to find the truth.

Another view, also investigated by Thibaut and Walker (1975), is that a trial should wash away pretrial views about a case. To study this, they created mock trials and gave jurors prejudicial information beforehand. They found that the adversary system was superior in terms of leading to decisions that did not reflect the prior bias, suggesting that the trial itself shaped the verdicts. Here the argument is that a trial should combat prior biases, and the adversary system can do that more effectively than the inquisitorial system.

Both of these studies illustrate the key point that we should not assume that truth and justice are the same thing, and will be reached through the same procedure. The public's belief in the adversarial jury trial remains strong in spite of this conflict. People recognize that inquisitorial trials are more likely to produce truth, but believe that adversary trials best establish justice (Austin & Tobiasen, 1984). When asked to choose, they choose adversary trials, suggesting that justice matters more than truth.

These findings reinforce those discussed earlier in suggesting that, while empirical research is a method for establishing truth, there are other values besides truth. People may be willing to tolerate error in determining the facts in the service of other goals. Accuracy is one goal, but it is balanced against others.

10.4 Psychological research and jury size

Some in the legal community in the United States, in contrast to the general public, believes that juries cost too much, take too long, and make poor decisions; and that, as a consequence, the use of juries should be more restricted than it is today. A series of Supreme Court opinions in the 1970s resulted in rulings lowering both jury size and the requirements for unanimity in jury verdicts. The opinions in these cases led to conflict with psychologists, who disagreed with the Court's interpretation of research findings referenced in the decisions.

This conflict is an example of the perceived power of psychological evidence to legitimate change, but also of the controversy legal decision-makers can generate through the misapplication of social science evidence. In *Williams v. Florida* (1970) the Supreme Court ruled that a six-person jury was adequate to convict a person of robbery. The majority opinion, written by Justice White, supported this outcome by indicating that there is no discernible difference between the results reached by different sized juries, all of which equally promoted deliberation and represented the community. Unfortunately, the social science research cited by the Court does not support this conclusion and actually suggests that group size does matter in terms of a variety of important dimensions related to the quality of deliberation. Simple statistics indicate that larger juries are more representative of the community.

The application of social science to support this proposed legal change led to sharp pushback from social scientists. Saks (1974), for example, refers to this use of social science evidence as reflecting remarkable incompetence and says that the Court "would not win a passing grade in a high school psychology class (p. 18)." The controversy led to a series of cases in which the Court sought to find a justification for changing the size of the jury and/or the requirement for a unanimous jury. The result, according to Monahan and Walker (2011), is "erroneous empirical fact-finding with mistaken history, producing an incoherent statement of the law which should be troubling to legal theorists of various perspectives—originalists, empiricists, and doctrinalists alike" (p. 77). In particular, the Court ended up concluding that six- and 12-person juries are equivalent from a legal perspective, a conclusion opposed by social science findings about how these different juries meet or fail to meet the stated objectives of the law. Subsequent social science research has continued to build a strong, fact-based case that 12-person unanimous-verdict juries both deliberate in better ways and are more representative of the community.

Beyond the specifics of the *Williams* case, this conflict highlights the issue of scientific facts in cases before appellate courts. At the trial level, the legal system has a mechanism of testimony and cross-examination to evaluate the credibility of evidence. Further, judges can hold pretrial hearings to decide if evidence is strong enough to be admitted. Appellate courts, even at the level of the Supreme Court, have lacked mechanisms to evaluate empirical evidence. In that situation, how will the justices evaluate empirical research? One approach is by inviting amicus briefs in which interested parties present evidence. These presentations are often non-neutral, although professional groups can present a "state of the evidence" brief. There is no opportunity for these briefs to be vetted for accuracy using the traditional trial procedure of cross-examination.

Justice Burger recognized these limits and encouraged the development of two institutions to aid the Supreme Court in this situation. One is the Federal Judicial Center, an in-house group of experts who advise the federal courts. The other is the National Center for State Courts, a similar institution, which provides assistance to state court judges. These agencies have the potential to do research that directly addresses the concerns of the Court before decisions are made, as well as acting as neutral investigators who summarize existing evidence.

A separate problem revealed by this situation is that there is often not enough time for research to be conducted before the Supreme Court hears a case. With the *Williams* case, there was no existing research directly addressing differences in how juries of varying sizes deliberated, and there was insufficient time to conduct studies on this issue between the time when the Court took the case and when it ruled. Unfortunately, the existing, indirect research was not correctly interpreted and applied by the Court. Social scientists had not conducted research on this issue because they had not been aware that it was going to be considered by the Court.

The irony of this conflict between law and psychology is that the Court could have avoided this problem by treating quality, representativeness, cost, and delay as values to trade off against one another. They could have noted (correctly) that some types of jury are better from a decision-making perspective, but that those juries take more time and cost more money. The Court could have said that the gains in quality of deliberation were not justified by the higher costs, a position that would be consistent with the evidence, since the social science evidence does not speak to value trade-offs.

In reality, neither the number 12 nor the number six as a jury size was originally derived from an empirical analysis. A cost-benefit analysis in civil trials—balancing the cost of falsely holding a defendant liable, failing to find a responsible defendant liable, and the time and cost of a jury deliberation—suggests that the ideal civil jury size is nine (King & Nesbit,

2009). It is easier to conduct this type of analysis with civil cases, since such cases involve monetary damages.

The Court may have avoided a cost-benefit analysis with criminal trials because it did not want to formally make a trade-off between economic issues and issues of false convictions. Performing a cost-benefit analysis in criminal cases would require putting a dollar value on false imprisonment, as well as the cost of letting a guilty person go free. It is hard to monetize justice in such cases. Social scientists refer to the public aversion to trading off monetary gain and human life as a taboo trade-off (Fiske & Tetlock, 1997).

10.5 Juries and group dynamics

Two distinct fields of psychology contribute to the study of juries: individual decision-making, since jurors are decision-makers, subject to the various heuristics and biases already outlined; and group dynamics, since the jury is a group which interacts and functions via social processes. The fact that the jury is a group is important in two ways. First, a group decision can balance out the various biases of the particular individuals on the jury. Second, the jury deliberates and discusses the case as a group. They correct individuals' misunderstandings about the evidence, a process that would generally be expected to produce a superior verdict.

It is an assumption of the legal system that juries actually do deliberate, and that this deliberation improves their decision-making. Psychological studies reveal that in the typical jury the mix of pre-deliberation preferences is a strong predictor of the final verdict. The Davis social decision model (Davis et al., 1975) argues that if two-thirds of the jury members or more are predisposed toward a particular verdict, that verdict is almost always the final outcome. There is also evidence that the jury can change, especially when there is disagreement pre-deliberation. This suggests that deliberation can matter in cases where the jury begins with disagreements about the right decision. Unanimous decisions particularly require deliberation when the jury begins more or less evenly split.

A key study of juries as groups can be found in Hastie et al. (1983), *Inside the Jury*. This was a sophisticated, empirical effort to understand jury deliberations. A core question, which makes jury research challenging, is explaining how we can know whether a deliberation is good or bad, since we seldom know for certain whether the verdict reached is the correct one. Hastie et al. videotaped and coded the deliberation of mock juries for quality, looking at issues such as how many facts are discussed, whether both sides of the facts are highlighted, etc.

The Hastie et al. research led to the "story model." That model argues that jurors use the evidence they see and hear to construct a plausible story explaining the events of the case. They do not simply combine pieces of evidence additively, but rather develop a plausible story to explain events. This story needs to be coherent and particularly needs to address questions of motive and intention, explaining why people did what they did. This model is consistent with the more general argument that juries focus on the character of the actors, seeking to infer a moral element in their actions. They want a coherent and compelling story organized around the character and motives of the people involved. Once a story is constructed, it is used to put the case into verdict categories.

An alternative but similar model is the Simon cognitive coherence approach (2019). This model suggests that, as evidence accumulates, people begin to form judgments about a case. They are then motivated to make later evidence consistent with their preexisting judgments, in order to maintain a coherent story line. Thus, cognitive distortions often occur as individual jurors seek to build and maintain a coherent view of the case. Jurors ignore or minimize evidence, such as statistical findings, that does not fit well within the story framework which seeks to model people's behavior based upon what they say and do.

More broadly, the story model aligns with general research on social perception, which emphasizes the effort to construct a model of people that includes an understanding of their character and motives, based upon what they say and do. Approaching their task as one of story construction is natural for juries since in their everyday lives this is one important way that people organize their understanding of other people. Trying to infer the character of others is central to the everyday task of interacting with them, so this is a problem that is very familiar to lay people.

It is easy to see why juries have trouble with statistical findings, and with social framework evidence in general. That evidence does not blend well into the story construction process. If we see a nerdy-looking person with poorly matched clothing and a pocket protector, we may infer that they are an engineer. Knowing that engineers are less than 2 percent of the workforce does not impact upon this heuristically driven process of creating a mental image of the person. It is also easy to see why juries underweight situations. A situational explanation is less compelling than one that tells a story about a person, their motives, and their actions. An important but little studied issue in legal psychology is when people either naturally focus on a situational explanation for behavior or find such an explanation compelling when it is presented to them in a trial setting.

The story model creates a framework for attorneys presenting their case in adversary proceedings. That framework draws upon the psychology of persuasion (Robbennolt & Sternlight, 2012). Research emphasizes that there are two elements that matter in influencing people: source credibility and message characteristics. This accords with the findings of Ivković, and Hans (2003) on the influence of experts. They found that 15 percent of juror comments about experts were about the content of their testimony, 23 percent about their credentials, 33 percent about their presentation style (clarity, enthusiasm), and 21 percent about impressions of them as people. This work highlights the important point that many issues besides the probative value of the information they provide shape the impact of both lawyers and experts on the jury.

10.6 Comparing juries to judges

A classic reference on judges and juries is *The American Jury* (Kalven & Zeisel, 1966), which compared the decisions made by these groups. Because of their legal education, specialized knowledge, and experience with many cases, judges are often presumed to make better legal decisions. This study of 3,576 criminal trials and 4,000 civil trials finds that judges and juries generally agree on the verdict 78 percent of the time. When they disagree, juries are usually more lenient. For example, in 19 percent of the criminal cases the judge would convict, but the jury acquits. This study makes the overall point that judges and juries are very similar.

A positive byproduct of the conflict over jury size in the *Williams* decision has been that psychologists have subsequently done considerable empirical research on juries trying to determine if juries are good decision-makers, either on intrinsic grounds or compared to judges. This research allows the quality of juries to be evaluated in several ways (Hans & Vidmar, 1986; Vidmar & Hans, 2007).

One dimension of jury evaluation is competence. Juries have been critiqued for being less competent than judges and, in particular, for having trouble with complex cases. How can competence be evaluated? The challenge is that the "truth" is seldom straightforward, making it difficult to identify a right answer in a case. Kalven and Zeisel (1966) addressed the problem of competence by comparing juries to judges, assuming that judges are correct, and counting jury deviations from what a judge would have decided as mistakes. Another approach has been to code jury deliberations directly.

Hastie et al. (1983) had jury pool members watch a videotape of a trial and then deliberate. Their deliberations were in turn videotaped and then coded. Using this approach, they report that juries correctly remember 90 percent of the evidence. Consistent with this conclusion, Kalven and Zeisel (1966) report that judges do not think that juries have difficulty understanding evidence.

It is important to remember that all decision-makers—juries as well as prosecutors and judges—frequently rely on evidence that is fragmentary and full of ambiguities, as well as on witnesses whose credibility may be uncertain. In addition, decision-makers often receive only a summary of the conclusions of an investigation, rather than detailed information about the acquisition of the evidence, so their deliberations revolve around making evaluations based upon the perceived credibility of the experts, not the quality of the evidence (Simon, 2019). Given the potential for error in these factors, many of the suggestions for improving the quality of decisions that come out of the legal system focus not on judges or juries, but on the police investigatory procedures or forensic practices that produce the evidence that is used in trials. At the same time, this literature supports the argument that juries are similar to judges in their decision-making abilities.

A separate question is whether juries can understand the law. Kalven and Zeisel (1966) argue that jurors differ from judges primarily in not understanding the law. Hastie et al. (1983) find that the jury correctly remembers 80 percent of judicial instructions. Ellsworth (1989) coded jury deliberations in a mock deliberation study, and found that jurors have more difficulty applying the law than they do remembering the facts. After coding actual deliberations of civil juries, Diamond & Salerno (2013) conclude that juries have an adequate understanding of judicial instructions. However, they noted that jurors have problems trying to fit different parts of their judicial instructions together into a coherent whole. Judges have advantages over jurors in terms of understanding the law.

Within the field of psychology there are a number of studies comparing individual and group decision-making, the results of which are complex (Cooper & Kagel, 2005; Kerr et al., 1996). While it is possible to argue that groups produce superior decisions that is not always actually the case. In this case the question has been whether a lay group is inferior to a professional acting alone.

Extensive reviews of the large literature on juries generally suggest that jurors, in spite of a challenging and unfamiliar decision-making environment, are broadly competent and make decisions based upon the preponderance of the evidence. Public support for juries is high, and a majority of Americans would prefer to have their fate determined by a jury if they were accused of a crime. From a legitimation perspective, therefore, juries have an important role in leading people to feel that they will receive justice from the legal system. In addition to receiving justice, people look to juries to show compassion and to uphold community values in the face of a set of laws that may or may not reflect those values. These different goals (Robbennolt et al., 2003) make it hard to decide how well the jury is fulfilling its function, and sometimes complicate the question of whether a jury is making a good decision.

Consider jury nullification, a situation in which, ignoring the judge's instructions, a jury relies on its own conscience to acquit (or convict) a defendant. Is it an acceptable function for a jury to acquit a defendant who is clearly guilty of drug possession because they believe that the mandatory sentence imposed would be too harsh? Is fulfilling the role of showing compassion and upholding community values, instead of convicting on the basis of clear evidence, a good decision? This is just one example of the many perspectives from which the legitimacy and quality of a jury's decisions can be evaluated.

One particularly important issue in assessing competence is the ability to ignore inadmissible evidence. Can judges do this, and in particular, are they better at doing this than jurors? Wistrich et al. (2005) conducted a series of experiments involving judges. They suggest that judges "struggled to perform this challenging mental task" (p. 1251). Although generally unable to ignore extra-judicial information, judges were able to do so in some situations.

What about jurors? The research establishes that the presence of inadmissible evidence has a significant impact on jury verdicts, in line with the evidentiary slant of the inadmissible information. The level of guilty verdicts rises with pro-prosecution evidence, and decreases with pro-defense evidence. Additionally, the research demonstrates that once inadmissible evidence is present, a corrective judicial admonition does not fully eliminate the impact of the inadmissible information. These conclusions come from a 2006 meta-analysis that summarized 175 experimental tests from 48 studies and 8,474 research participants (Steblay et al., 2006). Overall, this analysis suggests that judges and juries both struggle with inadmissible evidence, but that judges can manage to ignore it in some situations.

Robbennolt (2004–2005) reviews the entire range of evidence on decision-making by judges and compares it to juries. She suggests that judges and juries make decisions in roughly similar ways. This is consistent with the argument that judges and juries generally agree in their verdicts (Kalven & Zeisel, 1966).

While judges and juries are similar in many ways, there are also some clear differences in their decision-making processes. Juries are groups that, at least in theory, deliberate. Such deliberation is expected to balance out biases, and to encourage reasoned thinking. In reality, studies suggest that it can both diminish and intensify the influence of biases on decisions (Peter-Hagene et al., 2019). In contrast to juries, judges do not deliberate in trial settings. However, unlike juries, they have legal training, as well as a history of other cases with which to compare the current case.

An important aspect of legal training is reasoning by analogy. Many legal arguments, for example, about appropriate damages for harm or appropriate sentences for wrongdoing, are made based on references to similar cases that have occurred in the past (Ellsworth, 2005). Judges are familiar with this type of reasoning, and lawyers are adept at framing their cases as similar to others whose outcomes would favor their side. Further, because they are repeat players, judges and lawyers have long personal histories of cases on which to draw for comparison. Jurors do not have access to such a history, and so are less able to determine independently what is appropriate based on similar cases in the past. This leaves juries open to suggestions of an anchor on which to form their judgment, in contrast to repeat players who have numerous anchors to choose from.

On the other hand, compared to juries, judges are much more attuned to and constrained by precedent, and are less likely to think it appropriate to ignore the rules for personal reasons. They try to be consistent with prior principles (Schauer, 2008). Although juries are also supposed to follow legal precedents as reflected in the law, overt jury nullification does occur, if rarely. Since juries do not explain their decisions, the extent of covert jury deviance from the law is difficult to assess as is the frequency of less strikingly minimizing or ignoring the law.

While these various comparisons show the potential for differences between judges and juries, the existing literature suggests that both are generally reasonable decision-makers, and more similar in their strengths and limitations than often believed. The literature also points to ways in which the performance of both could be improved. In particular, juries struggle with legal rules which are often presented to them in complex and non-intuitive ways.

10.7 Jury decision-making

From a research perspective, the primary factor affecting the quality of jury deliberations is whether an evidence-driven or verdict-driven approach is used (Hastie et al., 1983). Evidence-driven approaches begin with a neutral review of the evidence. Verdict-driven approaches begin with a public ballot, in which people express a verdict preference (guilty/innocent) before discussion. An evaluation of the content of the jury's later deliberation indicates that an evidence-driven deliberation is of higher quality. The key to this research is that it does not focus on whether an accurate or even a fair verdict is arrived at, or even whether the jury reaches a verdict. The quality of the deliberations is separately rated by coding videotapes. This is necessary because the truth is usually not known so there is no way to evaluate verdicts by classifying them as accurate or inaccurate.

Showing that how a deliberation is conducted matters suggests that a way to improve decision-making by juries is to change trial procedures. This includes not only evidence-driven deliberation, but also explaining the law at the beginning of the trial, allowing jurors to take notes, and simplifying legal explanations and instructions throughout. In addition, as outlined in a prior chapter, jurors would benefit from expert testimony or written information in areas where they lack common knowledge, such as the potential for error in eyewitness and confession evidence. Earlier in the volume the importance of empirically based system level analysis was emphasized. The finding about evidence driven deliberation is an excellent example of how psychological studies can improve law. This analysis is similar to the earlier discussion of line up procedures in that it suggests a structuring of a legal task that improves performance. In this case the improvement is in the quality of the deliberation, so both prosecutors and defense attorneys would support efforts to incorporate this information into trials. Judges might, for example, simply suggest that a jury follow this procedure.

Another issue potentially affecting the quality of jury deliberations and decisions is the influence of non-evidentiary factors. Two such factors are prejudice and sympathy. The review of research by Hans & Vidmar (1986) suggests that extra-legal factors related to prejudice, like the race, age, and gender of the defendant, generally have little impact upon juries and sympathy is only a plausible factor in a very small number of cases. This is not to say that these types of influences are not sometimes found, but, in general, they are not a major factor in decisions. Rather, evidence strength is the primary factor shaping decisions. In addition, research suggests that, at the group level, deliberation both helps facilitate jury information processing, and often, but not always, cancels out preexisting biases (Peter-Hagene, 2019).

10.8 Decision-making by judges

The psychological literature focuses more on juries than on judges, for several reasons. The jury is a highly visible part of popular culture and has a key role in legitimating the legal system, but a more pragmatic reason is that it is difficult to obtain permission to study judges and prosecutors, who have traditionally been reluctant to be interviewed or to participate in experiments. Research on judges has therefore focused on the sentences they impose and their judicial opinions, while prosecutors, who do not create a public record of their reasoning, are even harder to investigate.

One standard that has been widely applied to judges, as well as juries, is disparate impact. If decisions are consistently different based on the race, gender, or age of the defendant, there is a suggestion that the decision-maker may hold prejudice or bias against the members of that group. The law is clear that decisions should be made based on the actions of individuals, and that their group memberships should not influence either verdicts of guilt/innocence or sentences when convicted. Minimizing possible disparate impact due to judges' bias was one motivation for a major policy change, the introduction of federal sentencing guidelines in 1987 (Stith & Cabranes, 1998).

The motivations for sentencing guidelines aside, as with juries, studies of judges generally find that, at least in recent years, the judge's race, gender, and age do not have clear and consistent influences upon their decisions (Mitchell, 2019). Rachlinski and Wistrich (2017) and Wistrich and Rachlinski (2018) argue that judges are aware of the problem of prejudice, and are able to limit or eliminate its influence because they can shift into decision-making by reasoning and by doing that they can counter the potential influence of extra-judicial motivations like bias. A core question has been whether people can, in fact, recognize and minimize the influence of biases on their decision-making. The fact that judges can minimize the influence of biases does not mean that they always do so, so a second question is whether bias influences everyday judicial decisions. Further, the crucial role of bias in prosecutorial charging decisions is not known.

A more widely studied extra-legal dimension of judges is their ideology. Clear evidence is found of the influence of judicial ideology on decisions (Epstein et al., 2013). Inferring a judge's ideology can be problematic, and studies typically use an indirect measure, such as the party of the appointing authority. Based on these indirect measures, ideology is found to have an influence, although it does not necessarily have a simple pattern.

It is not the case, for example, that conservative judges are always more punitive in criminal cases. However, Epstein et al. advocate for requiring judges to sit in panels balanced for ideology, to eliminate any aggregate influence of ideology on the decisions made.

Beyond the influence of prejudice or ideology is the empirical question of general quality of decision-making by judges. Wistrich & Rachlinski (2018) addressed the question of whether judges' expertise and experience lead them to make them better decisions. Drawing on the distinction between reasoning and acting based upon heuristics and biases they conducted a series of studies of judges, seeking to evaluate the quality of judicial decision-making. Their work suggests that judges are affected by anchoring influences, do not always disregard inadmissible evidence, and are influenced by framing effects. There is mixed evidence on whether they show hindsight bias. Overall, this evidence suggests that judges often use the same heuristics and are influenced by the same biases that are common to all decision-makers (Wistrich & Rachlinski, 2018). Unlike racial bias, judges are less aware of such cognitive limits and therefore are not trying actively to combat them.

10.9   Improving decision-making in trials

The last several decades of empirical research on decision-makers have not been kind to the self-confidence of experts. The evidence shows that a variety of heuristics and other non-rational elements underlie much of human decision-making, and that expertise and experience do not necessarily lead to better decisions. The legal system depends heavily on the quality of the discretionary judgments of experts such as police officers, prosecutors, judges, probation and parole officers, etc., so these findings are potentially troubling.

Several implications for the legal system result from the research. Procedures that guide both juries and experts toward high-quality decision-making would be one improvement. For example, legal authorities should be constrained by the existence of guidelines, checklists, and other mechanisms for making decisions more thoughtful and less reliant on intuition. When decisions are framed in terms of facts which can be objectively determined, decisions are also better. When decision-makers believe that they will have to account for their decisions they also make better decisions.

When legal actors have discretion, they should be required to account for their decisions. Mechanisms that involve explaining the decision-making process facilitate analytical, rather than intuitive, reasoning. In addition, people's own intuitions about the quality of their decisions should not be accepted, since the operation of both heuristics and biases is often outside their awareness. Their accounts should be independently reviewed and compared to evidence. This review can more easily occur when people are required to outline how they make decisions.

An interesting challenge for the legal system is whether to apply this reasoning to juries. Historically, jury deliberations have been secret, and juries do not need to account for their decisions. The assumption is that secrecy protects jurors who are in the complex position of representing the community, but also being kept separate from community influences. Jurors announce a verdict but do not explain it. This practice, no matter the reasons for it, is problematic, given the evidence that accountability improves decision-making. The lack of transparency also makes appeals more difficult, since there is no information to determine whether an improper decision has been made. This issue is addressed by Burd & Hans (2018) and Sood (in press).

Kahan & Braman (2006) highlights the tendency of decision-makers to evaluate information in the light of their prior views. One way to counter this tendency is to aggregate across people with varying prior views—as is the case in the dynamics of a jury. Epstein et al. (2013) suggest that the influence of judges' prior views can be managed by using balanced panels of judges, as do Wistrich & Rachlinski (2018).

Another proposed approach is that of a trial in which judges view evidence and decide whether to include or exclude it, before it is presented to a jury. Jurors see only admissible evidence, and their decision-making is insulated from the influence of any excluded information. Judges see the information but do not make the decision. This design does not control for material seen prior to a trial or outside the courtroom, but it does provide a way to control the trial environment. Another suggestion is to videotape trials, edit out the inadmissible evidence, and then show a jury the video, rather than having them present during the actual proceeding.

At various points in this discussion the fact that most cases are settled outside trial settings has been highlighted. While concerns have been expressed about the way discretion is exercised in these settings, it is also possible to view such informal settings as an ideal focus for efforts to reform the legal system. They are less constrained by formal legal rules and procedures, so they are more open to the possibility of experimentation. Restorative justice conferences prior to a trial are an example. This possibility has already been highlighted in the area of civil justice where the forums used to manage disputes can be diverse and are rapidly evolving. It is important to consider alternatives that might be incorporated into traditional adjudication such as drug or problem-solving courts.

10.10 Managing ambiguity

Irrespective of whether decisions are being made by prosecutors, judges, or jurors, the legal system asks them to make difficult decisions in an environment which is inherently ambiguous and filled with conflicting information that varies in its quality. Further, the legal system asks decision-makers to try to achieve multiple, sometimes conflicting goals. While it is possible to point to errors and the impact of extra-judicial factors, the overall conclusion of research is that both professional and lay decision-makers do a reasonably good job at the tasks the system asks them to perform. Studies further suggest that the general public is aware of the imperfect nature of this process but nonetheless accords legal decision-makers, jurors in particular, with considerable legitimacy.

This focus on legitimacy highlights a key difference between the literature on juries and the prior literature on evidence, for example the eyewitness. That literature has been almost totally focused on the question of accuracy. As the literature on juries makes clear the public distinguishes between accuracy and justice. It would be interesting to consider issues of evidence not from the perspective of accuracy, but through a framework of legitimacy. Doing so focuses on the issue of just procedures, not accurate procedures. The work on juries shows that, while these issues are related, the public does not view them as synonymous (Clark, Moreland & Larson, 2018).

11 Freedom, consent and subjective harm

Choice and freedom are important ideas in both law and in psychology. Psychologists have shown that people are strongly motivated to believe that they should be free to choose whatever they want to read, watch, listen to, or buy (Glasser, 2007; Maslow, 1943). Psychological research further demonstrates that having the opportunity to make free choices enhances well-being (Langer & Rodin, 1976). Psychologists recognize that people resist efforts to restrict their actions. Positive mental health is associated with feelings of freedom to make choices about one's life, while constraint causes psychological stress.

America's founding documents are framed in terms of protecting people's freedom from encroachment by the government. They guarantee civil liberties like the right to free speech and the right to privacy, and create a structure under which the meaning of those freedoms is defined and interpreted by legislatures and the courts. In recent years, the courts have turned to social science research findings for guidance when defining and limiting people's freedoms and rights in areas including free speech, consent, and privacy.

11.1 Restricting freedom

Traditionally, the issue of freedom has involved a fundamental right to free speech and association. "It is a cardinal constitutional principle that speech may not be suppressed merely because it is unpopular or offensive to the community" (Boyce, 2008, p. 300). People perceive their freedoms as including the right to watch, read, publish, and speak as they wish.

These freedoms are not, however, absolute. The state can seek to restrict people's freedom to act when there is a clear, compelling need—in particular, when someone's freedoms lead to harm to others (social harms). The classic example is Justice Holmes' statement that you are not entitled to shout "fire" in a crowded theater (*United States v. Schenck*, 1919; see also Aichele, 1989).

One way that psychology has been involved in legal discussions about government restrictions on freedom of expression involves the issue of erotic content, i.e., questions of the meaning of "obscenity" and "pornography" and reasons for their restriction. Historically, obscenity has been an anomaly in the free expression universe, because the Supreme Court has supported limits on the right to possess, read, or view material with explicit depictions of sexual behavior (i.e., "obscene material").

In discussing potentially harmful content it is important to distinguish two issues. One is the depiction of erotic activity. Another is the depiction of violence. Historically these have sometimes been intertwined, with a particularly pernicious type of content depicting violence toward people, usually women, in the context of erotic activity.

It is equally important to distinguish among various forms of potential harm. This discussion has been central to the literature on erotic material. The classic liberal view is that harm should be narrowly construed as involving content that leads readers/viewers to commit violence toward themselves or others in the real world. A frequent focus is on whether particular content facilitates criminal activity. Other perspectives emphasize harm to the world view, or values, of the consumer of such content which may then lead to behavior that hurts others. Prominent feminist scholars have emphasized that some types of erotic material reinforce patriarchal control, and promote the objectification and subjugation of women. This is harm in and of itself and may also lead to antisocial behaviors such as rape. Conversely, conservatives argue that erotic content can undermine support for traditional marriage and monogamy, leading to behaviors like divorce. In the case of depicting violence the emphasis has been on social harms like promoting violence toward others. For example, recently media violence has been suggested to be a factor behind mass shootings.

11.2 Obscenity

In the past, there have been strong moral views about the danger of allowing people free access to various depictions of sexual activity. The government's moral perspective is reflected in the use of pejorative terms like smut, obscenity, and pornography, rather than the more neutral term, erotica. This reflects the Puritan moral heritage of America and its view that sexual behavior is susceptible to lust, which overrides the boundaries of appropriate moral behavior, and thus needs to be controlled (Baker, 2005).

Prior to the internet era, it was more realistic for the government to believe that it could restrict access to erotic content, since people had to receive such content via mail, purchase or rent it from a store, or go to a movie theater to watch erotic films. The arrival of the internet has made censorship more complex. However, modern autocratic governments have shown that internet content can indeed be controlled, so the lack of recent government efforts to restrict access to erotica does not only reflect implementation challenges. It also reflects a change in the moral climate in America.

The depiction of sexual activity in literature and films has long been controversial. In discussions of such material a set of related issues are typically involved. Material can simply explicitly depict sex. It can also depict acts of sex that some people might label "deviant," such as interracial sex, sodomy, homosexual acts of any type, sex outside marriage or in groups, and sex involving different forms of violence, sadism, and dominance and submission. The traditional image of sex is that it is only acceptable when it occurs between two people of different genders who are married. This reflects a particular moral vision and is inconsistent with the actual sexual behavior of many adults, both historically and in the present (Kinsey et al., 1948, 1998). However, the values of the dominant culture have led much of that "deviant" behavior to remain publicly unacknowledged, leading to a private world of sexual behavior, often defined as illegal by the prevailing legal codes.

Can the freedom to experience erotica be banned? In *Roth v. United States* (1957) the Supreme Court indicated that "obscenity is not within the area of constitutionally protected speech or press" (p. 481). This raises the question of defining the criteria that make something obscene. Here the court says that the relevant issue is, "whether to the average person, applying contemporary community standards, the dominant theme of the material taken as a whole appeals to the prurient interest" (p. 488).

11.3 Community standards

Early on the Supreme Court sought to define obscenity as a violation of community standards, which led to a series of decisions around the question of what community standards are and how to determine them. The concept of community standards, defined empirically, raises several questions for legal authorities and social scientists, questions such as: What are community standards of unwholesome interest or sexual desire? Who is the community? Do people object to other people having access to material that they might personally not want to view/read? All of these issues have been addressed in a series of Supreme Court cases. Social scientists research such questions through surveys of members of the community. A factor in the design of those surveys is the legal decision that the relevant standards can be local standards. Consequently, every case invites a new survey of the relevant local community (see *Miller v. California*, 1973).

In theory, it would not be necessary to use a social science survey to determine community standards, since a jury is (at least in theory) a random sample of the community. However, courts have allowed defendants to present survey research evidence to address this question. The argument is that members of a jury may not know the standards in their community, so "Expert testimony based on a public opinion poll is uniquely suited to a determination of community standards. Perhaps no other form of evidence is more helpful or concise." (p. 1181, *Saliba v. State*, 1985)

11.4 Social harm

A further question is what justification the government claims for the right to restrict freedom in this particular way. This issue was not addressed by the Supreme Court, but in the decision of the U.S. Court of Appeals (2nd circuit) (1956) leading to the Supreme Court decision in *Roth* Justice

Clark argued that one reason to ban such material is that it is connected to social harm in the form of juvenile delinquency. He cited "the views of those with competence" (p. 799), who indicated that exposure to sexual content led to criminal behavior, particularly juvenile delinquency. This opinion suggests that there is a "very direct connection of this traffic with the development of juvenile delinquency" (p. 799) (Heins, 2007). This is the question of demonstrated social harm, i.e., harm to others as reflected in committing crimes.

Social scientist Marie Jahoda was cited in the appeals court-level Roth decision (1956). She told the justices that psychological/criminological research on this issue did not reach a clear conclusion (footnote 4). Following this argument, the court ruled that in the absence of clear evidence, the prudent action was to ban the material. Essentially the court conducted a cost–benefit analysis and decided that the risk of accepting material that might cause harm was greater than the benefit to the community of allowing people access. In this same Court of Appeals opinion, Justice Frank considers the same facts but emphasizes that there is "no evidence to justify the assumption that reading about sexual matters or about violence leads to delinquent acts" (p. 804). He argues that in the absence of evidence of harm, banning erotic material is not justified.

Decades of social science research on the connection between reading/ viewing sexual content and various forms of harm have followed. This includes a large psychological research literature. Early examinations focused upon erotic content, while more recent studies have considered the intersection of erotic content and violence. A series of national commissions have reviewed this evolving literature, and it has been addressed in a variety of social science meta-analyses. The overall conclusion is that the evidence does not support the argument that exposure to erotic material leads to changes in real-world criminal behavior. For example, in 1970, the President's Commission on Obscenity and Pornography (Lockhart Commission) concluded that there is "no evidence to date that exposure to explicit sexual materials plays a significant role in the causation of delinquent or criminal behavior among youth or adults (p. 27)." These efforts focus on erotic content, not violence.

The initial Supreme Court decision in *Roth* does not follow the Court of Appeals and cite social harm as an issue. The more recent *Miller v. California* case (1973) which established the current standard on obscenity is less dismissive of the potential "redeeming" value of erotica, but similarly does not focus on social harm. Nonetheless legislative and popular discussions about this issue have often addressed the question of whether such harm occurs. The consistent conclusion of research is that there is no evidence supporting the belief that there is a link between sexual content and criminal behavior.

Despite the lack of research evidence that erotica causes social harm, legislative efforts to restrict access to such content have continued. One reason for this is the weight that people place on their own experiences and intuitions. In *Jacobellis v. Ohio* (1964), Supreme Court Justice Potter Stewart commented about obscenity that "I know it when I see it" (p. 184). This accords with the view of political leaders that such material can be read or watched and seen to be or not be obscene based upon common sense. Once people have made this intuitive judgment it is difficult to dissuade people from imagining a linkage to various types of undesirable impact from exposure to the "obscene" material. As an example, the Final Report of the Attorney General's Commission on Pornography (1986), often called the Meese Report, simply included examples of obscene material as an appendix and appealed to face validity, arguing that the link between obscenity and harm should not be totally predicated on scientific data and is justified by our common sense based upon reading or viewing erotic material. The Meese Commission concluded that pornography contributes to sexual violence, disputing the findings of the 1970 Lockhart Commission. However, it is itself the subject of a strong critique, including from some of its own members, for distorting research findings.

The issue of whether there is social harm from engaging with erotica highlights the importance of how a legal question is framed. Psychologists use statistics, which are normally framed around the null hypothesis. This means that they begin with a baseline assumption that two concepts are not related. As evidence accumulates it can make it increasingly unlikely that this null hypothesis is true. So, for example, we might say that the level of association that appears in our study would occur 1 in 1,000 times if caused only by chance. We would then say that this makes the null hypothesis of "no association" extremely unlikely to be true, and we reject the null hypothesis with some degree of certainty. We conclude that there is a statistically significant connection, even if it is a small one in terms of magnitude.

While rejecting the null hypothesis is accurate as a statistical statement, it is poor politics. In this case, decision-makers have repeatedly asked whether there is an association between erotica and social harm. In response, psychologists say they cannot make such a statement. Research can never show that there is no harm, only that there is no evidence that any harm occurs. In the legal arena, an argument is that without proof that there is no harm, it is safer to ban the material.

A second point is that behavioral science research interacts with law within a larger political-social framework. Although civil liberties groups welcome regulation that requires clear evidence of a behavioral harm, as noted earlier other political actors have evaluated obscene content against different standards. Conservative groups have been concerned about its impact on social values like the sanctity of marriage and behaviors like monogamy. Liberals make a similar argument but with a focus on attitudes about objectification and actions such as rape. Neither group has readily acquiesced to the argument that, absent compelling empirical research linking exposure to either type of real-world behavioral harm to others, crime in particular, people should be allowed to read and view material (Linz & Malamuth, 1993).

It is important to note that these conservative and liberal perspectives do point to possible behavioral social harms, in particular an increased propensity to cheat on one's spouse or to rape women, but again research has not supported the argument that there is a behavioral impact of either type from viewing erotica. In the case of rape, this may also reflect problems with the evidence, including the generally low rate of self-reports of rape, as well as the high standards laws have for establishing that the crime of rape has occurred. It is hard to test an empirical argument when it is difficult to do appropriate research. But the bottom line is that evidence of a connection between exposure to erotica and rape has not been found.

This discussion of the political controversy over erotica is important because it highlights the challenges of trying to define cultural questions as empirical issues. In situations in which there is a clash of cultural values, it is tempting to try to defuse the conflict by defining a clear empirical behavioral (i.e., objective) question that at least in theory can be resolved with facts (Kahan, 1999). However, in each of these areas it has been found that those whose cultural values are at stake resist defining their issues as a set of empirical questions, and controversies persist even when the empirical evidence seems clear. Exposure to erotica does not promote anti-social behavior. This conclusion flows from extensive bodies of research and reviews by national commissions (except, as noted, the Meese Commission, which is controversial) and reviews of the empirical literature, yet these results did not settle the legal conflict, because they do not address the underlying cultural values out of which the legal conflict flows.

A parallel case is the effort of the Supreme Court to defuse debates about the morality of the death penalty in *Furman v. Georgia* (1972) by suggesting that this issue is an empirical one: whether the death penalty deters crime. This empirical framing reflects both of the problems noted with erotica. First, it is not possible to prove a negative (that executions do not deter crime) and, second, that empirical evidence may be insufficient to settle a conflict that reflects a larger value conflict within American society.

Beyond the issues noted, this literature also highlights the importance of how a question is defined. Historically the focus on regulation has been on sexual content. Studies show that such content does not produce anti-social behavior. Broadening the question to include violence leads to different conclusions about impact on attitudes and, possibly, behaviors.

Recent efforts to control what people can see or do have been related to violence, while efforts to regulate erotic content have largely dwindled. As noted, psychological research on obscenity finds that one situation in which there do appear to be behavioral effects of watching erotic content is when that material includes depictions of aggression against women. This has led researchers to draw upon the psychological literature on aggression, and to use research to show that media depictions of violence influence people's real-world behavior (Robertson et al., 2013).

11.5 Violence

More recently, violent content, particularly in video games played by minors, has been directly addressed. This has led to government efforts to restrict people's freedom to do what they want, in this case playing violent video games. What does research on media violence show? It suggests that media violence motivates social harm (Huesmann & Eron, 1986; Huesmann et al., Eron, 2003; Murray, 1973). As has been noted, to the degree that erotica includes violence toward women, social harm is more likely to be found. However, violence is the key, not erotic content. Erotica alone does not motivate harm, violence alone does.

Research in the area of media violence raises many of the textbook issues about methodology that are central to broader discussions within psychology, and which influence whether legal psychology research is taken seriously by the legal system. One issue is the distinction between laboratory and field research. Laboratory studies are more likely to find media influences than are field studies. Another issue is the importance of psychological impact vs. behavioral impact. It is easier to change what people think and feel, than what they do. A third is the value of experimental vs. correlational studies. It is more difficult to show cause and effect outside an experiment. Longstanding discussions within psychology about the quality of different methodologies become important to the legal community when psychological findings are drawn into a policy discussion. As with any use of evidence in adjudication, there are disagreements about what constitutes strong evidence, and whether efforts to summarize a field of research should exclude weak studies, or attempt to consider all evidence but weight each study by its validity.

Another important issue to consider is the distinction between statistical significance and strength of influence (effect size). This involves assessing the importance of a particular factor among the many influences that shape a person's behavior, contemporaneously and over time. Something could be statistically significant, but be only a minor factor in comparison to other elements in a person's life. We have already seen this in the case of many behaviors which are more strongly impacted by the situation than by the dispositions of the people in the situation. Dispositions may matter, but situational factors are more impactful in many cases.

In the case of erotica policy, decision-makers have frequently used this strength of impact argument, in two distinct ways. First, they note that law seeks to regulate depictions of erotic behavior, but ignores evidence that unregulated depictions of violence have much stronger behavioral effects. On the other hand, this same research suggests that neither erotica nor media violence are the strongest factors shaping whether a person commits crimes. Violence in video games has a similar or lesser effect size than watching violence on television or in movies—so why ban one and not others?

As empirical evidence of the harm of violence has developed, the attention of some public interest groups has shifted toward the regulation of violent content. The political problem they encounter is that violence sells commercial products, including video games, films, television series, and books. Thus, there is tremendous resistance to its restriction. The evidence that suggests media violence causes social harm has generally had little impact on law, and there have been only a few efforts to ban violent content beyond video games, and in the video game case only among juveniles. Violence is deeply enmeshed in American culture, and efforts to restrict it would likely meet the same type of widespread cultural resistance seen in efforts to regulate access to firearms. Societal values and commercial interests, not research evidence, drive public policy in this arena.

Emerging efforts to manage the content of online platforms have encountered similar problems. Whatever are the potential harms of hate filled or inaccuracy laden posts are, they are found to be widely viewed. This poses a problem for profit oriented companies who would undermine their business model by restricting such content in the same way movie studies would if they stopped making violent films.

The most recent manifestation of efforts to regulate people's activities comes specifically via the issue of juvenile access to video games, the topic of the *Brown v. Entertainment Merchants Association* (2011) decision. As background, legal authorities have always been more willing to consider restricting the freedom of juveniles, because the law does not regard them as entitled to full adult rights. The concept of in loco parentis in the juvenile justice system sees legal authorities acting as benevolent caretakers, rather than being punitive.

As Justice Scalia notes in *Brown v. Entertainment Merchants Association* (2011), it does not make much sense to focus on trying to ban violent video games based upon research evidence that exposure to violent content may damage them when children are generally exposed to violence in books and other media. Justice Scalia interestingly mentions not the violent culture of modern America, but the violence in children's fairy tales (e.g.

Snow White). He notes that research evidence suggests that these various forms of exposure to violence have a similarly strong influence on people.

In *Brown v. Entertainment Merchants Association* (2011), the Supreme Court rejected the regulation of the sale of violent video games to minors. This opinion is important because it includes efforts to deal with the social science literature, and accepts empirical research findings on social harm as being legally relevant. Justice Scalia dismissed the social science evidence, suggesting that it is primarily correlational. Justice Breyer is positive about the evidence and includes a lengthy appendix citing numerous studies by psychologists and other social scientists. He cites two types of evidence: research studies which suggest a link between playing violent video games and social harms, and opinions of professional organizations, such as the American Psychological Association (APA), which also suggest a link. The Court's use of these studies reflects a high level of willingness to engage with social science research findings, but also points to some of the challenges of using that evidence to reach a conclusion.

Justice Breyer notes that the APA concluded that playing violent video games has a damaging impact on people and changes their behavior. A report from the APA (August, 2015) suggests that violent video game play is linked to increased aggression. However, the report notes that insufficient evidence exists about whether the link extends to criminal violence or delinquency. The issue, therefore, is what type of impact matters from a policy point of view. Is it psychological change, for example, becoming less empathetic? Or is it behavioral change? And if it is behavioral change, is it bullying in the schoolyard or heightened criminal activity?

Most of the studies on video games look at the impact on people's attitudes. A few studies look at interpersonal aggression (e.g., bullying), and only one study was found in the American Psychological Association meta-analysis that looks at delinquent behavior. Further, there are issues of effect size. Mathur and VanderWeele (2019) suggest in a review of meta-analyses that "all of the meta-analyses do in fact point to the conclusion that, in the vast majority of settings, violent video games do increase aggressive behavior but that these effects are almost always quite small" (p. 705). The size of impact can be assessed both directly, in terms of effect sizes, or relative to other factors. Is playing violent video games, as Justice Scalia notes, the same thing as reading "Snow White"?

In the *Brown* decision, Justice Breyer cites a number of studies of the association between playing violent video games and aggressive behavior. He declines to evaluate the studies, but cites the opinion of professional groups, an example of which is the brief by the American Psychological Association. This approach had been used by the Court since the time of the earlier decision in *Brown v. Board of Education* (1954), where the justices similarly cited the opinions of social scientists, gathered in a survey, to support their arguments. This is similar to the *Frye* model for admitting scientific evidence into trials after establishing a consensus of the scientific community, although this is a consensus not about methodological validity but about an overall conclusion about the findings. It assumes that such briefs reflect a neutral and balanced evaluation of evidence on the question, something that is not always true (Rustad & Koenig, 1993).

Justice Breyer lists a number of studies to make his argument that violence in the media influences behavior. However, he does not take advantage of the newer methodology of meta-analysis, which combines research findings (Glass et al., 1981; Lipsey & Wilson, 2001; Sohn, 1995). It converts multiple findings to a common metric of impact, while weighting studies by the quality of their methodology. As we have seen it has the advantage of taking a large literature and reducing it to a single, overall conclusion. As an example, Prescott et al. (2018) summarize all of the studies (there are 24) they could identify that look at the impact of violent video game playing on subsequent, real-world, overt physical aggression. They conclude that there is a statistically significant impact. However, they also note that the impact, while reliably found, is small in magnitude. A second meta-analysis was conducted by an APA task force (Calvert et al., 2017). They similarly found that violent video game exposure was associated with increases in aggressive thought and action. However, they conclude that there is no evidence of a link to "delinquency or criminal behavior" (p. 126). One reason for this latter non-finding is the lack of sufficient research on this issue. From a legal point of view it is impact on criminal behavior that has been the traditional justification for restrictions.

The question of what target behavior is appropriate for a study of social harm has recently emerged as some lawmakers and public interest groups have sought to link violent video games to the adolescents who commit mass shootings, using their playing of video games as the default explanation for their later violent behavior. There are political reasons for this, such as deflecting attention from the violence in movies and the availability of guns as key American cultural issues. However, the pattern has been the same as that seen with other legal issues: assertions of a connection between violent video games and mass shooting involvement without empirical support.

The relevance to law and psychology is that the rise of the issue of whether violent video game use impacts on mass shootings motivated the American Psychological Association (2020) to highlight the distinction made above between interpersonal aggression and violence. They point out that, when the earlier studies were reviewed by the American Psychological Association task force, they defined aggression as including insults, threats, hitting, pushing, hair pulling, biting and other forms of verbal and physical aggression. There is no psychological research evidence connecting video game use to real-world mass shootings, just as there is no evidence connecting it to juvenile delinquency. In the case of mass shootings there is the further question of how such research evidence could be collected.

In thinking about video games, it is important to note the rapid advances in game technology. In particular, virtual reality allows players to participate in games with heightened immersion, literally feeling that they are in the space of the game. This is being experienced in combination with technologies that allow actors to have their physical movements represented in the virtual space. It is unclear how these changes in games will affect their influence on those who play them. Because these changes involve the psychology of experiencing video games, they are an obvious target for psychological research. Many of these changes in the structure of games bring them closer to the training methods used by the military to desensitize soldiers to engaging in aggressive actions such as killing (Grossman, 2009).

It is also worth noting that psychological research does not need to be directed only at the harms of playing video games. Studies suggest that playing video games produces many of the positive effects of other forms of playing among children. Such game playing is linked to developing higher IQs and other cognitive strengths (Bediou et al., 2018), as well as to greater general problem-solving ability (Granic et al., 2014). Games

also often provide social benefits because there are ways to play coop-
eratively with other children. By focusing only on possible harm, the
legal system does not confront the more complex problem of weighing
costs and benefits associated with video games. Legal regulation needs an
evidence-informed understanding of which aspects of video games are
associated with benefits and which with harms. It is likely that the content
of the game is key, suggesting another important research agenda for the
future.

11.6 Giving up freedom

Psychology has also intersected with law in another area involving personal freedom: the issue of consent and why people "willingly" give away
their privacy. Legal authorities gain the right to intrude into people's lives
when people "willingly and knowingly" consent to those intrusions. This
can occur when a police officer asks for permission to search someone's
car, an internet website asks to collect cookies detailing a person's search
history, or a scientist asks someone to agree to participate in a medical
experiment. The legal perspective on consent is that people are able to
make decisions about whether to give away their right to autonomy, so
evidence that they have done so "willingly and voluntarily" is a defense
against claims of harm resulting from actions for which they have given
consent.

Consent has several benefits. Psychologically, it leads a person to feel that
they have chosen what happens, and simultaneously leads observers and
authorities to believe that the person has chosen to accept the results of
what they do. Legally, it makes it harder for people to object to and seek
redress for consequences flowing from their choices. People assume
responsibility and risk by freely choosing to engage in conduct, as demonstrated by their consent. For that reason, people are often asked to express
consent verbally or in writing before moving forward.

The classic example of consent involves police requests to engage in
various types of investigatory action, for example, "May we search your
car?" Psychologists note that people often feel tremendous social pressure
to defer to the police. As was true in the earlier case of confessions during
an interrogation, research suggests that in later legal proceedings object-

ing to the results of such searches, judges and juries do not recognize this social pressure, or factor it adequately into legal decisions about whether the person "truly consented" to the search. This "voluntary" consent then supersedes the normal requirement that the police need to have probable cause that a crime is being committed to justify a search.

The aspect of consent which intersects law and psychology is the suggestion that consent has to be given "voluntarily" and is not due to duress. This implies some understanding of why a person consented, which is a psychological question. It requires an observer to infer the state of mind of the actor. In legal proceedings a judge decides whether, considering the totality of the circumstances, a reasonable person would feel free to refuse consent. The courts take a similar approach to whether someone has been seized by law enforcement. Would a reasonable person believe that they were free to leave?

The Supreme Court has ruled that, from a legal perspective, if officers are polite and ask for permission, any ensuing consent is valid. The Court has not chosen to consider the social context of authority relations that psychologists would suggest puts situational pressure on people to acquiesce (Nadler & Trout, 2012). Here the Court argues that the implied coercive authority of armed officers disappears when they ask for permission. For example:

> He spoke to the passengers one by one and in a polite, quiet voice. Nothing he said would suggest to a reasonable person that he or she was barred from leaving the bus or otherwise terminating the encounter .... There was ... no threat, and no command, not even an authoritative tone of voice. (*United States v. Drayton*, 2002, p. 204)

The opposite of free choice is compulsion. When do people feel compelled to accede? Do people feel that they can walk away if a police officer stops them on the street? Kessler (2009) surveyed the public to answer this question. He found that 80 percent of those interviewed did not feel free to decline to be questioned. Nadler (2002) refers to the tone of the police as "hollow politeness." She notes that studies show such searches are viewed as negative by citizens and undermine public views about the police. Finally, Nadler makes it clear that citizens may well accurately understand the reality of modern policing. Those who refuse were often searched anyway, and delayed or threatened by officers.

A study of suppression hearings reinforces the finding that judges have a very high standard for rejecting police behavior and only question voluntariness when there is clear evidence of the threat or use of physical force (Kessler, 2009). These findings intersect with the observation made before that people have a hard time factoring social pressure into their conception of free choice, and observers similarly do not recognize the social pressures that may lie behind a "free choice." It is primarily the evidence of physical menace or harm that raises flags among observers, just as was the case earlier with interrogations. If a suspect was physically beaten during an interrogation, jurors are less inclined to put weight on their confession. Consistent with a theme in this volume observers under-weight the power of situations to shape behavior.

More recently Sommers (2020) and Sommers & Bohns (2019) have conducted a series of studies mapping out the psychology of consent. Their particular argument is that perceived consent can still be seen as freely chosen even when obtained via fraud. They note that philosophical ideas of consent focus upon "knowing, competent, and free" consent. The public believes that overt physical coercion, but not deception, undermines consent. If a person consents to an operation because it was explained deceitfully by the doctor and they are injured, can they go to court and win? This research suggests that juries will regard consenting, even after being deceived, as accepting the consequences of the choice made. It will be hard to recover damages.

This finding highlights the value of identifying gaps between public understandings of law and the content of legal doctrine. A conse-quence of this gap is illustrated in their studies of litigation over harm after deceit-linked consent. This study might be described as modern Stanley Milgram. In his classic study on obedience to authority, already described, Milgram showed the strikingly powerful impact of social pres-sure. Sommers first shows that people acquiesce to intrusive requests such as allowing someone to gain access to their cell phone content with very little hesitation. She further demonstrates that people asked to judge the actions of others are insensitive to the impact of situational forces. As in many areas of the law, situational forces are in the perceptual background for both actors and observers.

A similar earlier discussion about Robinson and Darley (1995) noted the possibility of looking across many areas of law and highlighting situations in which there is a gap between the written law and public views about what is appropriate. This volume makes the general point that it is important to map the areas in which public views depart from legal rules and recognize that in such areas of law problems of public acceptance of legal authority are more likely to occur.

11.7 Psychological impact: nothing more than feelings?

In the case of erotica and violent video games, many people argue that there should be a high standard for restricting individual behavior. That standard should be that the behavior has to hurt others (social harm) and there has to be some real-world behavioral manifestation of such harm, in particular, evidence of criminal behavior. The issue that has arisen more recently is whether this same high standard should be maintained for other types of behavior, ranging from sexual harassment to bullying, where the actor is intentionally directing their negative actions at others.

The question of harming others returns us to examining what constitutes harm. One clear example of behavioral harm is criminal behavior, because other people are the victims. An expanded list of harms includes a variety of possible impacts on victims, including victim suicide, damage to the victim's success in life (e.g., through lower school achievement), social withdrawal and declines in victim's community engagement or other prosocial behavior, and poor victim physical health due to stress. These are some of the impacts that being bullied and harassed can have on the target person.

A distinct form of harm, which might lead to these changes in behavior, is psychological impact. This can include acute or chronic anxiety and stress, depression, suicidal ideation, social withdrawal, fear, and symptoms of post-traumatic stress disorder. The issue is whether these psychological harms are legally recognized harms in themselves, or only become relevant if they are shown to be linked to behavior.

Studies suggest that various forms of social behavior, including sexual/race-based harassment, bullying, and verbal abuse lead to psychological harm (Jay, 2009; Juvonen & Graham, 2014). However, the connection to damaging behavior among victims is less clear, partly due to the lack of studies, and also to the intrinsic problems associated with measuring behavioral changes compared with psychological changes. An important question for the legal system is the degree to which psychological harm matters.

Jay (2009) argues that research on the impact of various forms of verbal abuse (hate speech, sexual harassment, obscene telephone calls) is indeterminate as to harm, in part because the legal system has not clearly articulated what constitutes harm. He suggests that it is important not to create restrictions where the evidence about harm is not clear or compelling. He calls for evidence of actual harm, and argues that "scientific evidence is useful where common sense fails." Instead, "courts need to abandon inaccurate commonsense views of offensive speech, and be more open to expert testimony and scientific evidence regarding the nature of offensive words" (p. 94).

11.8 The reasonable person

Taking people's subjective states into account raises a series of issues for the law. One is which subjective states matter (emotional distress, pain and suffering, etc.) and how these subjective states will be measured. The other is how to evaluate any reaction that is psychological, rather than physical or behavioral. Do jurors, for example, simply award damages based upon how much emotional distress a defendant says they feel, or is there some reasonable amount of distress that a victim should feel in a particular situation? Legal theories attempt to deal with this latter issue by reference to the fictional idea of a reasonable person. Because this idea is typically not defined, it is unclear whether decision-makers view it as descriptive, as in an average person, or prescriptive, reflecting the response that the average person ought to have. This idea of reasonableness is used both in judging the conduct of a defendant, and the reaction of the plaintiff.

The idea of a reasonable person has an important role in civil trials, where jurors are asked to evaluate the defendant by considering whether they took the precautions that would be expected from a reasonable person. Similarly, legal arguments for psychological damages invoke the idea of a reasonable level of pain and suffering. In legal instructions, jurors are given only limited guidance concerning what it means to act as a reasonable person, so psychological research on the question of how reasonableness is understood is very important (Votruba, 2013).

This issue has recently arisen in the area of litigation involving hostile work environments, where the plaintiff's reaction is compared to the standard of reasonableness. The law considers two issues in evaluating whether a work environment is hostile. One is the perception of the "victim." If the victim does not feel harassed, the environment is not harassing. As an example, experiments in which men objectify women are not found to have a negative influence on women who like being objectified by men (Kimble et al., 2016).

The second factor in defining a hostile environment is whether a reasonable person would view the environment as hostile. Here studies indicate that, in contrast to the intention of the law, observer judgments about reasonableness are shaped by a variety of extra-legal factors. These include misunderstandings about the impact of environments on victims (Wiener et al., 2013), the gender of the person doing the rating, and attitudes about objectification among men (Wiener & Vardsveen, 2018). The lack of general agreement about the features of a non-hostile vs. a hostile workplace makes it difficult to create a single reasonable person standard. This is where a diverse jury, reflecting community values, can consider what is appropriate or inappropriate behavior.

11.9 Intrusions into a person's privacy

Another type of potential psychological harm to an individual is an intrusion into their lives by state actors. Discussions of intrusions, via police stops for example, often involve a consideration of the presumed impact on the person's psychology. The literature on the justification of police stops contains much conjecture about how such stops might influence the well-being of the people who are stopped, particularly members of minority groups. For example, in *United States v. Martinez-Fuerte* (1976) the Supreme Court considered highway stops at a fixed checkpoint set up to question occupants to determine if they are illegal immigrants. In writing an opinion, Justice Powell considered the psychological consequences of such stops, and suggested that they are not "frightening or offensive"

(p. 543), even if they are based largely upon membership in a particular ethnic group (in this case apparent Mexican ancestry). In dissent, Justice Brennan argues that such stops are inherently upsetting and humiliating. He concludes that it seems likely that deep resentment will be stirred by a sense of unfair discrimination.

Cases in this area raise several psychological questions. One is whether it is the intrusion per se, or the inference that the intrusion is based upon ethnicity, as in "the police stopped me because I appear to be Mexican," that is psychologically damaging. Court cases in this area have emphasized that intrusions must be based on some reasonable evidence and should not be open to the possibility of being, or being seen as, arbitrary, capricious, or based on group membership. Research has made it clear that the inferences people make about why they have been stopped shape their psychological reaction (Tyler & Wakslak, 2004), but less is known about how to prevent those inferences from occurring. Even avoiding the use of ethnicity as a profile criterion for a police stop will not be effective unless people actually believe that such criteria are not being used.

An example of a broader effort to use psychology to construct legal doctrine in the area of intrusions is the work of Slobogin and Schumacher (1993a, 1993b). This study details a series of ways in which legal authorities can intrude into people's lives (wiretapping, going through a person's garbage, surveilling someone's home). Respondents are asked to rate those intrusions both in terms of their personal feelings about being intruded upon in this way, and by the intrusiveness of this practice as a general law enforcement policy. The authors then compare people's feelings on intrusiveness to legal standards about the legality of these behaviors, and argue that there needs to be a closer alignment.

The Slobogin and Schumacher approach to intrusion is consistent with the efforts of the Court to define community standards in cases of erotica. The legal system can define its rules through an understanding of how they are perceived by people in the community, but then must answer the question of which community is relevant. In the case of the police, actions are typically directed disproportionately toward minorities. Does it matter whether the majority population views this impact as appropriate, or should the focus be on the views of the most impacted groups?

The Slobogin and Schumacher findings are further important because they indicate that people's views are influenced by the circumstances of the moment. For example, standards change when people are more afraid of crime. Is it appropriate for standards to change depending on conditions? And if so, is public opinion a suitable signaling tool to guide such changes?

This question illustrates an important challenge in policy research, namely how to incorporate public opinion, which is sometimes based on a misunderstanding of the facts. In this arena attention to public views can be concerning. Moral panics, for example, public fear of widespread violence when there is no evidence that it is actually occurring, can lead to (bad) public policy being enacted. Of broader concern is the finding that people often have a vague and erroneous understanding of facts about their community, their country, and the world in general. Efforts to pay attention to people's views need to be balanced against evidence about the relationship that those views have to actual conditions.

It is equally true that the law must balance subjective feelings, for example, the belief that one is in a hostile work environment, against some standard of reasonable reactions to a particular environment. Law cannot be driven simply by a person's feelings, especially when different people may have different feelings in the same situation. People in legal situations have a clear motivation for exaggerating their feelings which makes it hard to evaluate self-report.

On the other hand, there are problems when the law does not pay attention to those feelings at all, as was noted in the discussion about settlements in civil cases (i.e., the problem of trying to solve nonmonetary problems with monetary payments). Problems are created when people feel that the issues that are important to them have not been addressed and a just disposition of their case has not occurred.

12 Conclusion

Law and psychology have been intertwined throughout the 20th century. This connection has sometimes reflected a happy marriage of science and law, and sometimes has fallen into conflict and acrimony. Bersoff (1986) notes:

> If [the relationship between experimental psychologists and the courts] were to be examined by a Freudian, the analyst would no doubt conclude that it is a highly neurotic, conflict-ridden ambivalent affair (I stress affair because it is certainly no marriage). Like an insensitive scoundrel involved with an attractive but fundamentally irksome lover who too much wants to be courted, the judiciary shamelessly uses the social sciences. (pp. 155–156)

Psychologists have frequently expressed frustration like those expressed by Bersoff because to the lack of research awareness reflected in legal decisions, and the generally intuition-based and politically driven nature of the American legal system. Although psychologists have sometimes expressed frustrations, the material outlined in this book illustrates the tremendous range of the areas where psychologists have been taken seriously and have influenced the law.

Ambivalence about the law and psychology relationship has two sides. Legal authorities find the unwillingness of psychologists to recognize that facts have to be considered within a larger system of trade-offs challenging to manage. As has been continually highlighted in this volume, the degree to which law should reflect facts versus values is an ongoing issue throughout law, as is the issue of which values—public values or the values of political leaders or legal scholars.

Further, the legal system needs to make decisions that resolve issues working in uncertain situations, and often with limited resources. The legal system must have a working system and cannot pause because psychologists feel that "further research is needed." There must be a way to resolve conflicts and enforce rules. The reality that mistakes are made is an underlying and accepted presumption of both legal authorities and the public. Stability, predictability and the need for generally acceptable ongoing procedures are central to governance and law.

Further, psychologists often stop after raising questions about existing evidence and procedures, without providing achievable solutions. In particular, psychologists often fail to frame their discussions with an eye to the political realities surrounding law. Legal authorities are unlikely to be enthusiastic in acknowledging errors that undermine confidence in the current legal system without having another approach they can put in place that addresses those errors. This reflects the general recognition among reformers that leaders are reluctant to acknowledge a problem unless they can simultaneously propose a viable improvement that solves that problem.

These issues aside, the growth in the number and sophistication of legal psychologists and the proliferation of high-quality research is striking (Monahan & Walker, 2011). In most of the areas discussed there are so many studies being conducted at this time that reaching overall conclusions now requires the use of a meta-analysis to summarize across multiple studies.

And, of course, with the growth of the field there has been an increase in controversies within psychology, with researchers disputing among themselves about the implications of the research. The question of when there is a consensus upon which policy recommendations can be based has become more important. Organizations such as the American Psychological Association have been encouraged to write briefs about issues before the courts and psychologists have participated in National Academy of Sciences panels and Presidential task forces.

Much of the importance of what psychology has to offer to law involves evidence regarding the everyday operation of the legal system. The two traditionally most-studied areas are eyewitness identification and jury decision-making. And, with both, extensive research has produced both theoretical and applied strides. It is further true that psychologists have learned a great deal about productive law–psychology collaboration through their efforts in these arenas and these lessons are and can be further applied across the entire field.

It is noteworthy that these areas focus on the trial context. As this volume makes clear, many of the important actions in the legal system, civil and criminal, occur prior to or outside the framework of formal trials. The courts are a symbolic representation of legal ideals and adjudicate difficult or high-profile cases, but such cases are very infrequent. Other key areas outside the formal trial system that are being productively studied include negotiation, mediation, and settlement, as well as criminal investigation, interrogation and plea bargaining.

One adjustment that the field of law and psychology can make is to focus less on jury decision-making (Lempert, 1993; Kadane, 1993) and the mechanisms for weighing evidence in trials. This would reflect a recognition that the processes of negotiation and mediation (Hollander-Blumoff, 2010, 2017; Robbennolt and Sternlight, 2012) as well as plea bargaining and settlement conferences (Smith, 2005), are important.

The lack of trials is particularly relevant in the case of scientific evidence, since the mechanisms for evaluating the quality of evidence are embedded in trial procedures. The system is based upon the belief that judicial scrutiny and the rigors of cross-examination during a trial vet the probative value of evidence. It is here that experts testify about eyewitnesses and other lay misunderstandings. The lack of adjudication means that this mechanism for evaluating evidence is used infrequently. A consequence is that the bulk of evidence considered in investigations, plea bargaining, and settlements is typically not subjected to a systematic evaluation of its quality, and it is easy for misconceptions about probative value to develop, both in particular cases and in relationship to entire classes of evidence (fingerprints, bite marks, eyewitness identifications, confessions, etc.).

Legal psychologists have increasingly recognized the importance of moving their focus away from trials and toward the overall operation of the criminal justice funnel. In the eyewitness arena this has more recently occurred through a refocus on initial lineups. There has also been increasing attention to investigatory and interrogation procedures, rather than on the impact of confessions during trials. In civil justice this same recognition leads to a focus on processes of mediation and other forms of informal conflict management.

Consistent with the move away from a focus on trials, a further important development in law and psychology has been the increasing research on the psychological dynamics involved in the decision-making of forensic scientists, police officers, prosecutors and judges. Like juries these actors all make decisions that balance facts and values in managing the many cases with which they deal. However, they do so outside of and usually before there is any traditional adjudication.

Psychologists have also increasingly recognized the need to develop social change strategies crafted through an understanding of the complex value trade-offs that guide legal decisions (Tanford, 1990). Psychologists such as Gary Wells or Craig Haney have moved from being focused only on science to taking on a broader role as advocates of social change.

The issues at stake for the legal system include preserving the existing adversary process, promoting efficiency by discouraging trials, avoiding retrials and managing the authority given to juries, supporting the ideals of evidence-based and accurate verdicts, reaching just decisions, and maintaining a system consistent with public goals and values. Research-informed evidence is relevant as well, but is not the only factor shaping what happens in this complex system.

These trade-offs are especially strong when important public values are intertwined with law. In these cases people whose values are at stake resist allowing decisions to be defined by and decided through empirical research. In the context of generally evidence-free policy debates, people often rely on commonsense popular wisdom. An ongoing challenge for researchers has been finding ways to inject evidence-informed policies into such highly charged political debates.

Wells (2005) suggests that influencing legal policy requires psychologists to consider how their research findings fit into the complex fabric of legal institutions and authorities. He argues that impact does not depend "solely on the quality and relevance of the research" (p. 499). It requires psychologists to grapple with the complexity of the factors that legal decision-makers are balancing. As an example, the legal system has considerable control over the form of lineups (a system variable) so arguing for changes in this procedure targets something which can be changed (Wells, 2020). Wells emphasizes that, because the legal system has to solve problems, simply raising doubts is not effective. Policy-makers need to see evidence that there is an alternative system that has clear advantages.

They also need to believe that the changes advocated will be accepted within the prevailing legal system.

A focus on non-trial contexts has the potential advantage of opening up the possibility of more experimentation in law. While unexamined discretion can be critiqued for being potentially shaped by poor decisions and allowing actions based on bias, it is also true that legal actors have more ability to vary how they treat cases in this less regulated arena. They are not constrained by the rules of equal treatment for all defendants that define trials. This means that progressive legal decision-makers can experiment with different procedures and enact different policies, examining the influence of each change on outcomes. They can demonstrate that new ideas will work.

A number of social scientists have suggested a greater focus on institutional reform. For example, Sherman (2018) suggests that rather than trying to manage police behavior via punishing a particular police officer for misconduct after it happens there ought to be a neutral professional investigation of police shootings aimed at changing police procedures to prevent a recurrence of any unnecessary use of violence. The call for institutional analysis has been particularly strong in the arena of civil justice where there is a long tradition of trying to identify and address people's legal needs and design system that meet those needs (Sandefur, 2009; Sandefur & Albiston, 2013; Sandefur & Smyth, 2011).

Institutional analysis requires a proactive and aggregate level focus on the overall dynamics of the legal system. The current legal system is built around a retrospective individual-level focus. People engage in actions that may violate rules and then the legal system engages in procedures to determine and implement accountability. This approach fits well with the case-based framework of American common law, and fits an individual level psychology focus. An institutional design framework differs in two key ways. The first is by addressing problems at an aggregate system level. Instead of looking at an individual, the issue is how the overall system functions. Second, an institutional-level model is proactive. Instead of letting bad behavior occur and then punishing the people who engage in it, the goal is to design the system in advance to minimize problems. While these are clear differences it is important not to overstate them. Legal authorities argue that the way that they punish bad conduct is a signal to society that shapes future behavior.

In order for the legal system to be more proactive in designing institutions, it needs to more systematically study its operations on an ongoing basis. Consistent with the tradition of intuition-based law, the legal system has not prioritized efforts to study itself empirically. An example of making such an effort is the COMPSTAT system, used by the police in cities such as New York. This system keeps real-time records of crime in different areas of a city. Those data are then used to shift the deployment of police officers. While it is reactive in responding to crime, this system demonstrates the possibility of gathering data and using it to determine how legal authorities should function to address problems.

Because of the fragmented and local nature of American legal institutions and the reality of local political control, there has been very little pressure to develop systematic data collection. The system has been largely an "evidence-free zone" that manages individual cases based upon the presumed expertise and wisdom of legal actors. As has been outlined, those actors face very little pressure to account for their actions and, even when individual authorities are sympathetic to reform efforts, they have difficulty obtaining good information. Researchers who go into police departments or courts are often directed to basements filled with piles of disorganized case files. As an example, one issue highlighted by recent public controversies is that America has no systematic records of when and how frequently the police use force.

It would not be possible for the legal system to continue as it does without the support of the society within which it is embedded. America has a long history of managing social order at the local level. There has been little systematic effort to articulate a national model of legal procedures and to subject it to empirical validation. For example, the courts have handled cases unsystematically through plea bargaining and, more recently, managerial justice (Kohler-Hausmann, 2014; Smith, 2005). There is a pernicious dynamic around these informal systems. Because of the nontransparent way they function there is very little information available about how the law is being enacted. And, because there is very little information available there is very little basis for evidence-informed evaluation and change. Change occurs in response to dramatic events, a heinous crime or an egregious police shooting, rather than through systematic observation of the everyday activities of law. There is a maxim in law that "hard cases make poor law" but in the policy arena extreme cases drive social change changes and not the much larger bulk of everyday cases that flow through the system.

This call for institutional analysis is consistent with the general recognition in legal psychology that the current legal system places too much weight on the belief that actions flow from individual dispositions, so the lever for shaping individual conduct is found in the person. As evidence reviewed in this volume repeatedly shows, situational forces also shape behavior. This is true in the literature on the antecedents of criminal conduct, a literature which implicates the environment in generating criminal conduct. It is true in the literature on risk prediction and management, which demonstrates that situational factors are more important in producing violence than people's predispositions. It is true of the role of situational forces in leading to false confessions, and in the role of situational pressure in cases where the police ask for consent to search. Hence, there needs to be a parallel effort to focus on redesigning situations.

The central point from a legal perspective is not that situations matter but that people systematically underweight situational forces, consistent with the fundamental attribution error. Legal decision-making ignores evidence of powerful environmental and situational influences in favor of an image of people as autonomous actors whose will determines their behavior and who can, therefore, be held responsible for their actions. What particularly matters here is the mismatch between the true sources of behavior and the perceived sources of behavior.

Another aspect of situational forces are the organizational factors shaping the actions of legal authorities. An example of this argument is the recent discussion of policing in America. There is no question that the killing of Black Americans such as George Floyd is a tragedy. However, discussions of police reform have been linked to outrage over these events, outrage which arises and dissipates (in a long tradition of reacting to "moral panics"). Consequently there has been a series of equally saddening killings over the years, without any systematic long-term reform of police practices. Such killings are not simply actions of a few "bad apples". They reflect a warrior style of policing that, even when less dramatic in its consequences than killings, influences many police-resident interactions. Changing this style is important, but is a less dramatic argument than trying to convict "bad apples" in response to public outrage over extreme events (Quattlebaum & Tyler, 2020; Stoughton, 2015).

Finally, it is always important to emphasize that psychological processes operate within the structural realities of our society. As an example, social psychology has established a set of principles through which direct contact between people from different racial or ethnic groups can be expected to reduce prejudice. This important psychological finding is limited in impact in our society because of the persistence of racial segregation in housing. People live in largely segregated neighborhoods, even in the 21st century. Psychological models of contact are not helpful in situations in which people do not have contact.

Another example is jury decision-making. In theory, juries balance perspectives and cancel out prejudices to achieve verdicts reflecting community values. But in some areas the system is set up to exclude certain groups, such as the poor and minorities, from jury pools. Even when people are in jury pools, they can be excluded during voir dire. People's perspectives can only shape deliberation if they are actually on a jury.

Structural factors shape the realities of the legal process and influence when and how evidence about psychology is relevant to law and legal policies. People who never meet cannot become friends, so segregation undermines the possibility of the positive effects psychologists have shown can occur due to interpersonal contact. Jury rules exclude some groups from being on juries. Those excluded from procedures cannot influence the outcome of jury deliberation.

Structural factors can conversely shape who is included in legal procedures. The police are known to overpolice minority neighborhoods, relative to their crime rates. This means that the police are more likely to see rule breaking by minorities, leading to more arrests. Risk prediction tools consider arrest records when recommending sentences, leading to a negative impact on minority sentences through a procedure that on the surface is "neutral". Similarly prediction tools consider factors such as whether someone has lived in public housing, something linked to being poor.

12.1 Evidence-informed policies

The research reviewed in this volume makes clear that the science of psychology and the culture of social science are not perfect. Even in areas in which there is considerable research evidence available, psychologists still struggle to provide authorities with a clear answer to their questions about the most desirable legal policies and practices. This is partly because of limits in the research and publication processes in psychological science, and partly due to the reality that psychology is a field with its own culture and institutions.

Part of the culture of psychology is continually recognizing that "more research is needed." There is seldom a point at which a complex issue has been addressed to everyone's satisfaction. There are more typically a variety of views about the meaning of the research findings, as is illustrated by studies in areas as varied as lineups and violent video games. As a field, psychology has a variety of ways of identifying a consensus among psychologists about a particular issue.

Of course, no consensus is ever total and there are frequently minority opinions and dissents. An important development has been the systemization of mechanisms for meta-analysis, organized ways to summarize across multiple studies and read an overall conclusion about some legal issue.

It is not the goal of psychological research to reach a final answer, in sharp contrast to the desire of the legal system to resolve problems. An example is the *Brown* decision on desegregation. By citing psychological evidence on the harm of segregation the Supreme Court seemed to be inviting a research debate. And opposed parties rapidly identified social scientists who would be willing to present opposing evidence. But the Court defined their factual findings as findings of law, precluding further research controversies. Using psychological research findings but not allowing them to undergo normal scientific evolution is problematic.

The inability to give definitive conclusions in psychology is amplified by the nature of psychological theory. There is no grand theory that covers every situation. Rather, psychology is a field of situational interactions. This means that different models are helpful in explaining thoughts, feelings and behaviors in different settings. The answer to a broad question, like whether viewing violence in the mass media motivates aggressive behavior, is that the correct conclusion depends on a number of factors. There is not one simple answer, and it is possible to specify circumstances under which different conclusions are reached.

The impact of psychology on law has also been less than it might have been because for many years applied research was considered a lesser task, and many major psychology departments would not hire scholars who focused on law and psychology. Today psychology is more focused on translational research, i.e., studies with real-world applications, making psychology a more important player in the legal world. Nonetheless, if psychology is compared to economics it is clear that other fields have been more central to the policy making process for decades.

Further, the centrality of laboratory experiments to psychological research has led to skepticism among legal authorities about whether its research findings applied in real-world settings. The famous undergraduate research subject is known to differ from adults behaving in natural settings in a number of ways (Sears, 1986). And experimental tasks can often seem highly artificial and unlikely to engage subjects in high-stakes decisions or behaviors. The differences between a group of college students acting as jurors in a fictional case and people on a real jury deciding the fate of a person who committed a crime is one example.

Many of the concerns about laboratory experiments can be addressed by field studies which are experiments conducted in natural settings (Gerber & Green, 2012). However, unlike other institutions, for example, companies, the legal system is still resistant to experiments because they deny people equal access to law. To do an experiment there has to be inequality of treatments. One approach that has been used in legal settings is not to create a control group through depriving some people of benefits, but rather to give everyone their normal benefits and then give an experimental group additional benefits that they would not normally receive.

12.2 Prospects for the future

In the early years of the 21st century the importance of the field of law and psychology is growing. The range and sophistication of research has also

expanded and developed. Psychology has offered the legal system important evidence-informed tools for dealing with issues ranging from police
lineups to the meaning of a hostile work environment. Psychologists have
at the same time become more sophisticated in their efforts to cooperate
with legal authorities in developing evidence that speaks directly to the
concerns of legal authorities and is therefore more likely to be adopted.
These are all optimistic and hopeful signs.

There are many areas in which progress can still be made. Psychologists
continue to work within an environment that is dominated by intuition
and commonsense wisdom. That system functions by granting large
amounts of discretionary authority to legal actors without mechanisms
of accountability or transparency. The broadly dispersed nature of legal
authority and the general use of informal procedures often leads to a lack
of information and makes the systematic study of legal processes difficult.

Law and psychology is also challenged, as is science in general, by the
decline in public trust in expertise. People are less willing to accept statements about "truth" provided by experts of all types. Psychologists are
advocating evidence-informed policy development at a time when the
neutrality of science as a source of truth, and social science in particular,
has been widely and increasingly criticized in American society. The core
assumption that there are facts, that they are distinct from values, and
that they can be determined through empirical research is increasingly
problematized. These developments raise questions about the future
of evidence-informed law of all types, including psychological research
findings.

References

Literature

Abbe, A., & Brandon, S. E. (2014). Building and maintaining rapport in investigative interviews. *Police Practice & Research: An International Journal, 15*(3), 207–220.

Aichele, G. (1989). *Oliver Wendell Holmes, Jr.: Soldier, scholar, judge.* Twayne.

Albiston, C. R., Edelman, L. B., & Milligan, J. (2014). The dispute tree and the legal forest. *Annual Review of Law and Social Science, 10,* 105–131.

Alder, K. (2007). *The Lie Detectors: The history of an American obsession.* Free Press.

Allen, F. (1981). *The decline of the rehabilitative ideal: Penal policy and social purpose.* Yale University Press.

Allport, G. (1954). *The nature of prejudice.* Addison-Wesley.

Alpert, G. P., MacDonald, J. M., & Dunham, R. G. (2005). Police suspicion and discretionary decision making during citizen stops. *Criminology, 43*(2), 407–434.

American Psychological Association. (2013). *Specialty guidelines for forensic psychology.*

American Psychological Association. (2015, August 15). *American Psychological Association review confirms link between playing violent video games and aggression* [Press release].

American Psychological Association (2017). *Position statement on segregation of prisoners with mental illness.* Washington, D.C.: APA.

American Psychological Association. (2020, March 5). *American Psychological Association warns against linking violent video games to real-world violence* [Press release].

Arnold Foundation. (2013). *Developing a national model for pretrial risk assessment.* www.arnoldventures.org.

Aronson, J. D. (2007). Brain imaging, culpability and the juvenile death penalty. *Psychology, Public Policy, and Law, 13*(2), 115–142.

Austin, W., & Tobiasen, J. M. (1984). Legal justice and the psychology of conflict resolution. In R. Folger (ed.), *The Sense of Injustice.* Plenum.

Baker, W. (2005). *America's crisis of values: Reality and perception.* Princeton University Press.

Baldus, D. C., Woodworth, G., & Pulaski, C. A., Jr. (1990). *Equal justice and the death penalty: A legal and empirical analysis.* Northeastern University Press.

Bandes, S. (2009). Victims, "closure," and the sociology of emotion. *Law and Contemporary Problems, 72*, 1–26.

Banks, D., Hendrix, J., Hickman, M., & Kyckelhahn, T. (2016). *National sources of law enforcement employment data*. Office of Justice Programs. U.S. Department of Justice.

Barclay, (2004). A new aspect of lawyer-client interactions: Lawyers teaching process-focused clients to think about outcomes. *Clinical Law Review, 11*, 1–13.

Baskin-Sommers, A. R., & Fonteneau, K. (2016). Correctional change through neuroscience. *Fordham Law Review, 85*(2), 423–436.

Beattey, R. A. & Fondacaro, M. R. (2017). The misjudgment of criminal responsibility. *Behavioral Science and Law, 36*, 457–469.

Bediou, B., Adams, D. M., Mayer, R. E., Tipton, E., Green, C. S., & Bavelier, D. (2018). Meta-analysis of action video game impact on perceptual, attentional, and cognitive skills. *Psychological Bulletin, 144*(1), 77–110.

Beijersbergen, K. A., Dirkzwager, A. J. E., Eichelsheim, V. I., Van der Laan, P. H., & Nieuwbeerta, P. (2015). Procedural justice, anger, and prisoners' misconduct: A longitudinal study. *Criminal Justice and Behavior, 42*(2), 196–218.

Beijersbergen, K. A., Dirkzwager, A. J. E., & Nieuwbeerta, P. (2016). Reoffending after release: Does procedural justice during imprisonment matter? *Criminal Justice and Behavior, 43*(1), 63–82.

Berkowitz, S. R., & Javaid, N. L. (2013). It's not you, it's the law: Eyewitness memory scholars' disappointment with *Perry v. New Hampshire*. *Psychology, Public Policy, and Law (19)*3, 369–379.

Bersoff, D. N. (1986). Psychologists and the judicial system. *Law and Human Behavior, 10*, 151–165.

Berwin, C. R. (2003). *Posttraumatic stress disorder: Malady or myth?* Yale University Press.

Bingham, L. B. (2008). Designing justice: Legal institutions and other systems for managing conflict. *Ohio State Journal on Dispute Resolution, 24*, 1–52.

Blader, S., & Tyler, T. R. (2003a). What constitutes fairness in work settings? A four-component model of procedural justice. *Human Resource Management Review, 12*, 107–126.

Blader, S., & Tyler, T. R. (2003b). A four-component model of procedural justice: Defining the meaning of a "fair" process. *Personality and Social Psychology Bulletin, 29*(6), 747–758.

Boeckmann, R. (1997). *An alternative conceptual framework for offense evaluation: Implications for a social maintenance model of retributive justice.* [Doctoral dissertation, UC, Berkeley].

Bond, C. F., & DePaulo, B. M. (2006). Accuracy of deception judgments. *Personality and Social Psychology Review, 10*, 214–234.

Bonnie, R. J., & Scott, E. S. (2013). The teenage brain. *Current Directions in Psychological Science, 22*, 158–161.

Bowers, J., & Robinson, P. H. (2012). Perceptions of fairness and justice: The shared aims and occasional conflicts of legitimacy and moral credibility. *Wake Forest Law Review, 47*, 211–284.

Boyce, B. (2008). Obscenity and community standards. *Yale Journal of International Law, 33*, 299–368.

Braithwaite, J. (1989). *Crime, shame and reintegration.* Cambridge University Press.

Braithwaite, J. (2002). *Restorative justice and responsive regulation.* Oxford University Press.

Brekke, N. (1991). The impact of non-adversarial versus adversarial expert testimony. *Law and Human Behavior, 15,* 451–475.

Brewer, N., & Palmer, M. A. (2010). Eyewitness identification tests. *Legal and Criminological Psychology, 15,* 77–96.

Breyer, S. (2010). *Making our democracy work.* Vintage.

Brigham, L. B. (2008). Designing justice: Legal institutions and other systems for managing conflict. *Ohio State Journal of Dispute Resolution, 24,* 1–51.

Brigham, J., & Bothwell, R. K. (1983). The ability of prospective jurors to estimate the accuracy of eyewitness identifications. *Law and Human Behavior, 7,* 19–30.

Bull, R., & Milne, B. (2004). Attempts to improve the police interviewing of suspects. In G. D. Lassiter (ed.), *Perspectives in law & psychology, Vol. 20. Interrogations, confessions, and entrapment* (pp. 181–196). Kluwer Academic/Plenum Publishers.

Burch, E. C. (2010). Aggregation, community, and the line between. *Kansas Law Review, 58,* 889–916.

Burch, E. C. (2011). Group consensus, individual consent. *George Washington Law Review, 79,* 506–542.

Burch, E. C. (2016). Calibrating participation: reflections on procedure versus procedural justice. *DePaul Law Review, 65,* 323–356.

Burd, K. A. & Hans, V. P. (2018). Reasoned verdicts: Oversold? *Cornell International Law Journal,* 51, 320-360.

Brunton-Smith, I., & McCarthy, D. J. (2016). Prison legitimacy and procedural fairness: A multilevel examination of prisoners in England and Wales. *Justice Quarterly, 33*(6), 1029–1054.

Calvert, S. L., Appelbaum, M., Dodge, K. A., Graham, S., Hall, G. C. N., Hamby, S., Fasig-Caldwell, L. G., Citkowicz, M., Galloway, D. P. & Hedges, L. V. (2017). The American Psychological Association Task Force assessment of violent video games. *American Psychologist, 72,* 126–143.

Campbell, C. (2018, March 10). A brief history of blaming video games for mass murder. *Polygon.*

Campbell, D. T., & Stanley, J. C. (1963). *Experimental and quasi-experimental designs for research.* McGraw-Hill.

Carlsmith, K. M., & Darley, J. M. (2008). Psychological aspects of retributive justice. In M. P. Zanna (ed.), *Advances in experimental social psychology: Vol. 40.* (pp. 193–236). Elsevier Academic Press.

Carlsmith, K. M., Darley, J. M., & Robinson, P. H. (2002). Why do we punish? Deterrence and just deserts as motives for punishment. *Journal of Personality and Social Psychology, 83*(2), 284–299.

Chalfin, A., & McCrary, J. (2014). Criminal deterrence: A review of the literature. *Journal of Economic Literature, 55*(1), 5–48.

Chein, J., Albert, D., O'Brien, L., Uckert, K. & Steinberg, L. (2011). Peers increase adolescent risk taking by enhancing activity in the brain's reward circuitry. *Developmental Science, 14*(2), F1–F10.

Chorn, J. A. (2019). Variations in reliability and validity do not influence judge, attorney, and mock juror decisions about psychological expert evidence. *Law and Human Behavior*, *43*, 542–557.

Clark, K. B., & Clark, M. P. (1947). Racial identification and preference among negro children. In E. L. Hartley (ed.), *Readings in social psychology*. Holt, Rinehart, and Winston.

Clark, S.E., Moreland, M.B. & Larson, R.P. (2018). Legitimacy, procedural justice, accuracy and eyewitness identification. *University of California Irvine Law Review*, 8, 41-82.

Cohen, A. O., Breiner, K., Steinberg, L., Bonnie, R. J., Scott, E. S., Taylor-Thompson, K., Rudolph, M. D., Chein, J., Richeson, J. A., Heller, A. S., Silverman, M. R., Dellarco, D. V., Fair, D. A., Galván, A., & Casey, B. J. (2016). When is an adolescent an adult? *Psychological Science*, *27*, 549–562.

Cole, S. A. (2005). More than zero: Accounting for error in latent fingerprint identification. *Journal of Criminal Law and Criminology*, *95*, 985–1078.

Cole, S. A. (2006). Is fingerprint identification valid? Rhetorics of reliability in fingerprint proponents' discourse. *Law and Policy*, *28*, 109–135.

Coleman, J. (1964). *Equality of educational opportunity*. National Center for Educational Statistics

Connecticut Eyewitness Identification Task Force (2012). www.cga.ct.gov.

Cooper, D. J., & Kagel, J. H. (2005). Are two heads better than one? Team versus individual play in signaling games. *American Economic Review*, *95*(33), 477–509.

Cooper, J. (2000). The hired gun effect: Assessing the effect of pay, frequency of testifying, and credentials on the perception of expert testimony. *Law and Human Behavior*, *24*, 149–171.

Correll, J., Hudson, S. M., Guillermo, S., & Ma, D. S. (2014). The police officer's dilemma: A decade of research on racial bias in the decision to shoot. *Social and Personality Psychology Compass*, *8*, 201–213.

Correll, J., Park, B., Judd, C. M., & Wittenbrink, B. (2007). The influence of stereotypes on decisions to shoot. *European Journal of Social Psychology*, *37*, 1102–1117.

Criminal Law Review Committee (1971). United Kingdom.

Cullen, F. T. (2005). The twelve people who saved rehabilitation: How the science of criminology made a difference—the American Society of Criminology 2004 Presidential Address. *Criminology*, *43*(1), 1–42.

Cullen, F. T. (2013). Rehabilitation: Beyond nothing works. *Crime and Justice*, *42*, 299–376.

Curran, B. (1977). *The legal needs of the public*. American Bar Foundation.

Darley, J. M., & Pittman, T. S. (2003). The psychology of compensatory and retributive justice. *Personality and Social Psychology Review*, *7*, 324–336.

Davis, J. H., Kerr, N. L., Atkin, R. S., Holt, R., & Meek, D. (1975). The decision processes of 6- and 12-person mock juries assigned unanimous and two-thirds majority rules. *Journal of Personality and Social Psychology*, *32*(1), 1–14.

Davis, J. P. & Valentine, T. (2009). CCTV on trial: Matching video images with the defendant in the dock. *Applied Cognitive Psychology*, *23*, 482–505.

Dawes, R. M. (1979). The robust beauty of improper linear models. *American Psychologist*, *34*(7), 571–582.

Delgado, R. (1985). Rotten social background: Should the criminal law recognize a defense of severe environmental deprivation? *Law and Inequality*, 3, 9–90.

DePaulo, B. M. (1992). Nonverbal behavior and self-presentation. *Psychological Bulletin*, 111(2), 203–243.

DePaulo, B. M., Charlton, K., Cooper, H., Lindsay, J. J., & Muhlenbruck, L. (1997). The accuracy-confidence correlation in the detection of deception. *Personality and Social Psychology Review*, 1, 346–357.

DePaulo, P. J., & DePaulo, B. M. (1989). Can deception by salespersons and customers be detected through nonverbal behavioral cues? *Journal of Applied Social Psychology*, 19, 1552–1577.

DePaulo, B. M., Lindsay, J. J., Malone, B. E., Muhlenbruck, L., Charlton, K., & Cooper, H. (2003). Cues to deception. *Psychological Bulletin*, 129, 74–118.

DePaulo, B. M., & Morris, W. L. (2004). Discerning lies from truths: Behavioral cues to deception and the indirect pathway of intuition. In P. A. Granhag & L. Strömwall (eds), *The detection of deception in forensic contexts* (pp. 15–40). Cambridge University Press.

Devine, D. J., Clayton, L. D., Dunford, B. B., Seying, R., & Pryce, J. (2001). Jury decision making. *Psychology, Public Policy, and Law*, 7(3), 622–727.

Devine, D. J. (2012). *Jury decision making: The state of the science*. NYU Press.

Devine, P. G. & Elliot, A. J. (1995). Are racial stereotypes fading? *Personality and Social Psychology Bulletin*, 21, 1139–1150.

Devlin Committee. (1976). *Report of the committee on evidence of identification in criminal cases*. UK: House of Commons.

Diamond, S. S. (2019). Empirical legal scholarship. *Northwestern University Law Review*, 113, 1229–1242.

Diamond, S. S. & Salerno, J. (2013). Empirical analysis of juries in tort cases. In J. Arlen (ed.). *Research Handbook on the Economics of Torts*. Elgar.

Diagnostic and Statistical Manual of Mental Disorders (DSM). Washington, D.C.: American Psychiatric Association.

Dobbin, F. (2009). *Inventing equal opportunity*. Princeton University Press.

Dobbin, S. A., Gatowski, S. I., Richardson, J. T., Ginsburg, G. P., Merlino, M. L., & Dahir, V. (2001–2002). Applying Daubert. How well do judges understand science and scientific method? *Judicature*, 85(2), 244–247.

Doherty, F. (2016). Obey all laws and be good: Probation and the meaning of recidivism. *Georgetown Law Review*, 104, 291–354.

Dressel, J., & Farid, H. (2018). The accuracy, fairness and limits of predicting recidivism. *Science Advances*, 4, eaao5580.

Eberhardt, J. L., Davies, P. G., Purdie-Vaughns, V., & Johnson, S. L. (2006). Looking deathworthy: Perceived stereotypicality of black defendants predicts capital-sentencing outcomes. *Psychological Science*, 17(5), 383–386.

Economou, N. R. (1991). Defense expert testimony on rape trauma syndrome: Implications for the stoic victim. *Hastings Law Journal*, 42, 1143–1173.

Eigen, Z. J. (2012). When and why individuals obey contracts. *Journal of Legal Studies*, 41, 67–93.

Eigen, Z. J. & Listokin, Y. (2012). Do lawyers really believe their own hype, and should they? *Journal of Legal Studies*, 41(2), 239–267.

Ekman, P. (1985). *Telling lies: Clues to deception in the marketplace, politics, and marriage*. Norton.

Ellsworth, P. (1989). Are twelve heads better than one? *Law and Contemporary Problems, 52*, 205–224.

Ellsworth, P. (2005). Legal Reasoning. In, Holyoak, K. J. & Morrison, R. G. (eds) *The Cambridge handbook of thinking and reasoning* (pp. 685–703). Cambridge University Press.

Emery, R. E., Matthews, S. G., & Kitzmann, K. M. (1994). Child custody mediation and litigation: Parents' satisfaction and functioning one year after settlement. *Journal of Consulting and Clinical Psychology, 62*(1), 124–129.

Epstein, L., Landes, W. M., & Posner, R. A. (2013). *The behavior of federal judges.* Harvard University Press.

Eyer, K. B. (2012). That's not discrimination: American beliefs and the limits of anti-discrimination law. *Minnesota Law Review, 96*, 1275–1362.

Faigman, D. L. (2005). Battered woman syndrome. In Faigman, D. L., Kaye, D. H., Saks, M. J. & Sanders, J. (2005). *Modern Scientific Evidence* (volume 2). Thomson West.

Faigman, D. L., Cheng, E. K., Mnookin, J., Murphy, E. E., Sanders, J., & Slobogin, C. (2020). *Modern scientific evidence: The law and science of expert testimony.* Thomson West.

Falk, P. (1996). Novel theories of criminal defense based upon the toxicity of the social environment. *North Carolina Law Review, 74*, 731–811.

Fazel, S., Singh, J. P., Doll, H. & Grann, M. (2012). Use of risk assessment instruments to predict violence and antisocial behavior in 73 samples involving 24,827 people. *British Medical Journal,* 345:e4692 doi: 10.1136/bmj.e4692.

Fiske, A. P., & Tetlock, P. E. (1997). Taboo trade-offs: reactions to transactions that transgress the spheres of justice. *Political Psychology, 18*, 255–297.

Fiske, S. T., Bersoff, D. N., Borgida, E., Deaux, K., & Heilman, M. E. (1991). Social science research on trial: Use of sex stereotyping research in Price Waterhouse v. Hopkins. *American Psychologist, 46*, 1049–1060.

Felker-Kantor, M. (2018). *Policing Los Angeles: Race, resistance, and the rise of the LAPD.* The University of North Carolina Press.

Felstiner, W. L. F., Abel, R. L., & Sarat, A. (1980–81). The emergence and transformation of disputes: Naming, blaming and claiming. *Law and Society Review, 15*, 631–654.

Findley, K., & Scott, M. (2006). The multiple dimensions of tunnel vision in criminal cases. *Wisconsin Law Review,* 2006(2), 291–397.

Fondacaro, M. R., & O'Toole, M. J. (2015). American punitiveness and mass incarceration: Psychological perspective on retributive and consequential responses to crime. *New Criminal Law Review, 18*, 477–509.

Frazier, P. A., & Borgida, E. (1992). Rape trauma syndrome: A review of case law and psychological research. *Law and Human Behavior, 16*, 293–311.

Gabel, J. D. (2014). Realizing reliability in forensic science from the ground up. *Journal of Criminal Law and Criminology, 104*, 283–352.

Galanter, M. (1983). Reading the landscape of disputes: What we know and don't know (and think we know) about our allegedly contentious and litigious society. *UCLA Law Review, 31*, 4–71.

Galea, S., Ahern, J., Resnick, H., Kilpatrick, D., Bucuvalas, M., Gold, J., & Vlahov, D. (2002). Psychological sequelae of the September 11 terrorist attacks in New York City. *New England Journal of Medicine, 346*, 982–987.

Galvan, A., Hare, T., Voss, H., Glover, G., & Casey, B. J. (2006). Risk-taking and the adolescent brain: Who is at risk? *Developmental Science, 10*, F8–F24.

Ganis, G., Rosenfeld, J. P., Meixner, J., Kievit, R. & Schendan, H. E. (2011). Lying in the scanner: covert countermeasures disrupt deception by functional magnetic resonance imaging. *Neuroimage, 55*, 312–319.

Garrett, B. (2011). *Convicting the innocent.* Harvard University Press.

Gerber, A.S. & Green, D.P. (2012). *Field experiments.* Columbia University Press.

Goetting, A. & Howsen, R.M. (1986). Correlates of prisoner misconduct. *Journal of Quantitative Criminology, 2*, 49-67.Gordon, N.S. & Fondacaro, M.R. (2017). Rethinking the voluntary act requirement. *Behavioral Science and Law, 36*, 426-436.

Geis, G., & Bienen, L. B. (1998). *Crimes of the century: From Leopold and Loeb to O.J. Simpson.* Northeastern University Press.

George, W. H., & Martinez, L. J. (2002). Victim blaming in rape: Effects of victims and perpetrator race, type of rape, and participant racism. *Psychology of Women Quarterly, 26*(2), 110–119.

Gerber, A., & Green, D. P. (2012). *Field experiments: Design, analysis, and interpretation.* NY: Norton.

Glass, G. V., McGaw, B., & Smith, M. L. (1981). *Meta-analysis in social research.* Sage.

Glaser, J. (2014). *Suspect race: Causes and consequences of racial profiling.* Oxford University Press.

Glasser, W. (2007). *Choice theory: A new psychology of personal freedom.* Harper Perennial.

Glover, J. M. (2015). Disappearing claims and the erosion of substantive law. *Yale Law Journal, 124*(8), 3052–3092.

Goetting, A., & Howsen, R. M. (1986). Correlates of prisoner misconduct. *Journal of Quantitative Criminology, 2*, 49–67.

Goff, P. A., Eberhardt, J. L., Williams, M. J., & Jackson, M. C. (2008). Not yet human: Implicit knowledge, historical dehumanization, and contemporary consequences. *Journal of Personality and Social Psychology, 94*(2), 292–306.

Goff, P. A., & Tyler, T. R. (2018). National survey of Americans concerning race. Unpublished paper. Russell Sage Foundation.

Goldstein, A. G., Chance, J. E., & Schneller, G. R. (1989). Frequency of eyewitness identification in criminal cases: A survey of prosecutors. *Bulletin of the Psychonomic Society, 27*(1), 71–74.

Goldstein, J. (2018, March 3). "Testilying" by police: A stubborn problem. *The New York Times.*

Gordon, N. S., & Fondacaro, M. R. (2017). Rethinking the voluntary act requirement. *Behavioral Science and Law, 36*, 426-436.

Gottfredson, D. C., Kearley, B. W., Najaka, S. S., & Rocha, C. M. (2007). How drug treatment courts work: An analysis of mediators. *Journal of Research in Crime and Delinquency, 44*, 3–35.

Granhag, P. A., & Hartwig, M. (2008). *Detecting deception.* In G. M. Davies, C. R. Hollin, & R. Bull (eds.), *Forensic psychology* (pp. 133–158). Wiley.

Granic, I., Lobel, A., & Engels, R. (2014). The benefits of playing video games. *American Psychologist, 69*, 66–78.

Granot, Y., Balcetis, E., Feigenson, N., & Tyler, T. R. (2018). In the eyes of the law: Perception versus reality in appraisals of video evidence. *Psychology, Public Policy, and Law, 24*, 93–104.

Granot, Y., Balcetis, E., Tyler, T. R., & Schneider, K. E. (2014). Justice is not blind: Visual attention exaggerates effects of group identification on legal punishment. *Journal of Experimental Psychology: General, 143*, 2196–2208.

Green, T. L., & Hagiwara, N. (2020). The Problem with Implicit Bias Training. Scientific American. *https://www. scientificamerican. com/article/ the-problem-with implicit-bias-training.*

Grisso, T., & Tomkins, A. J. (1996). Communicating violence risk assessments. *American Psychologist, 51*, 928–930.

Grossman, D. (2009). *On killing: The psychological cost of learning to kill in war and society.* Boston: Little, Brown.

Gunderson, C. A., & ten Brinke, L. (2019). Deception detection. Chapter 4 in N. Brewer & A. B Douglass (eds.), *Psychological science and the law.* Guilford.

Hadfield, G. (2008). Framing the choice between cash and the courthouse. *Law and Society Review, 42*, 645–682.

Hamilton, M. (2017). Briefing the Supreme Court: Promoting science or myth? *Emory Law Journal Online, 67*, 2016–2043.

Haney, C. (2018). Restricting the use of solitary confinement. *Annual Review of Criminology, 1*, 285–310.

Haney, C., & Lynch, M. (1997). Regulating prisons of the future: A psychological analysis of supermax and solitary confinement. *New York University Review of Law and Social Change, 23*(4), 477–570.

Hans, V. P., (2000). *Business on trial: The civil jury and corporate responsibility.* Yale University Press.

Hans, V. P. (2014). What's it worth: Jury damage awards as community judgments. *William & Mary Law Review, 55*, 935–969.

Hans, V.P. & Saks, M.J. (2018). Improving judge and jury evaluation of scientific evidence. *Daedalus, 147*, 164–180.

Hans, V. P., & Vidmar, N. (1986). *Judging the jury.* Plenum.

Hanson, J., & Yosifon, D. (2004–05). The situational character: A critical realist perspective on the human animal. *Georgetown Law Journal, 93*, 1–180.

Hanson, R. K., & Morton-Bourgon, K. E. (2009). The accuracy of recidivism risk assessments for sexual offenders. *Psychological Assessment, 21*, 1–21.

Harris, D. A. (2012). *Failed evidence: Why law enforcement resists science.* NYU Press.

Hartwig, M., & Bond, C. F. (2014). Lie detection from multiple cues: A meta-analysis. *Applied Cognitive Psychology, 28*(5), 661–676.

Hartwig, M., Granhag, P. A., Stromwall, L. A., & Vrij, A. (2004). Police officers' lie detection accuracy: Interrogating freely versus observing video. *Police Quarterly, 7*, 429–456.

Hartwig, M., Granhag, P. A., Stromwall, L. A., & Vrij, A. (2005). Detecting deception via strategic disclosure of evidence. *Law and Human Behavior, 29*, 469–484.

Hastie, R., & Dawes, R. M. (2001). *Rational choice in an uncertain world: The psychology of judgment and decision making* (3rd ed.). Sage.

Hastie, R., Penrod, S., & Pennington, N. (1983). *Inside the jury*. Harvard University Press.

Hastorf, A. H., & Cantril, H. (1954). They saw a game: A case study. *Journal of Abnormal and Social Psychology, 49*(1), 129–134.

Heckman, K., & Happel, M. D. (2007). Mechanical detection of deception. In *Educing information: Interrogation: Science and art*. National Defense Intelligence College.

Heins, M. (2007). *Not in front of the children: "Indecency," censorship, and the innocence of youth* (2nd ed.). Rutgers University Press.

Henry, P. J., & Sears, D. O. (2002). The symbolic racism 2000 scale. *Political Psychology, 23*, 253–287.

Heuer, L., & Penrod, S. (1994). Juror note taking and question asking during trials: A national field experiment. *Law and Human Behavior, 18*, 121–150.

Heuer, L., Penrod, S. & Kattan, A. (2008). The role of societal benefits and fairness concerns among decision makers and decision recipients. *Law and Human Behavior, 31*(6), 573–610.

Hewstone, M., Rubin, M., & Willis, H. (2002). Intergroup bias. *Annual Review of Psychology, 53*, 575–604.

High value detainee interrogation groups. Interrogation best practices. (2016). Washington, D.C.: Interagency body.

Hilbert, J. (2019). The disappointing history of science in the courtroom: Frye, Daubert, and the ongoing crisis of "junk science" in criminal trials. *Oklahoma Law Review, 71*, 759–821.

Hofstadter, R. (1963). *Anti-intellectualism in American life*. Vintage.

Hollander-Blumoff, R. (2017). Formation of procedural justice judgments in legal negotiation. *Group Decision and Negotiation, 26*, 19–43.

Hollander-Blumoff, R. (2010). Just negotiation. *Washington University Law Review, 88*, 381–432.

Holmes, O. W. (1881). *The common law*. Project Gutenberg EBook.

Hoy, A. Q. (2017). Fingerprint Source Identity Lacks Scientific Basis for Legal Certainty. News report. American Association for the Advancement of Science. https://www.aaas.org/news.

Hritz, A. C. (in press). Parole board decision making and Constitutional rights. *Annual Review of Law and Social Science*.

Huber, P. W. (1991). *Galileo's revenge: Junk science in the courtroom*. BasicBooks.

Huesmann, L. R., & Eron, L. D. (1986). *Television and the aggressive child: A cross-national comparison*. Erlbaum.

Huesmann, L. R., Moise-Titus, J., Podolski, C.-L., & Eron, L. D. (2003). Longitudinal relations between children's exposure to TV violence and their aggressive and violent behavior in young adulthood: 1977–1992. *Developmental Psychology, 39*(2), 201–221.

Hurst, J. W. (1956). *Law and the conditions of freedom in the nineteenth-century United States*. University of Wisconsin Press.

Hurst, W. (1964). *Law and economic growth: The legal history of the lumber industry in Wisconsin, 1836–1915*. Harvard University Press.

Inbau, F. E., Reid, J. E., Buckley, J. P., & Jayne, B. C. (2013). *Criminal interrogation and confessions* (5th ed.). Jones & Bartlett Learning.

Ivković, K., Diamond, S., Hans, V. P. & Marder, N. (2021). *Juries, law judges, and mixed courts: A global perspective*. Cambridge University Press.

Ivković, S. K., & Hans, V. (2003). Jurors' evaluations of expert testimony: Judging the messenger and the message. *Law and Social Inquiry, 28*, 441–482.

Jackson, J., Tyler, T. R., Bradford, B., Taylor, D., & Shiner, M. (2010). Legitimacy and procedural justice in prisons. *Prison Service Journal, 191*, 4–10.

Jay, T. (2009). Do offensive words harm people? *Psychology, Public Policy, and Law, 15*, 81–101.

Johnson, R. R., & Morgan, M. A. (2013). Suspicion formation among police officers: An international literature review. *Criminal Justice Studies, 26*, 99–114.

Johnstone, G. (2011). *Restorative justice: Ideas, values, debates* (2nd ed.). Routledge.

Jones, J. M., Dovidio, J., & Vietze, D. L. (2013). *The psychology of diversity: Beyond prejudice and racism*. Wiley.

Jost, J. T., & Banaji, M. R. (1994). The role of stereotyping in system-justification and the production of false consciousness. *British Journal of Social Psychology, 33*, 1–27.

Jost, J. T., Banaji, M. R., & Nosek, B. A. (2004). A decade of system justification theory. *Political Psychology, 25*, 881–919.

Jost, J. T., Blount, S., Pfeffer, J., & Hunyady, G. (2003). Fair market ideology: Its cognitive and motivational underpinnings. *Research in Organizational Behavior, 25*, 53–91.

Justice in the Balance 2020: Report of the Commission on the Future of the California Courts (1993). Administrative office of the California Courts. San Francisco.

Juvonen, J., & Graham, S. (2014). Bullying in schools: The power of bullies and the plight of victims. *Annual Review of Psychology, 65*, 159–185.

Kadane, J. B. (1993). Sausages and the law: Juror decisions in the much larger justice system. In R. Hastie (ed.), *Inside the juror*. Cambridge University Press.

Kahan, D. (1999). The secret ambition of deterrence. *Harvard Law Review, 113*, 413–500.

Kahan, D., & Braman, D. (2006). Cultural cognition and public policy. *Yale Law and Policy Review, 24*, 147–170.

Kahan, D., Hoffman, D. A., & Braman, D. (2009). Whose eyes are you going to believe? Scott v. Harris and the perils of cognitive illiberalism. *Harvard Law Review, 122*, 837–906.

Kahan, D. M., Hoffman, D. A., Braman, D., Evans, D., & Rachlinski, J. J. (2012). They saw a protest: Cognitive illiberalism and the speech-conduct distinction. *Stanford Law Review, 64*, 851–906.

Kahneman, D. (2011). *Thinking, fast and slow*. Farrar, Straus & Giroux.

Kalven., H. K., Jr., & Zeisel, H. (1966). *The American jury*. Boston: Little, Brown.

Kanwar, V. (2002). Capital punishment as closure: The limits of a victim-centered jurisprudence. *NYU Review of Law and Social Change, 27*(2), 215–255.

Kassin, S. M. (2015). The social psychology of false confessions. *Social Issues and Policy Review, 9*(1), 25–51.

Kassin, S. M., & Fong, C. T. (1999). "I'm innocent!": Effects of training on judgments of truth and deception in the interrogation room. *Law and Human Behavior, 23*, 499–516.

Kassin, S. M., Meissner, C. A., & Norwick, R. J. (2005). "I'd know a false confession if I saw one": A comparative study of college students and police investigators. *Law and Human Behavior, 29,* 211–227.

Katsh, E., & Rabinovich-Einy, O. (2017). *Digital justice: Technology and the internet of disputes.* Oxford University Press.

Kay, A. C., Jost, J. T., & Young, S. (2005). Victim derogation and victim enhancement as alternate routes to system justification. *Psychological Science, 16*(3), 240–246.

Keltner, D., Gruenfeld, D. H., & Anderson, C. (2003). Power, approach, and inhibition. *Psychological Review, 110*(2), 265–284.

Kerner Commission Report (1968). *Report of the national advisory commission on civil disorders.* Washington, D.C.

Kerr, N. L., MacCoun, R. J., & Kramer, G. P. (1996). When are two heads better (or worse) than one? Biased judgments in individuals and groups. In E. H. Witte & J. H. Davis (eds), *Understanding group behavior: Consensual action by small groups* (pp. 105–136). Erlbaum.

Kessler, D. K. (2009). Free to leave? An empirical look at the Fourth Amendment's seizure standard. *Journal of Criminal Law and Criminology, 99,* 51–88.

Kimble, K. M. K., Farnum, K. S., Weiner, R. L., Allen, J., Nuss, G. D. & Gervais, S. J. (2016). Differences in the eyes of the beholders: The roles of subjective and objective judgments in sexual harassment claims. *Law and Human Behavior, 40,* 319–336.

King, E. B., Dunleavy, D. G., Dunleavy, E. M., Jaffer, S., Morgan, W. B., Elder, K., & Graebner, R. (2011). Discrimination in the 21st century: Are science and law aligned? *Psychology, Public Policy, and Law, 17,* 54–75.

King, K. A., & Nesbit, T. M. (2009). The empirical estimation of the cost-minimizing jury size and voting rule in civil trials. *Journal of Economic Behavior & Organization, 71,* 463–472.

Kinsey, A., Pomeroy, W., & Martin, C. (1948). *Sexual behavior in the human male.* W.B. Saunders.

Kinsey, A. C., Pomeroy, W. B., Martin, C. E. & Gebhard, P. H. (1998). *Sexual behavior in the human female.* Indiana University Press.

Kleiman, M. (2009). *When brute force fails: Strategic thinking for crime control: How to have less crime and less punishment.* Princeton University Press.

Kluger, R. (1975). *Simple justice.* Vintage.

Kohler-Hausmann, I. (2014). Managerial justice and mass misdemeanors. *Stanford Law Review, 66*(3), 611–694.

Kovera, M. B., McAuliff, B. D., & Hebert, K. S. (1999). Reasoning about scientific evidence: Effects of juror gender and evidence quality on juror decisions in a hostile work environment case. *Journal of Applied Psychology, 84*(3), 362–375.

Kramer, A. (2007). William H. Parker and the thin blue line: politics, public relations and policing in postwar Los Angeles. [Doctoral Dissertation, American University.]

Kraus, M. W., Onyeador, I. N., Daumeyer, N. M., Rucker, J. M., & Richeson, J. A. (2019). The misperception of racial economic inequality. *Perspectives on Psychological Science, 14,* 899–921.

Kritzer, H. M. (2010). Claiming behavior as legal mobilization. In P. Cane & H. Kritzer (eds), *The Oxford handbook of empirical legal research*. Oxford University Press.

Lambert, E. (2003). The impact of organizational justice on correctional staff. *Journal of Criminal Justice, 31*(2), 155–168.

Lambert, E. G., Hogan, N. L., & Allen, R. I. (2006). Correlates of correctional officer job stress: The impact of organizational structure. *American Journal of Criminal Justice, 30*(2), 227–246.

Lambert, E. G., Hogan, N. L., & Griffin, M. L. (2007). The impact of distributive and procedural justice on correctional staff job stress, job satisfaction, and organizational commitment. *Journal of Criminal Justice, 35*(6), 644–656.

Lambert, E. G., Hogan, N. L., Jiang, S., Elechi, O. O., Benjamin, B., Morris, A., Laux, J. M., Dupuy, P. (2010). The relationship among distributive and procedural justice and correctional life satisfaction, burnout, and turnover intent: An exploratory study. *Journal of Criminal Justice, 38*(1), 7–16.

Lanfear, C. C., Matsueda, R. L., & Beach, L. R. (2020). Broken windows, informal social control, and crime. *Annual Review of Criminology, 3*, 97–120.

Langer, E., & Rodin, J. (1976). The effects of choice and enhanced personal responsibility for the aged: A field experiment in an institutional setting. *Journal of Personality and Social Psychology, 34*, 191–198.

Langleben, D. D., Hakun, J. G., Seelig, D., Wang, A.-L., Ruparel, K., Bilker, W. B., & Gur, R. C. (2016). Polygraphy and functional magnetic resonance imaging in lie detection. *Journal of Clinical Psychiatry, 77*(10), 1372–1380.

Larcom, S. (2015). Internalizing legal norms: An investigation into the legitimacy of payback killings in the New Guinea Island. *Law and Society Review, 49*, 179–208.

Lassiter, G. D., Ware, L. J., Ratcliff, J. J., & Irvin, C. R. (2009). Evidence of the camera perspective bias in authentic videotaped interrogations. *Legal and Criminological Psychology, 14*, 157–170.

Lee, H., & Hicken, M. T. (2016). Death by a thousand cuts: The health implications of black respectability politics. *Souls, 18*(2), 421–445.

Lee, M. Y. H. (2015, July 7). Yes, U.S. locks people up at a higher rate than any other country. *The Washington Post*.

Lempert, R. (1993). Why do jury research? In R. Hastie (ed.), *Inside the juror*. Cambridge University Press.

Leo, R. (2008). *Police interrogation and American justice*. Harvard University Press.

Levett, L. M., & Kovera, M. B. (2008). The effectiveness of opposing expert witnesses for educating jurors about unreliable expert evidence. *Law and Human Behavior, 32*, 363–374.

Lidz, C. W., Mulvey, E. P. & Gardner, W. (1993). The accuracy of predictions of violence to others. *JAMA, 24*, 1007–1011.

Liebling, A. (2004) *Prisons and their moral performance: A study of values, quality and prison life*. Oxford University Press.

Lilienfeld, S. O. (2020). Public skepticism of psychology. *American Psychologist, 67*, 111–129.

Lind, E. A., Kulik, C. T., Ambrose, M., & de Vera Park, M. V. (1993). Individual and corporate dispute resolution: Using procedural fairness as a decision heuristic. *Administrative Science Quarterly, 38*(2), 224–251.

Linz, D., & Malamuth, N. (1993). *Pornography.* Sage.

Lipsey, M. W., & Cullen, F. T. (2007). The effectiveness of correctional rehabilitation: A review of systematic reviews. *Annual Review of Law and Social Science, 3,* 297–320.

Lipsey, M. W., & Wilson, D. B. (2001). *Practical meta-analysis.* Sage.

Liptak, A. (2011, August 22). 34 years later, the Supreme Court will revisit eyewitness IDs. *The New York Times.*

Liu, P. P., & Quezada, L. (2019). Associations between micro-aggression and adjustment outcomes: A meta-analytic and narrative review. *Psychological Bulletin, 145,* 45–78.

Loftus, E. (1979). *Eyewitness testimony.* Harvard.

Loftus, E., & Greenspan, R. L. (2017). If I'm certain, is it true? Accuracy and confidence in eyewitness memory. *Psychological Science in the Public Interest, 18*(1), 1–2.

Lvovsky, A. (2017). The judicial presumption of police expertise. *Harvard Law Review, 130,* 1997–2077.

Lum, C., Koper, C. S., Wilson, D. B., Stoltz, M., Goodier, M., Eggins, E., Higginson, A., & Mazerolle, L. (2020). Body-worn cameras' effects on police officers and citizen behavior. *Campbell Systematic Reviews, 16*(3), e1112.

Lykken, D. T. (1981). *A tremor in the blood: Uses and abuses of the lie detector.* McGraw.

MacCoun, R. J. (2013). Moral outrage and opposition to harm reduction. *Criminal Law and Philosophy, 7,* 83–98.

MacCoun, R. J. (2015). The epistemic contract: Fostering an appropriate level of public trust in experts. *Nebraska Symposium on Motivation, 62,* 191–214.

MacCoun, R. J., & Tyler, T. R. (1988). The basis of citizens' preferences for different forms of criminal jury. *Law and Human Behavior, 12,* 333–352.

Mamalian, C. A. (2011). *State of the science of pretrial risk assessment.* Bureau of Justice Assistance.

Martinson, R. (1974). What works? Questions and answers about prison reform. *The Public Interest, 35,* 22–54.

Maslow, A. H. (1943). A theory of human motivation. *Psychology Review, 50*(4), 370–396.

Mathur, M. B., & VanderWeele, T. J. (2019). Finding common ground in meta-analysis: "Wars" on violent video games. *Perspectives on Psychological Science, 14,* 705–708.

McEwen, C. A., & Maiman, R. J. (1981). Mediation in small claims court. *Law and Society Review, 18*(1), 11–50.

McNulty, J. (2018, February 1). *Canada's landmark ruling against solitary confinement.* University of California News. https://www.universityofcalifornia.edu/news/canadas-landmark-ruling-against-solitary-confinement.

Meehl, P. (1954). *Clinical versus statistical prediction: A theoretical analysis and a review of the evidence.* University of Minnesota Press.

Meissner, C. A., & Kassin, S. M. (2002). "He's guilty!": Investigator bias in judgments of truth and deception. *Law and Human Behavior, 26,* 469–480.

Meissner, C., Redlich, A. D., Michael, S. W., Evans, J. R., Camilletti, C. R., Bhatt, S., & Brandon, S. (2014). Accusatorial and information-gathering interrogation methods and their effects on true and false confessions: A meta-analytic review. *Journal of Experimental Criminology, 10*, 459–486.

Meissner, C. A., Surmon-Böhr, F., Oleszkiewicz, S., & Alison, L. J. (2017). Developing an evidence-based perspective on interrogation: A review of the U.S. government's high-value detainee interrogation group research program. *Psychology, Public Policy, and Law, 23*(4), 438–457.

Meixner, J. B., & Diamond, S. S. (2014). The hidden Daubert factor: How judges use error rates in assessing scientific evidence. *Wisconsin Law Review, 2014*(6), 1063–1133.

Memon, A., Meissner, C. A., & Fraser, J. (2010). The cognitive interview: A meta-analytic review and study space analysis of the past 25 years. *Psychology, Public Policy, and Law, 16*(4), 340–372.

Mentovich, A., & Rabinovich-Einy, O. (2019). Is judicial bias inevitable? Empirical insights from online courts. *International ODR Forum.*

Merry, S. E. (2016). *The seductions of quantification.* University of Chicago Press.

Michell, J. (1999). *Measurement in psychology.* Cambridge University Press.

Milgram, S. (1974). *Obedience to authority.* Basic books.

Mitchell, G. (2019). Judicial decision-making. Chapter 16. Neil Brewer and Amy Bradford Douglass (eds), *Psychological science and the law.* (pp. 395–416) Guilford.

Moffitt, T. E. (1993). Adolescent-limited and life-course-persistent antisocial behavior. *Psychological Review, 100*, 674–701.

Monahan, J. (2007). The scientific status of research on clinical and actuarial predictions of violence. In D. Faigman et al. (eds), *Modern Scientific Evidence: The Law and Science of Expert Testimony.* Thomson West.

Monahan, J. (2013). Violence risk assessment. In Otto, R. K. & Weiner, I. B. (eds), *Handbook of psychology* (2nd ed.). Wiley. John Wiley & Sons.

Monahan, J., Steadman, H. J., Silver, E., Appelbaum, P. S., Robbins, P. C., Mulvey, E. P., Roth, L. H., Grisso, T., & Banks, S. (2001). *Rethinking risk assessment: The MacArthur Study of Mental Disorder and Violence.* Oxford University Press.

Monahan, J., & Walker, L. (2011). Twenty-five years of social science in law. *Law and Human Behavior, 35*, 72–82.

Monahan, J., & Walker, L. (2018). *Social science in law* (9th ed.). Foundation Press.

Monteleone, G. T., Phan, K. L., Nusbaum, H. C., Fitzgerald, D., Irick, J.-S., Fienberg, S., & Cacioppo, J. T. (2009). Detection of deception using fMRI: Better than chance, but well below perfection. *Social Neuroscience, 4*, 528–538.

Monterosso, J., Royzman, E. B. & Schwartz, B. (2005). Explaining away responsibility: Effects of scientific explanation on perceived causality. *Ethics and Behavior, 15*, 139–158.

Montesquieu. (1754). *The spirit of the laws.*

Morgan, R. D., Gendreau, P., Smith, P., Gray, A. L., Labrecque, R. M., MacLean, N., Van Horn, S. A., Bolanos, A. D., Batastini, A. B., & Mills, J. F. (2016). Quantitative syntheses of the effects of administrative segregation on inmates' well-being. *Psychology, Public Policy, and Law, 22*(4), 439–461.

Münsterberg, H. (1908). *On the witness stand: Essays on psychology and crime.* Doubleday.

Murphy, J. (2003). *Getting even: Forgiveness and its limits*. Oxford University Press.

Murray, J. P. (1973). Television and violence. *American Psychologist, 28*, 472–480.

Murray, P. (1987). *Song in a weary throat*. Liveright.

Murrie, D., & Boccaccini, M. T. (2015). Adversarial allegiance among expert witnesses. *Annual Review of Law and Social Science, 11*, 37–55.

Nadler, J. (2002). No need to shout: Bus sweeps and the psychology of coercion. *The Supreme Court Review*, 154–222.

Nadler, J., & Trout, J. D. (2012). The language of consent in police encounters. In P. M. Tiersma and L. M. Solan (eds), *The Oxford handbook of language and law* (pp. 326–339). Oxford University Press.

National Academy of Sciences. (2009). *Strengthening forensic science in the United States: A path forward*.

National Alliance on Mental Illness. (2020). *Mental Health Facts in America*.

Neil, R., & Winship, C. (2019). Methodological challenges and opportunities in testing for racial discrimination in policing. *Annual Review of Criminology, 2*, 73–98.

Neal, T. M. S., Slobogin, C., Saks, M. J., Faigman, D. L., & Geisinger, K. F. (2019). Psychological assessments in legal contexts: Are courts keeping junk science out of the courtroom? *Psychological Science in the Public Interest, 20*, 135–164.

Needs, A., & Towl, G. (2004). *Applying psychology to forensic practice*. Blackwell.

Neil, R., & Winship, C. (2019). Methodological challenges and opportunities in testing for racial discrimination in policing. *Annual Review of Criminology, 2*, 73–98.

Nisbett, R., & Ross, L. (1980). *Human inference: Strategies and shortcomings of social judgment*. Prentice-Hall.

O'Brien, T. C., & Tyler, T. R. (2020). Authorities and communities: Can authorities shape cooperation with communities on a group level? *Psychology, Public Policy, and Law, 26*, 69–87.

O'Brien, T. C., Tyler, T. R., & Meares, T. L. (2020). Building popular legitimacy with reconciliatory gestures and participation. *Regulation and Governance, 14*, 821–839.

Office of Technical Assistance. (1983). Scientific validity of polygraph testing: A review of research and evaluation. Office of Technical assistance. U.S. Congress. Washington, D.C.

Okimoto, T. G., Wenzel, M., & Feather, N. T. (2012) Retribution and restoration as general orientations towards justice. *European Journal of Personality, 26*(3), 255–275.

Oreskes, N., & Conway, E. M. (2010). *Merchants of doubt: How a handful of scientists obscured the truth on issues from tobacco smoke to global warming*. Bloomsbury Press.

Parkin, F. (1971). *Class inequality and political order*. Granada.

Paternoster, R., (2010). How much do we really know about criminal deterrence? *Journal of Criminal Law and Criminology, 100*, 765–824.

Paternoster, R. & Deise, J. (2011). A heavy thumb on the scale. *Criminology, 49*(1), 129–161.

Payne, B. K., Vuletich, H. A., & Lundberg, K. B. (2017). The bias of crowds: How implicit bias bridges personal and systemic prejudice. *Psychological Inquiry, 28*, 233–248.

Pearson, K. (1900). On the criterion that a given system of deviations from the probable in the case of a correlated system of variables is such that it can be reasonably supposed to have arisen from random sampling. *Philosophical Magazine*, Series 5, *50*(302), 157–175.

Peirce, C. S. (1877–78). Illustrations of the logic of science. *Popular Science Monthly, 12–13.*

Peter-Hagene, L. C., Salerno, J. M., & Phalen, H. (2019). Jury decision-making. In N. Brewer & A. B. Douglass (eds), *Psychological Science and the Law*. Guilford.

Petrosino, A., Turpin-Petrosino, C., Hollis-Peel, M. E., & Lavenberg, J. G. (2013). "Scared straight" and other juvenile awareness programs for preventing juvenile delinquency. *Campbell Systematic Review.*

Petrucci, C. J. (2002). Apology in the criminal justice setting: evidence for including apology as an additional component in the legal system. *Behavioral Science and Law, 20*, 337–362.

Pettigrew, T., & Tropp, L. R. (2011). *When Groups Meet*. Psychology Press.

Pew Research Center. (May 6, 2020). Black imprisonment rate in the U.S. has fallen by a third since 2006.

Pfungst, O. (1911). *Clever Hans (The horse of Mr. von Osten): A contribution to experimental animal and human psychology* (C. L. Rahn, Trans.). Henry Holt. (Originally published in German, 1907).

Phillips, S. W. (2020). The formation of suspicion: A vignette study. *International Journal of Police Science and Management, 22*, 274–284.

Plato. *The Republic.*

Plaut, V. C., & Bartlett, R. P. (2011). Blind consent? A social psychological investigation of non-readership of click-through agreements. *Law and Human Behavior, 36*, 293–311.

Porter, S., Woodworth, M., & Birt, A. R. (2000). Truth, lies, and videotape. *Law and Human Behavior, 24*, 643–658.

Poythress, N. G., Bonnie, R. J., Monahan, J., Otto, R. & Hoge, S. K. (2002). *Adjudicative competence*. Kluwer Academic/Plenum.

Prescott, A. T., Sargent, J. D., & Hull, J. G. (2018). Meta-analysis of the relationship between violent video game play and physical aggression over time. *Proceedings of the National Academy of Sciences, 115*, 9882–9888.

President's Council of Advisors on Science and Technology. (2016). Forensic science in the criminal courts: Ensuring scientific validity of feature-comparison methods. Washington, D.C.

Pruitt, D. G., Peirce, R. S., McGillicuddy, N. B., Welton, G. L., & Castrianno, L. M. (1993). Long-term success in mediation. *Law and Human Behavior, 17*(3), 313–330.

Quattlebaum, M. & Tyler, T.R. (2020). Beyond the law: An agenda for policing reform. Boston University Law Review, 100, 1017-1046.

Quintanilla, V. D. (2017). Human-centered civil justice design. *Pennsylvania State Law Review, 121*, 745–806.

Quintanilla, V. D., & Yontz, M. A. (2018). Human-centered civil justice design. *Tulsa Law Review, 54*, 113–148.

Rachlinski, J. J. (2011). Evidence-based law. *Cornell Law Review, 96*, 901–924.

Rachlinski, J. J. & Wistrich, A. J. (2017). Judging the judiciary by the numbers. *Annual Review of Law and Social Science, 13*, 203–229.

Reisig, M., & Mesko, G. (2009). Procedural justice, legitimacy, and prisoner misconduct. *Psychology, Crime and Law, 15*(1), 41–59.

Reitz, K. R., & Rhine, E. E. (2020). Parole release and supervision: Critical drivers of American prison policy. *Annual Review of Criminology, 3*, 281–298.

Redfield, S. E. (ed.). (2017). *Enhancing justice: Reducing bias.* American Bar Association.

Relis, T. (2006–2007). It's not about the money: A theory of misconceptions of plaintiffs' litigation aims. *University of Pittsburgh Law Review, 68*, 341–385.

Reyna, V. F., Hans, V. P., Corbin, J. C., Yeh, R., Lin, K., & Royer, C. (2015). The gist of juries: A model of damage award decision making. *Psychology, Public Policy, and Law, 21*, 280–294.

Robbennolt, J. K. (2004–2005). Evaluating juries by comparison to judges. *Florida State University Law Review, 32*, 469–509.

Robbennolt, J. K. (2009). Apologies and medical error. *Clinical Orthopaedics and Related Research, 2*, 376–82.

Robbennolt, J. K. (2010). Apologies and settlement. *Court review, 45*, 90–97.

Robbennolt, J. K. (2008). Apologies and civil justice. In B. H. Bornstein, R. L. Wiener, R. Schopp, & S. L. Willborn (eds), *Civil juries and civil justice: Psychological and legal perspectives.* Springer.

Robbennolt, J. K., Darley, J. M., & MacCoun, R. J. (2003). Symbolism and incommensurability in civil sanctioning. *Brooklyn Law Review, 68*, 1121–1159.

Robbennolt, J. K., & Hans, V. P. (2016). *The psychology of tort law.* NYU Press.

Robbennolt, J. K., & Sternlight, J. R. (2012). *Psychology for lawyers.* American Bar Association.

Robertson, C. T., & Kesselheim, A. S. (eds.). (2016). *Blinding as a solution to bias.* Academic Press.

Robertson, L. A., McAnally, H. M., & Hancox, R. J. (2013). Childhood and adolescent television viewing and antisocial behavior in early adulthood. *Pediatrics, 131*, 439–446.

Robinson, P. H. (2011). Are we responsible for who we are? *Alabama Civil Rights and Civil Liberties Law Review, 2*, 53–77.

Robinson, P. H. (2017). Democratizing criminal law: Feasibility, utility, and the challenge of social change. *Northwestern University Law Review, 111*, 1565–1596.

Robinson, P. H., & Darley, J. M. (1995). *Justice, liability and blame.* Westview.

Rosenthal, R., & Jacobson, L. (1968). Pygmalion in the classroom. *Urban Review, 3*, 16–20.

Rottman, D. B., & Tyler, T. R. (2014). Thinking about judges and judicial performance. *Oñati Socio-legal Series, 4*(5), 1046–1070.

Rustad, M., & Koenig, T. (1993). The Supreme Court and junk social science: Selective distortion in amicus briefs. *North Carolina Law Review, 72*, 91–162.

Ruva, C. L., & Coy, A. E. (2020). Your bias is rubbing off on me: The impact of pretrial publicity and jury type on guilt decisions, trial evidence interpretation, and impression formation. *Psychology, Public Policy, and Law, 26*(1), 22–35.

Saks, M. J. (1974). Ignorance of science is no excuse. *Trial, 10*, 18–20.

Saks, M. J., & Koehler, J. J. (2005). The coming paradigm shift in forensic identification science. *Science, 309*, 892–895.

Saks, M. J., & Spellman, B. A. (2016). *The psychological foundations of evidence law.* NYU Press.

Sandefur, R. L. (ed.). (2009). *Sociology of Crime, Law, and Deviance: Vol. 12. Access to Justice.* Emerald/JAI Press

Sandefur, R. L., & Albiston, C. R. (2013). Expanding the empirical study of access to justice. *Wisconsin Law Review*, 101–120.

Sandefur, R. L., & Smyth, A. C. (2011) Access across America: First report of the Civil Justice Infrastructure Mapping Project. American Bar Foundation.

Sauer, J. D., Palmer, M. A., & Brewer, N. (2019). Eyewitness identification. In N. Brewer & A. B. Douglass (eds), *Psychological science and the law.* Guilford.

Schauer, F. (2008). Why precedent in law (and elsewhere) is not totally (or even substantially) about analogy. *Perspectives on Psychological Science, 3*(6), 454–460.

Scheff, T. J. (1990). *Microsociology: Discourse, emotion, and social structure.* Chicago: University of Chicago Press.

Scheff, T. J. (1994). *Bloody revenge: Emotions, nationalism and war.* Boulder, Colo.: Westview.

Scheff, T. J., & Retzinger, S. M. (1991). *Emotions and violence: Shame and rage in destructive conflicts.* Lexington, Mass.: Lexington Books.

Schofield, P. (2013). The legal and political legacy of Jeremy Bentham. *Annual Review of Law and Social Science, 9*, 51–70.

Schofield, W. J., & Hausmann, L. R. M. (2004). School desegregation and social science research. *American Psychologist, 59*(6), 538–546.

Schuller, R. A., & Hastings, P. A. (1996). Trials of battered women who kill: The impact of alternative forms of expert evidence. *Law and Human Behavior, 20*, 167–187.

Schuller, R. A. & Rzepa, S. (2002). Expert testimony pertaining to battered woman syndrome: Its impact on jurors' decisions. *Law and Human Behavior, 26*(6), 655–673.

Schuller, R. A., & Vidmar, N. (1992). Battered woman syndrome evidence in the courtroom. *Law and Human Behavior, 16*, 273–291.

Schweitzer, N. J., Saks, M. J., Murphy, E. R., Roskies, A. L., Sinnott-Armstrong, W., & Gaudet, L. M. (2011). Neuroimages as evidence in a mens rea defense: No impact. *Psychology, Public Policy, and Law, 17*(3), 357–393.

Scott, E. S., & Steinberg, L. (2010). *Rethinking juvenile justice.* Harvard University Press.

Scurich, N., & Krauss, D. A. (2020). Public's views of risk assessment algorithms and pretrial decision making. *Psychology, Public Policy, and Law, 26*(1), 1–9.

Sela, A. (2018). Can computers be fair? How automated and human-powered online dispute resolution affect procedural justice in mediation and arbitration. *Ohio State Journal on Dispute resolution, 33*, 91–148.

Sears, D. O. (1986). College sophomores in the laboratory. *Journal of Personality and Social Psychology, 51*, 515–530.

Semmler, C., Brewer, N., & Wells, G. L. (2004). Effects of postidentification feedback on eyewitness identification and nonidentification confidence. *Journal of Applied Psychology, 89*(2), 334–346.

Sevier, J. (2014). The truth-justice tradeoff: Perceptions of decisional accuracy and procedural justice in adversarial and inquisitorial legal systems. *Psychology, Public Policy, and Law, 20*(2), 212–224.

Sevier, J. (2019–2020). A [relational] theory of procedure. *Minnesota Law Review, 104*, 1987–2060.

Sherman, L. W. (2018). Reducing fatal police shootings as system crashes: Research, theory and practice. *Annual Review of Criminology, 1*, 421–449.

Sherman, L. W., & Strang, H. (2007). *Restorative justice: The evidence.* Smith Institute.

Sherman, L. W., Strang, H., Mayo-Wilson, E., Woods, D. J., & Ariel, B. (2015). Are restorative justice conferences effective in reducing repeat offending? Findings from a Campbell systematic review. *Journal of Quantitative Criminology, 31*(1), 1–24.

Shultz, M. M., & Zedeck, S. (2009). Predicting lawyer effectiveness. *Law and Social Inquiry, 36*, 620–661.

Sidanius, J., & Pratto, F. (1999). *Social dominance.* Cambridge University Press.

Silver, E., Cirincione, C., & Steadman, H. J. (1994). Demythologizing inaccurate perceptions of the insanity defense. *Law and Human Behavior, 18*(1), 63–70.

Simon, D. (2019). On juror decision making. *Annual Review of Law and Social Science, 15*, 415–435.

Simon, D., Ahn, M., Stenstrom, D. M., & Read, S. J. (2020). The adversarial mindset. *Psychology, Public Policy, and Law, 26*, 353–377.

Simon, J. (2005). Reversal of fortune: The resurgence of individual risk assessment in criminal justice. *Annual Review of Law and Social Science, 1*, 397–421.

Simpson, J. (2008). Functional MRI lie detection: Too good to be true? *Journal of the American Academy of Psychiatry and the Law, 36*, 491–498.

Skeem, J. L., & Monahan, J. (2011). Current directions in violence risk assessment. *Current Directions in Psychological Science, 20*, 38–42.

Skeem, J., Scurich, N., & Monahan, J. (2020). Impact of risk assessment on judges' fairness in sentencing relatively poor defendants. *Law and Human Behavior, 44*, 51–59.

Slobogin, C. (2006). *Minding justice: Laws that deprive people with mental disability of life and liberty.* Oxford University Press.

Slobogin, C. (2007). *Proving the unprovable: The role of law, science, and speculation in adjudicating culpability and dangerousness.* Oxford University Press.

Slobogin, C. (2010). Psychological syndromes and criminal responsibility. *Annual Review of Law and Social Science, 6*, 109–127.

Slobogin, C., & Fondacaro, M. R. (2011). *Juveniles at risk: A plea for preventive justice.* Oxford University Press.

Slobogin, C., Hafemeister, T., Mossman, D., & Reisner, R. (2013). *Law and the mental health system* (6th ed.) West.

Slobogin, C., & Schumacher, J. E. (1993a). Rating the intrusiveness of law enforcement searches and seizures. *Law and Human Behavior, 17*, 183–200.

Slobogin, C., & Schumacher, J. E. (1993b). Reasonable expectations of privacy and autonomy in fourth amendment cases: An empirical look at understandings recognized and permitted by society. *Duke Law Journal, 42*(4), 727–775.

Smith, B. P. (2005). Plea bargaining and the eclipse of the jury. *Annual Review of Law and Social Science, 1*, 131–149.

Sohn, D. (1995). Meta-analysis as a means of discovery. *American Psychologist*, *50*(2), 108–110.

Sommers, R. (2020). Commonsense consent. *Yale Law Journal*, *129*, 2232–2320.

Sommers, R., & Bohns, V. K. (2019). The voluntariness of voluntary consent. *Yale Law Journal*, *128*, 1062–2033.

Sommers, S. (2011). *Situations matter: Understanding how context transforms your world*. Riverhead.

Sood, S. (in press). What's so special about general verdicts? Empirically unexplored questions about verdict format in criminal law. *Theoretical Inquiries in Law*.

Sparks, J. R., & Bottoms, A. E. (1995). Legitimacy and order in prisons. *The British Journal of Sociology*, *46*(1), 45–62.

Sparks, J. R., Bottoms, A. E., & Hay, W. (1996). *Prisons and the problem of order*. Oxford University Press.

Stanley, T. D., Carter, E. C., & Doucouliagos, H. (2018). What meta-analyses reveal about the replicability of psychological research. *Psychological Bulletin*, *144*, 1325–1346.

Steblay, N. M., Besirevic, J., Fulero, S. M., & Jimenez-Lorente, B. (1999). The effects of pretrial publicity on juror verdicts: A meta-analytic review. *Law and Human Behavior*, *23*(2), 219–235.

Steblay, N., Hosch, H., Culhane, S., & McWethy, A. (2006). The impact on juror verdicts of judicial instruction to disregard inadmissible evidence: A meta-analysis. *Law and Human Behavior*, *30*, 469–492.

Steinberg, L. (2007). Risk taking in adolescence. *Current Directions in Psychological Science*, *16*, 55–59.

Steinberg, L. (2014). *Age of opportunity: Lessons from the new science of adolescence*. Houghton Mifflin Harcourt.

Steller, M., & Koehnken, G. (1989). Criteria-based statement analysis. In D. C. Raskin (ed.), *Psychological methods in criminal investigation and evidence* (pp. 217–245). Springer Publishing Company.

Stith, K., & Cabranes, J.A. (1998). *Fear of judging: Sentencing guidelines in the federal courts*. University of Chicago Press.

Stochholm, K., Bojesen, A., Jensen, A. S., Juul, S., & Gravholt, C. H. (2012). Criminality in men with Klinefelter's syndrome and XYY syndrome: A cohort study. *British Medical Journal open*, *2*(1), e000650.

Stoughton, S. (2015). Law enforcement's warrior problem. Harvard Law Review Forum,128, 225-234.

Stryker, R., Docka-Filipek, D., & Wald, P. (2012). Employment discrimination law and industrial psychology: Social science as social authority and the co-production of law and science. *Law and Social Inquiry*, *37*, 777–814.

Sue, D. W. (2010). *Micro-aggressions in everyday life*. Wiley.

Swencionis, J. K., & Goff, P. A. (2017). The psychological science of racial bias and policing. *Psychology, Public Policy, and Law*, *23*(4), 398–409.

Tajfel, H. (1974). Social identity and intergroup behavior. *Social Science Information*, *13*, 65–93.

Talesh, S. A. (2009). The privatization of public legal rights. *Law and Society Review*, *43*, 527–562.

Tanford, J. A. (1990). The limits of a scientific jurisprudence. *Indiana Law Journal*, 66(1), 137–173.

Taxman, F. S., & Gordon, J. A. (2009). Do fairness and equity matter?: An examination of organizational justice among correctional officers in adult prisons. *Criminal Justice and Behavior*, 36(7), 695–711.

Taylor, S. E., & Brown, J. D. (1988). Illusion and well-being: A social psychological perspective on mental health. *Psychological Bulletin*, 103(2), 193–210.

Telesh, S. (2009). The privatization of public legal rights. *Law and Society Review*, 43, 527–562.

Terrill, R. J. (2009). *World criminal justice systems* (7th ed.). Elsevier.

Thibaut, J., & Walker, L. (1975). *Procedural justice*. Erlbaum.

Thibaut, J., & Walker, L. (1978). A theory of procedure. *California Law Review*, 66, 541–566.

Thurston, R. C., Chang, Y., Matthews, K. A., von Känel, R., & Koenen, K. (2019). Association of sexual harassment and sexual assault with midlife women's mental and physical health. *Journal of the American Medical Association: Internal Medicine*, 179(1), 48–53.

Tonry, M. (2014). Legal and ethnical issues in the prediction of recidivism. *Federal Sentencing Review*, 26, 167–176.

Tyler, T. R. (1988). What is procedural justice?: Criteria used by citizens to assess the fairness of legal procedures. *Law and Society Review*, 22, 103–135.

Tyler, T. R. (1989). The quality of dispute resolution processes and outcomes: Measurement problems and possibilities. *Denver University Law Review*, 66, 419–436.

Tyler, T. R. (2006a). *Why people obey the law: Procedural justice, legitimacy, and compliance*. Princeton University Press.

Tyler, T. R. (2006b). Legitimacy and legitimation. *Annual Review of Psychology*, 57, 375–400.

Tyler, T. R. (2012). *Results of a national survey on criminal justice*. Unpublished manuscript. Yale Law School.

Tyler, T. R., & Boeckmann, R. (1997). Three strikes and you are out, but why? The psychology of public support for punishing rule breakers. *Law and Society Review*, 31, 237–265.

Tyler, T. R., & Huo, Y. J. (2002). *Trust in the law: Encouraging public cooperation with the police and courts*. Russell-Sage Foundation.

Tyler, T. R., & Jackson, J. (2014). Popular legitimacy and the exercise of legal authority: Motivating compliance, cooperation and engagement. *Psychology, Public Policy, and Law*, 20, 78–95.

Tyler, T. R., & McGraw, K. M. (1986). Ideology and the interpretation of personal experience. *Journal of Social Issues*, 42, 115–128.

Tyler, T. R., & Trinkner, R. (2018). *Why children follow rules: Legal socialization and the development of legitimacy*. Oxford University Press. (http://www.oxfordscholarship.com)

Tyler, T. R., & Wakslak, C. (2004). Profiling and the legitimacy of the police: Procedural justice, attributions of motive, and the acceptance of social authority. *Criminology*, 42, 13–42.

U.S. Department of Justice. (2016). *Report and recommendations concerning the use of restrictive housing*.

Vallone, R., Ross, L., & Lepper, M. (1985). The hostile media phenomenon: Biased perception and perceptions of media bias in coverage of the Beirut massacre. *Journal of Personality and Social Psychology, 49*, 577–585.

Vidmar, N. (1995). *Medical malpractice and the American jury.* University of Michigan Press.

Vidmar, N., & Hans, V. P. (2007). *American juries: The verdict.* Prometheus.

Vidmar, N., & Laird, N. (1983). Adversary social roles: Their effects on witnesses' communication of evidence and the assessments of adjudicators. *Journal of Personality and Social Psychology, 44*, 888–898.

Votruba, A. M. (2013). Will the reasonable person please stand up? *Arizona Law Journal, 45*, 703–732.

Vrij, A. (2000). *Detecting lies and deceit.* Wiley.

Vrij, A., Akehurst, L., & Knight, S. (2006). Police officers', social workers', teachers' and the general public's beliefs about deception in children, adolescents and adults. *Legal and Criminological Psychology, 11*, 297–312.

Vrij, A. (2008). *Detecting lies and deceit* (2nd ed.). Wiley.

Vrij, A., Fisher, R. P., & Blank, H. (2017). A cognitive approach to lie detection: A meta-analysis. *Legal and Criminological Psychology, 22*, 1–21.

Vrij, A., Hartwig, M., & Granhag, P. A. (2019). Reading lies: Nonverbal communication and deception. *Annual Review of Psychology, 70*, 295–317.

Vrij, A., Meissner, C. A., Fisher, R. P., Kassin, S. M., Morgan, A., III, & Kleinman, S. (2017). Psychological perspectives on interrogation. *Perspectives on Psychological Science, 12*, 927–955.

Walker, L. (1979). *The battered woman.* Harper & Row.

Wall, T. (2019). The police invention of humanity: Notes on the "thin blue line." *Crime, Media, Culture, 16*, 319–336.

Weisberg, R. (2005). The death penalty meets social science. *Annual Review of Law and Social Science, 1*, 151–170.

Wells, G. L. (2005). Helping experimental psychology affect legal policy. In N. Brewer & K. Williams (eds), *Psychological Science and the Law.* Guilford.

Wells, G. L. (2020). Psychological science on eyewitness identification and its impact on police policies and practices. *American Psychologist, 75*, 1316–1329.

Wells, G. L., Smalarz, L., & Smith, A. M. (2015). ROC analysis of lineups does not measure underlying discriminability and has limited value. *Journal of Applied Research in Memory and Cognition, 4*, 313–317.

Wells, H. (2012). *The fast and the furious: Drivers, speed cameras and control in a risk society.* Ashgate.

Wenzel, M., & Okimoto, T. G. (2010). How acts of forgiveness restore a sense of justice: Addressing status/power and value concerns raised by transgressions. *European Journal of Social Psychology, 40*(3), 401–417.

Wenzel, M., Okimoto, T. G., Feather, N. T., & Platow, M. J. (2008) Retributive and restorative justice. *Law and Human Behavior, 32* (5), 375–389.

Wenzel, M., Okimoto, T. G., Hornsey, M. J., Lawrence-Wood, E., & Coughlin, A. M. (2017). The mandate of the collective. *Personality and Social Psychology Bulletin, 43*, 758–771.

Wheatcroft, J. M., Wagstaff, G. F., & Kebbell, M. R. (2010). The influence of courtroom questioning style on actual and perceived eyewitness confidence and accuracy. *Legal and Criminological Psychology, 9*, 83–101.

Wiener, R. L., Gervais, S. J., Allen, J., & Marquez, A. (2013). Eye of the beholder: Effects of perspective and sexual objectification on harassment judgments. *Psychology, Public Policy, and Law, 19,* 206–221.

Wiener, R. L., & Vardsveen, T. C. (2018). The objective prong in sexual harassment: What is the standard? *Law and Human Behavior, 42,* 545–557.

Wilkinson-Ryan, T., & Hoffman, D. A. (2010). Breach is for suckers. *Vanderbilt Law Review, 63,* 1003–1045.

Wilkinson-Ryan, T., & Hoffman, D. A. (2015). Common sense of contract formation. *Stanford Law Review, 67,* 1270–1301.

Williams, M. T. (2020). Micro-aggressions: Clarification, evidence, and impact. *Perspectives on Psychological Science, 15,* 3–26.

Wistrich, A. J., Guthrie, C., & Rachlinski, J. J. (2005). Can judges ignore inadmissible information? *University of Pennsylvania Law Review, 153,* 1251–1345.

Wistrich, A. J., & Rachlinski, J. J. (2018). Implicit bias in judicial decision making: How it affects judgment and what judges can do about it. Chapter 5 in S. E. Redfield (ed.), *Enhancing justice: Reducing bias* (pp. 87–130). American Bar Association.

Witkin, H. A., Mednick, S. A., Schulsinger, F., et al. (1976). Criminality in XYY and XXY men. *Science, 193*(4253), 547–555.

Wixted, J. T., & Wells, G. L. (2017). The relationship between eyewitness confidence and identification accuracy. *Psychological Science in the Public Interest, 18,* 10–65.

Wrightsman, L. S. (2001). *Forensic psychology.* Wadsworth Thomson Learning.

Yaffe, G. (2012). Intoxication, recklessness, and negligence. *Ohio State Journal of Criminal Law, 9,* 545–583.

Yokum, D., Ravishankar, A., & Coppock, A. (2019). A randomized control trial evaluating the effects of police body-worn cameras. *Proceedings of the National Academy of Sciences, 116,* 10229–10332.

Yong, J. C., Li, N. P., & Kanazawa, S. (2020). Not so much rational but rationalizing: Humans evolved as coherence-seeking, fiction-making animals. *American Psychologist.* Advance online publication. https://doi.org/10.1037/amp0000674

You can't change what you can't see: Interrupting racial and gender bias in the legal profession (2018). American Bar Association.

Cases

Barefoot v. Estelle, 463 U.S. 880 (1983)
Brown v. Board of Education of Topeka, 347 U.S. 483 (1954)
Brown v. Board of Education II, 349 U.S. 294 (1955)
Brown v. Entertainment Merchants Association, 564 U.S. 786 (2011)
Daubert v. Merrell Dow Pharmaceuticals, 509 U.S. 579 (1993)
Frye v. United States, 293 F. 1013 DC Cir. (1923)
Furman v. Georgia, 408 U.S. 238 (1972)
Griggs v. Duke Power Co., 401 U.S. 424 (1971)
Jacobellis v. Ohio, 378 U.S. 184 (1964)
Kahler v. Kansas, 140 S. Ct. 1021 (2020)
Kansas v. Hendricks, 521 U.S. 346 (1997)
Kumho Tire Co. v. Carmichael, 526 U.S. 137 (1999)
Manson v. Brathwaite, 432 U.S. 98 (1977)
McCleskey v. Kemp, 481 U.S. 279 (1987)

Miller v. California, 413 U.S. 15 (1973)
Muller v. Oregon, 208 U.S. 412, 28 S.Ct. 324, 52 L. Ed. 551 (1908)
New Jersey v. Henderson (2011) State v. Henderson, 27 A.3d 872 (N.J. 2011)
Perry v. New Hampshire, 565 U.S. 228 132 S.Ct. 716. (2012)
Plessy v. Ferguson, 163 U.S. 537 (1896)
Price Waterhouse v. Hopkins, 490 U.S. 228 (1989)
Roper v. Simmons, 543 U.S. 551 (2005)
Roth v. United States, 354 U.S. 476 (1957)
Saliba v. State, 1985 475 N.E.2d 1181 (1985)
Schall v. Martin, 467 U.S. 253 (1984)
Schenck v. United States, 249 U.S. 47 (1919)
Scott v. Harris, 550 U.S. 372 (2007)
Shelby County v. Holder, 570 U.S. 529 (2013
Simmons v. United States, 390 U.S. 377 (1968)
State v. Chapple, 135 Ariz. 281, 660 P.2d 1208, 1983 Ariz. LEXIS 153 (Ariz. Jan. 11, 1983)
State of Louisiana v. Heads, 1980; State v. Heads 385 So. 2d 230 (1980) No. 63311. Supreme Court of Louisiana
State v. Cocuzza, 1484-79 (New Jersey superior court (1981)
State of Oregon v. Lawson, 352 Or. 724, 291 P.3d 673 (2012)
Tarasoff v. Regents of University of California, 17 Cal. 3d 425, 551 P.2d 334, 131 Cal. Rptr. 14 (Cal. 1976)
United States v. Drayton, 536 U.S. 194 (2002)
United States v. Lopez, 328 F. Supp. 1077 (E.D.N.Y. 1971)
United States v. Martinez-Fuerte, 428 U.S. 543 (1976)
United States v. Salerno, 481 U.S. 739 (1987)
United States v. Sokolow, 490 U.S. 1 (1989)
Williams v. Florida, 399 U.S. 78 (1970)

Index

Titles in the **Elgar Advanced Introductions** series include:

Elgar Advanced Introductions are stimulating and thoughtful introductions to major fields in the social sciences, business and law, expertly written by the world's leading scholars. Designed to be accessible yet rigorous, they offer concise and lucid surveys of the substantive and policy issues associated with discrete subject areas.

Leading scholar Tom R. Tyler provides a timely and engaging introduction to the field of law and psychology. This *Advanced Introduction* outlines the main areas of research, their relevance to law and the way that psychological findings have shaped – or failed to shape – the corresponding areas of law.

Key features include:

- broad coverage of the key topics in the field
- accessible, non-technical presentation of research findings
- focus on the relevance of psychological theories to topics in law
- emphasis on the institutional realities within which law functions
- discussion of the problems of bringing research findings into the legal system.

Presenting an informative overview of this rapidly developing area, the *Advanced Introduction to Law and Psychology* will be a key resource for students and scholars of law, psychology and the social sciences. It will also be of benefit to psychologists and legal practitioners.

Tom R. Tyler is the Macklin-Fleming Professor of Law and
Professor of Psychology at Yale University. His research concerns
authority dynamics in groups, organizations, communities and
societies. He has studied these issues in legal, political and
managerial settings. His books include: *Why People Obey the
Law*; *Cooperation in Groups*; *Why People Cooperate*; *Trust in the
Law*; *The Social Psychology of Procedural Justice*; *Social Justice
in a Diverse Society*; and *Why Children Follow Rules*. He earned
his Ph.D. in Social Psychology from UCLA.